The Changing Dynamic of Cuban Civil Society

CONTEMPORARY CUBA

UNIVERSITY PRESS OF FLORIDA

Florida A&M University, Tallahassee
Florida Atlantic University, Boca Raton
Florida Gulf Coast University, Ft. Myers
Florida International University, Miami
Florida State University, Tallahassee
New College of Florida, Sarasota
University of Central Florida, Orlando
University of Florida, Gainesville
University of North Florida, Jacksonville
University of South Florida, Tampa
University of West Florida, Pensacola

Contemporary Cuba
Edited by John M. Kirk

Afro-Cuban Voices: On Race and Identity in Contemporary Cuba, by Pedro Pérez-Sarduy and Jean Stubbs (2000)

Cuba, the United States, and the Helms-Burton Doctrine: International Reactions, by Joaquín Roy (2000)

Cuba Today and Tomorrow: Reinventing Socialism, by Max Azicri (2000); first paperback edition, 2001

Cuba's Foreign Relations in a Post-Soviet World, by H. Michael Erisman (2000); first paperback edition, 2002

Cuba's Sugar Industry, by José Alvarez and Lázaro Peña Castellanos (2001)

Culture and the Cuban Revolution: Conversations in Havana, by John M. Kirk and Leonardo Padura Fuentes (2001)

Looking at Cuba: Essays on Culture and Civil Society, by Rafael Hernández, translated by Dick Cluster (2003)

Santería Healing: A Journey into the Afro-Cuban World of Divinities, Spirits, and Sorcery, by Johan Wedel (2004)

Cuba's Agricultural Sector, by José Alvarez (2004)

Cuban Socialism in a New Century: Adversity, Survival, and Renewal, edited by Max Azicri and Elsie Deal (2004)

Cuba, the United States, and the Post–Cold War World: The International Dimensions of the Washington-Havana Relationship, edited by Morris Morley and Chris McGillion (2005)

Redefining Cuban Foreign Policy: The Impact of the "Special Period," edited by H. Michael Erisman and John M. Kirk (2006)

Gender and Democracy in Cuba, by Ilja A. Luciak (2007)

Ritual, Discourse, and Community in Cuban Santería: Speaking a Sacred World, by Kristina Wirtz (2007)

The "New Man" in Cuba: Culture and Identity in the Revolution, by Ana Serra (2007)

U.S.-Cuban Cooperation Past, Present, and Future, by Melanie M. Ziegler (2007)

The Changing Dynamic of Cuban Civil Society, edited by Alexander I. Gray and Antoni Kapcia (2008)

The Changing Dynamic
of Cuban Civil Society

EDITED BY
ALEXANDER I. GRAY AND ANTONI KAPCIA

University Press of Florida
Gainesville/Tallahassee/Tampa/Boca Raton
Pensacola/Orlando/Miami/Jacksonville/Ft. Myers/Sarasota

Copyright 2008 by Alexander I. Gray and Antoni Kapcia
Printed in the United States of America on acid-free paper
All rights reserved

13 12 11 10 09 08 6 5 4 3 2 1

Library of Congress Cataloging-in-Publication Data
The changing dynamic of Cuban civil society / edited by Alexander I. Gray
and Antoni Kapcia.
p. cm.—(Contemporary Cuba)
Includes bibliographical references and index.
ISBN 978-0-8130-3192-7 (alk. paper)
1. Civil society—Cuba. 2. Non-governmental organizations—Cuba.
I. Gray, Alexander Ian. II. Kapcia, Antoni.
JL1016.C45 2008
300.972919-dc22   2007038095

The University Press of Florida is the scholarly publishing agency for the State
University System of Florida, comprising Florida A&M University, Florida
Atlantic University, Florida Gulf Coast University, Florida International Uni-
versity, Florida State University, New College of Florida, University of Central
Florida, University of Florida, University of North Florida, University of South
Florida, and University of West Florida.

University Press of Florida
15 Northwest 15th Street
Gainesville, FL 32611–2079
http://www.upf.com

Contents

List of Tables and Figures   vii
List of Abbreviations   ix

Introduction. Responding to Crisis at the Grass Roots   1
ALEXANDER I. GRAY AND ANTONI KAPCIA

1. Setting the Stage for a Discussion of Cuban Civil Society: The Nature of
Cuban "Communism" and the Revolution's Political Culture   20
ANTONI KAPCIA

2. Civil Society: The Cuban Debate   40
MICHELLE MARÍN-DOGAN

3. The Rise of the Private Sector in Cuba   65
FRANCISCO DOMÍNGUEZ

4. Rediscovering *Lo Local*: The Potential and the Limits of Local
Development in Havana   90
MIREN URIARTE

5. Solidarity Organizations and Friendship Groups: Internationalist
Volunteer Work Brigades and People-to-People Ties   116
NINO PAGLICCIA

6. "A Space within the Revolution": Religious Cubans and
the Secular State   140
CHRISTINE AYORINDE

7. The Genesis of NGO Participation in Contemporary Cuba: Perceptions
from the Field, as Reported by Local and Foreign NGO Representatives   160
ALEXANDER I. GRAY

Conclusion   183
ALEXANDER I. GRAY AND ANTONI KAPCIA

Glossary   189
About the Contributors   191
Index   193

Tables and Figures

Tables

3.1. Number of associations with foreign capital in Cuba 68

3.2. Economic associations by economic sector 69

3.3. Economic associations by country of origin 70

3.4. Origin and destination of FDI in Cuba 71

3.5. Associations with foreign capital in the food and beverage industry 72

3.6. Foreign trade 73

3.7. Number of UBPCs in 1996 74

3.8. Contribution of UBPCs and CPAs in cattle and agricultural production 76

3.9. Selected production indicators of CPAs, 1996–2001 77

3.10. Sales in agricultural markets per type of supplier, in percentage 78

3.11. Evolution of output in Cuban agriculture 78

3.12. *Cuentapropistas* according to economic activity, in percentage 80

3.13. Proportion of licenses granted of the total requested 80

3.14. Approximate number of Cubans under mercantilist or semi-mercantilist relations 81

Figures

5.1. Three-dimensional solidarity-charity space 123

7.1. The role of new NGOs within Cuban civil society 174

Abbreviations

ACRC	Asociación de Combatientes de la Revolución Cubana (Association of Veterans of the Cuban Revolution)
ACY	Asociación Cultural Yoruba (Yoruba Cultural Association)
AE	*asociación económica* (joint venture)
AIFLD	American Institute for Free Labor Development
ANAP	Asociación Nacional de Agricultores Pequeños (National Association of Small Farmers)
CAM	Consejo Administrativo Municipal (Municipal Administrative Council)
CAP	Consejo Administrativo Provincial (Provincial Administrative Council)
CCFA	Canadian Cuban Friendship Association
CCS	Cooperativa de Crédito y Servicios (Credit and Service Cooperative)
CDR	Comité de Defensa de la Revolución (Committee for the Defense of the Revolution)
CEA	Centro de Estudios de América (Center for American Studies)
CEE	Centro de Estudios Europeos (European Studies Center)
CIERIC	Centro de Intercambio y Referencia sobre Iniciativas Comunitarias (Center for Exchange and Information on Community Initiatives)
CMEA	Council for Mutual Economic Exchange (Comecon)
CNC	Canadian Network on Cuba
CPA	Cooperativa de Producción Agrícola (Agricultural Production Cooperative)
CTC	Central de Trabajadores de Cuba (Cuban Workers' Confederation)
DESR	Departamento de Estudios Socioreligiosos (Department of Socioreligious Studies)
FDI	foreign direct investment
FEEM	Federación de Estudiantes de la Enseñanza Media (Federation of Secondary School Students)
FEU	Federación de Estudiantes Universitarios (Federation of University Students)

x / Abbreviations

FMC	Federación de Mujeres Cubanas (Federation of Cuban Women)
GALEES	Grupo de Acción para la Libre Expresión de Elección Sexual (Action Group for the Free Expression of Sexual Choice)
GDIC	Grupo de Desarrollo Integral de la Capital (Group for the Integrated Development of the Capital)
ICAIC	Instituto Cubano de Arte e Industria Cinematográficos (Cuban Film Institute)
ICAP	Instituto Cubano de Amistad con los Pueblos (Cuban Institute for Friendship with the Peoples)
ICRT	Instituto Cubano de Radio y Televisión (Cuban Institute of Radio and Television)
MINAG	Ministerio de Agricultura (Ministry of Agriculture)
MINVEC	Ministerio de Inversión Extranjera y Cooperación Económica (Ministry for Foreign Investment and Economic Cooperation)
NAFTA	North American Free Trade Agreement
NNOC	National Network on Cuba
ONE	Oficina Nacional de Estadísticas (National Statistical Office)
ORI	Organizaciones Revolucionarias Integradas (Integrated Revolutionary Organizations)
PCC	Partido Comunista de Cuba (Communist Party of Cuba, therefore also given as CCP)
PSP	Partido Socialista Popular (People's Socialist Party)
TTI	Taller de Transformación Integral del Barrio (Neighborhood Transformation Workshop)
UBPC	Unidad Básica de Producción Cooperativa (Basic Unit of Cooperative Production)
UJC	Unión de Jóvenes Comunistas (Union of Communist Youth)
USAID	U.S. Agency for International Development

Introduction

Responding to Crisis at the Grass Roots

ALEXANDER I. GRAY AND ANTONI KAPCIA

Most analyses of Cuba since 1990 focus on the big issues. Broadly, they tend to address the challenges to and the changes in Cuba (most notably the economic crisis, the tightened embargo, the external political pressures, the impact of the dollar, or the increasing social divisions) or the growth of a "civil society" (as necessarily in conflict with the Communist state) and dissident challenges to the system and that system's response. This book, however, focuses on a secondary layer of change, equally important in its implications, that is, the effects on civil society of the Cuban state's necessary adaptation to the effects of those dramatic changes. This adaptation has meant, for example, an opening to new actors (such as NGOs and international donor agencies), a broadening of perspectives, and a tolerance of new activities (cultural and economic), but with a caution and an uncertainty about the resultant organic changes, within a context of the need to preserve the "essence" of the Revolution and the basics of social provision.

Through this focus, this book hopes to provide a framework for discussion and a possible reconceptualization of the whole question of civil society within a political system whose long-standing characteristic has been the juxtaposition of a high level of centralization with remarkably high levels of grass-roots participation.

Background to the Crisis of the 1990s

Between 1961 and 1990, the Cuban economy went through several incarnations and crises, but, broadly, it remained a centrally planned command economy. After 1965, that centralization increased, being especially influenced by Che Guevara's radical ideas and culminating in the Revolutionary Offensive of 1968 (when some 56,000 small businesses and self-employment activities were taken over by the state) and what was supposed to have been the 10–million ton sugar harvest of 1970. It was, however, the failure of that harvest that generated a redirection of the economy after 1972, when Cuba was at last allowed into the Council for Mutual Economic Exchange (CMEA), thus entering a protective network of bilateral trade agreements and barter-swap arrangements, exchanging Cuban primary products for eastern European consumer and industrial goods. After 1975 the whole process of economic institutionalization led to the more decentralized operation that largely characterized the Cuban system until the 1990s.

This was the resource context for the changes in social provision and structure that the Revolution wrought from the earliest days. Those changes were fundamental, involving an immediate and accelerating transformation of the social fabric as thousands of middle-class Cubans left the island and many thousands more moved into the vacated properties of the departed from their slums or shanties, as the Literacy Campaign of 1961 reduced illiteracy (from 23 percent to 3 percent in one year), thus socializing and integrating thousands of poor and mostly rural Cubans, and as health reforms and social security provisions steadily improved the daily lives of most Cubans. In the more staid 1970s and 1980s those changes accelerated, funded by economic improvement and based on the effects of the early investments in education, leading to rising expectations among the young. This process was paralleled by comparable drives toward cultural democratization, broadening the hitherto confined cultural spaces and popularizing the definitions of culture to include the popular in every sense.

From the outset, all of this was driven by a political vanguard whose radicalization since 1956 caused its commitment to revolution to become greater and less compromising. After the early flirtation with social-liberal reformism (1959–60), and after the relationship with the United States worsened (through the trade embargo after 1960, the break in relations in January 1961, and the traumatic Bay of Pigs invasion in April 1961), that vanguard gravitated increasingly leftward. After an initial attraction toward Soviet and Communist definitions of change (1961–63), a series of internal disputes (especially with the Communists of the Partido Socialista Popular [People's Socialist Party, or PSP] prior to 1959), and external differences with a Soviet Union that was less willing to support Cuba than many had hoped, the vanguard moved toward home-grown models of organization and ideology. It was now that the characteristically energetic and unorthodox image of the Revolution was shaped, as the population was mobilized regularly for defense and labor, and as increasingly radical definitions of economy, socialization, and political structure were tried. All of that ended after 1970, when economic, Soviet, and popular pressure forced the leaders to institutionalize: in 1975 the Communist Party had its first congress and expanded massively to become a more recognizable political force; in 1976 a new Soviet-style pyramidal electoral system, Poder Popular (People's Power), was introduced, and the Revolution's first Constitution was enacted. All of that meant a decline in active mobilization and a consolidation of the hitherto rapid process of change. It also meant a return to influence for those marginalized in the 1960s, notably the former activists of the PSP, and the rise of a new generation of Soviet-trained technocrats whose ideological patterns and political interpretations and goals were less radical than those of the ex-guerrillas who still formally led the Revolution but whose power was more circumscribed. In particular, leaders of the PSP such as Carlos Rafael Rodríguez and Blas Roca, who had always been a minority part of the inner circle, now began to exercise more influence, and the ideas of the now dead Guevara (which had dominated so much of the 1965–70 period) were marginalized.

Only in foreign policy was there any semblance of the old radicalism, where the characteristically challenging policies of the 1960s (when Havana saw itself as the active base for the Latin American armed revolution and when Guevara took that policy to its personally fatal conclusion in Bolivia) were continued in Africa, especially in Angola with staggering success. Indeed, the years after 1975 saw a boom in an "internationalism" that saw thousands of young Cubans dispatched all over the Third World as soldiers, doctors, technicians, and teachers.

After 1985, however, the combined threats from a stagnant economy, excessive expectations, increased evidence of privilege in a more bureaucratized party, and Gorbachev's plans to put Cuban-Soviet relations on a commercial footing, all led to a crisis that was addressed, characteristically, by the campaign of "Rectification" ("of past errors and negative tendencies"). Much misunderstood outside Cuba, the campaign was a multifaceted process of economic reform (laying the basis for many of the emergency reforms that reacted to the crisis of 1990) and political "cleansing" (of the party) and redefinition of many aspects of the Revolution, as the political costs of overdependence on Soviet links, models, and personnel were countered by a return to the principles of the 1960s, by a purging of thousands of "opportunists" who had used the party for personal advancement, and by a debate about the essence of the whole process. That debate and those changes were already under way when the crisis of 1989–91 struck Cuba and forced both their intensification and their reassessment.

The Economic Crisis

The economic crisis of the 1990s changed Cuba fundamentally. Trade with the Soviet Union, which had accounted for 80 percent of all Cuban trade, disappeared overnight, the implications of that loss being catastrophic for the Cuban economy, which was now suddenly more vulnerable than ever to international neoliberal market forces. As a result, the gross domestic product

4 / Alexander I. Gray and Antoni Kapcia

(GDP) plummeted by about one-third, personal consumption declined rapidly, and black market, employment, and emigration problems all escalated, lending an urgency to a range of problems of a social, political, ideological, and security nature.

The system's response was to declare an emergency period of adjustment, the Período Especial en Tiempos de Paz (Special Period in Peacetime), popularly known thereafter as the "Special Period."[1] This meant austerity measures aimed at maintaining Cuba's egalitarian division of (now scarce) resources in the face of visible social tensions and increasing and informal competition between government policies and the requirements of market forces. Hence, in the absence of old certainties, the leaders and ordinary Cubans alike had little choice but to put ideology aside while searching out immediate solutions to urgent problems; the 1990s were clearly not to be a time for the continued "building of the Revolution," but were rather to be dedicated to protecting the "gains of the Revolution" so as to ensure the continued survival of social advances, especially in the fundamental pillars of the Revolution: education, nutrition, and healthcare.

In addition to austerity, a sustained campaign of urgent and often unprecedented reforms was launched in 1993, which in turn risked creating a different crisis, a "crisis of change"; this was felt at all levels of society from the state down to the individual, since the sudden and unexpected nature of the reforms caught the country by surprise and left many reeling as they struggled to comprehend the significance of the country's new economic condition. At the macro level, there was the rapid emergence of mixed and private enterprise, and at both the macro and micro levels the dollar became the most significant currency for everyday transactions.[2] This period effectively ushered in Cuba's partial reinsertion into a world economy and the reluctant adoption of certain market mechanisms in the national economy, mechanisms that might well have been previously avoided due to their association with market-led economies.

The resulting emergence of a layer of petty entrepreneurs in an otherwise state-led economy, and the activities, economic dynamics, and social objectives associated with this layer, contradicted the socialist direction toward which the Cuban economy was still firmly geared (as argued in Francisco Domínguez's essay) and brought into focus the tensions between an economy based on semi-mercantilist principles of personal gain and one based on socialist principles of solidarity and the greater good of society as a whole. At the same time, the state legalized the holding of foreign currencies, rapidly making access to the dollar an important method for solving daily needs; indeed, all Cubans were now permitted, and arguably encouraged, to shop at the state-run *diplotiendas* (hard currency shops) where all products were sold

Introduction: Responding to Crisis at the Grass Roots / 5

in dollars. However, this so-called "dollarization" of the Cuban economy, and the ensuing inequalities in and importance of access to the dollar became more and more apparent. Purchasing power became the decisive factor in the acquisition of goods and services, providing increased social influence, and arguably importance, to those who excelled in the newly emerging economy.

What have such fundamental economic changes meant at the local level? Most clearly, they meant that the significance of the formal economy, historically so important to individual Cubans, was partly replaced by the growing informal economy, as the state's inability to satisfy all of the population's needs (beyond the very basic needs, which were largely met by a return to rationing and a recourse to traditional systems of social support) resulted in a mushrooming of black market and other related informal or "illegal" activities. Cubans quickly became accustomed to what became commonly known as the act of *resolver* (resolve, that is, to find a way around) shortages or a lack of goods or services through means outside the state apparatus. The patterns of local economic life were altered. Some opted to take advantage of the opportunities offered by the new economy and opened *paladares* (private restaurants) or *casas particulares* (guest houses), both options working at both the formal and informal levels, given the costs of official license and taxation requirements. Others chose to resolve their daily needs by engaging in *jineterismo* (hustling), which, covering a broad spectrum of activity and carried out by both men and women, could involve anything from hustling tourists to outright prostitution and introduced a phenomenon almost absent before 1990. While the prevalence of *jineteros* has been exaggerated by some media and academics, their presence has unquestionably grown significantly since the start of the Special Period.

All of these changes, challenges, and policies gave civil society a fundamental role as the theater in which were enacted the grass-roots reactions of Cubans and their individual and organized forms of combat against the new difficulties. It is indeed that reaction with which this book deals, highlighting the dynamism and versatility of the (often authoritative) state and the creativity (and not always subordinate attitudes) of ordinary Cubans.

Thus while in 1985 Cuba might have been one of the most egalitarian societies in the world, by the 1990s the state found it increasingly difficult to maintain this equality, and inequalities started to re-emerge for the first time since 1959. As the quantity of goods available on the *libreta* (ration book) began to diminish, those without access to dollars saw their standard of living diminish; this was especially true for the most vulnerable segments of the population, including the elderly, who became reliant on the assistance of family and friends as state provisions could no longer cover all of their needs. This situation was particularly unsettling for Cuban youth as, for three generations, they had grown up under the watchful eye of the state, unable to countenance the idea of a state no longer able to respond to their needs.

The External Dimension

Before 1991 the external context defined Cuba: the politics of the Cold War, the hostility of relations between the United States and Cuba, and the implications of the post-1960 links with the Soviet Union all played their part in determining the direction, character, and survival of the Revolution. On the one hand, the isolation or "siege" of Cuba, which U.S. hostility created, intensified Cuban nationalism, justified a defensive attitude to dissent and conformity, and drove much of Cuba's foreign policy, especially in the 1960s. On the other hand, Cuba enjoyed a special relationship with the Soviet Union, due in large part to Cuba's geo-strategic importance in the Cold War; in addition to the benefits of the economic link, the strong political link between the two (especially after a partial détente from 1972) helped to create an external image of Cuba that also affected how Cubans perceived themselves internationally. However, by the mid-1980s, this and other aspects of the traditionally close relationship between the two ideologically aligned nations were open to question, as, coinciding with a more aggressive U.S. posture under Reagan, Gorbachev's moves to put Cuba's relations with the Soviet bloc on a commercial footing were profoundly disturbing to Cuba's sense of security.

It was within this context that the disintegration of the Soviet bloc came about, accompanied by the simultaneous tightening of the U.S. embargo. The two processes combined to create a nightmare scenario of Armageddon for the Revolution's survival. Quite apart from the economic consequences, the dissolution of the Soviet bloc signaled the loss of a valuable ideological ally, not so much a point of reference as a companion in solidarity. Without the prospect of Soviet protection, economically and diplomatically, Cuba now faced an onslaught from the United States, now rampant in a world more committed than ever to neoliberal economic and political policies.

Indeed, identifying Cuba's economic weakness, the United States moved quickly and decisively to increase its pressure on the island's economy. The Cuban Democracy Act of 1992 made it illegal for foreign subsidiaries of U.S. firms to trade with Cuba; the potentially more damaging Helms-Burton law of 1996 included a controversial provision allowing U.S. citizens to sue foreign firms and individuals who "traffic" in their former properties nationalized by the Cuban government after 1959; the USAID report of 1997, *Support for Democratic Transition in Cuba*, offered financial and other assistance to dissident elements in Cuban civil society; and the President's Commission for Assistance to a Free Cuba, headed by the then secretary of state, Colin Powell,

Introduction: Responding to Crisis at the Grass Roots / 7

issued in June 2004 a 500–page report containing hard-line recommendations that were immediately adopted as official U.S. policy. As a result, U.S. support for the "pro-democracy" movement increased from seven million to thirty-six million dollars, funding being channeled toward the training, development, and empowerment of a Cuban "democratic opposition and civil society," although this meant in practice favoring the less compromising elements of the illegal opposition over the more moderate elements, the latter represented especially by Osvaldo Payá, the author of the Proyecto Varela, who viewed this latest U.S. drive with some disappointment, arguing that it contaminated the opposition, making its task more difficult.

However, beyond Washington, most Western countries have tended to maintain an approach to relations with Cuba based on what the Canadians term "constructive engagement." This is an interactive, rather than exclusionary, approach, which allows for dialogue and exchange in commercial and public spheres. This constructive approach did go through an awkward period between April 2003 and June 2005, however, as, in response to Cuban arrests of seventy-five U.S.-backed dissidents and in response also to U.S. pressure, the European Union (EU) shifted toward a policy of non-cooperation and partial boycott; it was only with the rise of a new socialist government in Spain and the awareness that this policy was counterproductive that this temporary change in policy was ended.

One way in which this "constructive dialogue" has displayed itself is through governmental and nongovernmental cooperation with the island's civil society sector, in the form of projects with international donor agencies and NGOs. Indeed, since 1991, participation of foreign actors in Cuba's social development has added a dimension that was largely absent during the Cold War. This participation has presented challenges to the system's traditional approach to external cooperation with such foreign actors and has led to a balancing of the concern that participation by foreign NGOs is not entirely conducive to maintaining the status quo in the Revolution's approach to social development with an awareness that Cuba's new needs demand a new consideration of distinct approaches to social development. These interventions by NGOs (welcomed in the darkest days of the crisis) have brought about a new context where the revolutionary socialist view of civil society comes into close contact with a more Western conception.

Political Response to the Crisis

As a result of the profound economic changes, the challenges to social cohesion, and the arrival of the NGOs, Cubans (both leaders and led) also had to respond politically, especially through a decentralization of decision-making power in such a way as to encourage local initiatives as a means of resolving those challenges. Two programs (both starting in the late 1980s, but only gaining significance in the 1990s) were received with particular enthusiasm and significant measure of success; the Talleres de Transformación Integral (Neighborhood Transformation Workshops) and the Consejos Populares (People's Councils) are unique in Cuba's experience in that they involve the participation of many diverse actors, including the mass organizations, Cuban and foreign NGOs, state-run academic institutions, independent academic centers, and, of course, the local residents (these programs are discussed in the essays of Miren Uriarte and Alexander Gray). These organizations lie at the heart of the changes to the Cuban system, since the implicit devolution of autonomy to the local level empowers citizens to search out solutions to their own problems, with the state relinquishing a degree of management of social development; hence, the organizations implementing the new programs enjoy a certain degree of independence while still representing the public face of the state-directed revolutionary project.

These changes, however, raise the vexed question of the nature of political participation in Cuba, a central issue in the constant debates about "democracy" and Cuba. Put simply, are the various mechanisms of political representation and involvement in Cuba mechanisms for political control and incorporation by a political elite or party, or are they mechanisms to allow for active and willing involvement with access to power and decision making? Clearly, this debate and these questions are fundamental to the continual polemic waged since 1961 between two opposing camps: those arguing that the Cuban system is essentially coercive, dictatorial, or totalitarian (essentially the position of the United States and émigrés) and those arguing that the Cuban system is essentially democratic, representative, and participatory (essentially those inside Cuba committed to the system and those in the "solidarity" camp). Because of the passions roused by the debate and the complete antagonism between these perspectives, and because of the assumptions that both sides make about the meaning of "democracy," it is perhaps best here to get away completely from the term itself in discussions of the internal political structures and popular involvement. Instead, it may be better to view this system through a different optic, which allows a more nuanced view to emerge: to see "participation" (the term preferred by Cubans themselves) as a long spectrum between, at the one end, empowerment (seen not just as the acquisition of power but the feeling of power) and, at the other, mobilization (of the people by the system). This approach is useful because it allows us to move away from the unhelpful dichotomy between inherently conflictive and contradictory processes (of "real" representation where people act as subjects and of a controlling organization of "the masses" as objects) to the idea that

Introduction: Responding to Crisis at the Grass Roots / 9

these are simply different ends of the same spectrum, with the two being capable of overlapping at any one time.

From this point of view, for example, the experiences in Cuba in the early 1960s might best be seen as a process of empowerment, since most of those Cubans who remained and chose to become actively involved in processes such as the Literacy Campaign or the militias genuinely felt that they were being involved, listened to, and given some worth, and that therefore they felt that they now counted. However, many of those same processes implied a campaign of active mobilization of occasionally reluctant Cubans by an emerging state and political apparatus, not to mention peer pressure, in ways that felt coercive at the time (occasionally leading the neutrals to leave Cuba). The point is that however coercive this participation might have been, it was effective at the level of giving people a stake in the system (as well as "delivering the goods"), of giving them a role and a purpose, of empowering them to some extent. Hence, they often became willing participants in a mass mobilization. Equally, one might argue that after 1975, when the mood and ethos of mobilization declined for various reasons (except at a somewhat ritual level), the emergence of a feeling of declining empowerment (one of the growing complaints of the 1980s, especially among the young) was not unrelated to this process; hence, the rise of the less active People's Power system coincided with the decline of the neighborhood "civil defense" and vigilance groups, the Committees for the Defense of the Revolution (CDRs), and contributed to an environment wherein Cubans had less of a sense of being actively involved. For this reason, while in the late 1980s young people might have felt that they were being dragooned into voluntary labor, May Day rallies, or mass organizations, the decline of these very experiences as the crisis of the 1990s set in played a part in making many Cubans feel alienated and disempowered. This is certainly one reason why the Cuban leaders felt the need to create new structures and bodies for involvement, such as the People's Councils, the Asociación de Combatientes de la Revolución Cubana (Association of Veterans of the Cuban Revolution) for older Cubans, who were potentially left out of the political structures of active participation, and the Tribunas Abiertas (Open Platforms) after 1999. Michelle Marín-Dogan's essay sets this debate regarding the political responses to the crisis within its historical and contemporary context.

Political and Social Spaces

One of the most evident features of the Cuban system, at any time since 1959, is how little it corresponds to preconceptions. This is especially true of those interpretations based on Eastern European perspectives prior to 1989 that have tended often to characterize the system as monolithic (focusing either on Castro's supposed personalistic domination or on the system's Communist structures and practices). However, any close familiarity with Cuba on a day-to-day basis immediately demonstrates the inaccuracy of such a reading. Although the political system may well from time to time, and perhaps even for most of the time for many Cubans, be restricting, controlling, and centralizing, the fact is that at the grass roots it is more frequently characterized not by monolithic patterns but rather by a range of spaces, areas of daily life where the supposedly long arm of the state simply does not reach, or reach effectively, and therefore, by not intruding as much as it might, allowing gaps for ordinary Cubans to operate independently.

Essentially, there are two ways of perceiving and interpreting these (political and social) spaces. On the one hand, they can be offered as evidence of the extent to which the whole system fails to work, either in controlling or in meeting people's needs; hence, they can be seen as the areas where a would-be civil society or an individualistic ethos develops, in the so-called interstices between the various state organizations. In Eckstein's view (Eckstein 1994), these are the spaces where resistance occurs, where "foot-dragging" operates, where the informal economy thrives and develops, and where ordinary Cubans escape the state and develop patterns of survival and adaptation. If true, then it is unquestionably the case that the Special Period increased such spaces, either as the formal state apparatus failed, contracted, or withered away, or as the struggle for survival after 1990 either shelved any communal spirit or blew away the spurious solidarity that had survived until 1989 (two common explanations offered), thus leading to an increasingly atomized society as every Cuban abandoned the state, his or her employment, and even his or her neighbors to pursue the daily individual battle for existence. At its most positive, such a perspective could foresee the seeds of a future civil society and a future capitalistic private enterprise in this process of disintegration, as indeed one might suggest had been the case in Eastern Europe after 1989 or Russia after 1990.

The alternative reading, however, is that such spaces are actually not so much against the system as within it, the result of several processes. The evolution of different and often experimental or at least empirical structures over the decades has created a pattern wherein each new structure or mechanism does not fully replace those that are already in existence but, instead, operates alongside them. The most outstanding examples are the successive creation of the CDRs, People's Power, and the People's Councils. While this evolution can produce a confusion of roles and responsibilities, and, at its worst, a frustrating inability to deliver, it also creates spaces between those roles and responsibilities, spaces wherein ordinary Cubans develop various means of making the

Introduction: Responding to Crisis at the Grass Roots / 11

system work practically (usually illegally or informally, but usually tolerated because they deliver) and where the state structures themselves also blur the edges of the formal and the informal. This certainly seems to be the pattern described in the essays of Alexander Gray, Christine Ayorinde, and Antoni Kapcia.

The point about these "positive" spaces is that, if they do exist, they are therefore mechanisms not just of resistance (although clearly they have the capacity to offer this function and frequently do for those Cubans who dissent) but also of adherence to the system. In other words, the fact that they exist and the manner in which Cubans use them means that the boundaries of the formal and informal structures are blurred to good effect, allowing passively supportive citizens to go outside the formal structures without challenging the system and allowing the state a space for solutions to be worked out creatively on the ground in ways that the more rigid structures cannot encompass. While this local tolerance can easily be dismissed as inefficiency and even low-level corruption (since all visitors encounter it in some form or another, as official rules are breached or bent to allow normal operations to proceed), it may also be part of the process of negotiation in which all Cubans have to engage daily and in which the whole Revolution has been engaged from the outset, as developments have come as much empirically as by (often flawed) design. Hence rather than (or perhaps as well as) being contested spaces, they are overlaps or spaces of fusion.

In 1992, indeed, the socialist Constitution of the National Assembly of 1976 was revised to some degree, partly to create such spaces for Cuban civil society organizations. For example, for the first time religious Cubans (*creyentes*, believers) were permitted membership in the Communist Party; with the official removal of religious intolerance there was an immediate increase in the number of religious organizations (as dealt with in Christine Ayorinde's essay). Discrimination based on sexual orientation was also removed from Article 7 of the Constitution; the release of the film *Fresa y Chocolate* (Strawberry and Chocolate) aided enormously in reforming public opinion with respect to homosexuals. At the same time, there are no gay or lesbian organizations in Cuba; such organizations are not permitted on the grounds that the rights of homosexuals are already laid out in the Constitution. However, there was a brief period in 1994 that saw the formation of the Gay and Lesbian Association of Cuba, which soon transformed itself to become the Action Group for the Free Expression of Sexual Choice (GALEES) (Lumsden 1996). However, neither of these groups, despite their enthusiasm, ever had large numbers, and GALEES soon disappeared.

Further changes occurred with the legalization of nongovernmental organizations. Until 1993, "associations" and "autonomous societies," including

12 / Alexander I. Gray and Antoni Kapcia

sports and cultural clubs, bird-watchers groups, and so on, were regulated by Law Number 54 of 1985. When Cuban NGOs began to appear many had difficulty registering under Law 54 as the existence of nongovernmental organizations was practically unknown. This prompted the revision of the old law, which reappeared in 1993 under the new Association Act. The new law still prohibits the registration of organizations whose goals violate the Cuban Constitution or involve activities that, according to the Ministry of Justice, "are properly the role of the state." This rule effectively bans the registration of political parties as the Cuban Constitution provides for a one-party system. As they are considered to be covert political parties, human rights organizations are denied registration. Some of these NGOs had been in existence for many years previous to 1993 but did not enjoy any official status until the Association Act. One of the newer and lesser known groups is the Asociación de Combatientes. At the same time, many NGOs are in existence but have for one reason or another not been able to attain official recognition. The current role of these and other increasingly significant civil society actors will be debated in the book, all seen within a system that, as Alexander Gray makes clear with his model of pyramids, is ever more complex and challenging to expectations.

Religion

The question of spaces for believers also of course introduces the role of religion in Cuban society. Approaching the topic of religion can be a perilous undertaking in any culture, especially where there is an organized desire to aspire to a culture of Communism; here there is a logical assumption that, in Cuba, the question is dominated by church-state relations. Closer inspection, however, reveals that expectation and reality are quite different, not least because religion in Cuba is more commonly associated with *santería*, the fusion of Catholic and African beliefs that has evolved over time to become, many would argue, the predominant belief system on the island, with most Cubans seeming to equate "religion" with *santería*. Never officially recognized by the church, and for long not recognized by either church or state, *santería* clearly constitutes part of the informal area of Cuban life, although in this sense the informal does not refer to illegal activity but rather to behavior that lies outside officially promoted norms. Having said that, the permission given in 1992 to *creyentes* to join the Communist Party probably applied more to adherents of *santería* than to mainstream Catholics.

Although Christine Ayorinde looks in passing at the Catholic Church and Judaism, the book does not actually look at the church per se as part of civil society, whereas some of the church's organizations, such as Caritas, may well belong in that category. One reason for this is that the church was socially

Introduction: Responding to Crisis at the Grass Roots / 13

weak before 1959 and did not have as large a following as might have been expected. Moreover, and perhaps more to the point, in some respects one might argue that large institutions, such as the Catholic Church, have power structures in place that would liken them more to a state organization than a civil society organization, especially given the church's organizational links to the Vatican, a state that upholds its own foreign policy (Kirk 1989). This is a deeply controversial and highly debatable point, and while it is not a main element of this book to argue whether or not the churches lie within the boundaries of civil society, this is a point that is touched upon in some of the essays.

Certainly, from the earliest days of the Revolution, social space was taken from the Catholic Church in an effort to decrease any influence it might wield in the counterrevolution both within and beyond Cuba. While many Cubans remained Christian, church attendance dropped steeply. However, perhaps almost conversely, Afro-Cuban religions (which had a tradition of resisting the church) were initially not viewed as posing such a threat, as their practitioners were considered those who had benefited the most from the country's social transformations and were therefore those who would be more likely to participate in revolutionary social tasks. Nonetheless, the 1970s saw attempts to apply theories of scientific atheism and people were encouraged to keep religion as a strictly private matter and to place their loyalties in the mass organizations. Believers were barred from the Communist Party and the Union of Communist Youth, membership in either of which became necessary to obtain a university place and certain posts within the bureaucracy.

What makes religion an especially relevant topic for this book, however, is the fact that, in addition to economic hardship, the Special Period ushered in an era of diminished expectations, low morale, and decreased consideration for accepted ideology. In confronting this general sense of helplessness, many Cubans turned to spirituality, increasing religious practice on the island. Therefore, religious tolerance took on new meaning in 1992 when the Constitution was modified and the Cuban state switched from being officially atheist to officially secular, which had the added effect of making discrimination against believers illegal. Identifying oneself as religious, whether Christian or Afro-Cuban, became somewhat more acceptable in social and professional circumstances. For ordinary Cubans the role of religion, especially *santería* and its historical ties, became more significant as this spiritual outlet served in some ways as consolation for the personal hardships of the country's then deepening economic crisis. At the same time, Christine Ayorinde points out that the Cuban government began to realize the importance of increasing religious recognition. Youth were beginning to join the Christian churches, some denominations of which were previously and technically illegal, in a search for social space. Some argue that the space offered by the churches was

14 / Alexander I. Gray and Antoni Kapcia

doubly appealing as it lay outside the confines of the state. Whether youth were identifying with Christianity, seeking protection from growing inequalities, or pursuing nonconformist attitudes, the churches clearly became more popular as the country headed into harder economic times and the state's ability to provide for the populace diminished. The state thus recognized the compatibility of Christianity with revolutionary ideals and therefore was able to appeal to Christian values as a mechanism to garnish public support in combating the difficult period that lay ahead. At the same time, the continued rise in popularity of Afro-Cuban religions was accompanied by state efforts toward forming official organizations associated with these religions. This enabled institutionalization of believers, bringing them closer to the state while allowing freedom of religious expression.

One of the underlying reasons for this entente was that in the 1990s both the churches and the Revolution were concerned with a *crisis de valores* (decline in moral values), which was associated with the ruined economy, the social challenges associated with increased tourism, and the "dollarization" of the economy. In this sense, perception and reality may not have been as far apart as expected, as the churches were actually a good deal closer to the Revolution than they may have appeared. It would be an exaggeration to imply that the churches and the state were working in tandem; however, both shared a desire to instill moral values and a sense of collective consciousness. These and other aspects of Cuban religiousness are explored in the essay by Christine Ayorinde.

Moreover, the increase in religious tolerance was a part of Cuba's general opening to the outside world, giving the churches and Afro-Cuban religions the opportunity to increase links with foreign counterparts. The culmination of this period of warming relations, in fact, came in 1998 with the pope's visit to the island, something that would have been unimaginable ten years earlier, which brought international attention and lent international support to the broadening of religious freedom on the island.

Ideology

One of the most contentious and perhaps least understood aspects of the Revolution is the vexed question of ideology. Superficially, of course, this is an easy matter, since, from 1961, the process has explicitly followed a socialist and then a Communist path, all confirmed by Cuba's alliances with the Soviet Union and then membership in the CMEA after 1972. Hence, the Revolution's ideology can be taken to be Marxist-Leninist. Nothing is, of course, ever that clear in Cuba, especially when one bears in mind some basic elements of the process's evolution, such as the fact that before 1961 the question of socialism only really existed in the minds and practices of a few individuals within the leadership or in the PSP, which, after 1958, allied with the guerrilla rebels of the 26 July Movement. Equally, this was a revolution that came to power without a Communist Party in a leading position and then went on to define itself as Communist at a time when the PSP was clearly in a secondary role.

Instead it is more useful and accurate to consider the process's ideology as stemming from its roots and beginnings, as the traditions of radical nationalism that can be summarized as the ideology of *cubanía rebelde* (rebel Cubanness; Kapcia 2000), that is, the belief in the attainment of the goal of an independent and socially reforming Cuba, the traditional Cuba Libre (Free Cuba). These traditions, which are traceable from the ideas, example, and figure of José Martí, the leader of independence and a *héroe nacional* (national hero), through generations of radicals of the 1920s and 1930s, culminated in 1953 in the challenge mounted by Castro's young rebels, a challenge whose *martiano* (following the ideas of Martí) imprint was all too clear, especially in its discourse and project. Those traditions were then developed, and radicalized, through the guerrilla experience of 1956–58 to become the blueprint for the victorious revolution of 1959. Throughout that trajectory, the coherence of the tradition was maintained by a seemingly unbroken series of symbolic events and figures (the Platt Amendment, Martí, Batista's coup of 1934, and so on), commemorated and ritually conserved as a cosmology or demonology of Cuba Libre but above all by a continuity of a number of codes and myths. These codes included, for example, a belief in the value and Cubanness of action, youth, culture and education, the countryside, and an abiding and all-encompassing concept of political morality.

After 1959, the whole experience of collective struggle, defense, and defiance, of popular participation and mobilization, of siege and isolation, and of survival and successful challenge to U.S. hegemony all combined to convert this *cubanía rebelde* into a more coherent but still essentially nationalist or patriotic *cubanía revolucionaria*. This was essentially the old dissident ideology of challenge, enhanced by success, empowerment, and struggle and shorn of its supposedly discordant elements (such as a pro-American bourgeoisie or a pluralist liberalism) to become a governing but still mobilizing ideology of transformation, challenging hegemonies (capitalist American and socialist Soviet) from a position of strength rather than marginal opposition. By 1970, this process had added new codes to the old, such as collectivism and internationalism, both of which could be subsumed under the broad concept of solidarity.

By the 1980s, solidarity, indeed, had become very much a governing principle of the system, referring to domestic patterns of voluntarism (in labor), political involvement, and social support, but also to the new experience of practical solidarity with the Third World. In the 1960s this solidarity had manifested itself as support for guerrilla attempts to overthrow regimes, but in the 1970s and 1980s it had become an extensive program of aid and service abroad. Hence, Cuba's welcome of others' manifestations of solidarity with Cuba (as outlined in Nino Pagliccia's chapter) was not just pragmatic but reflected a wider code and guiding principle.

Understanding the System

Discussion of ideology naturally leads to the related question of how to understand the system itself, or, put another way, to discussion of the models that have conventionally been applied to the Cuban case. Here, of course, the variations are myriad, given the length of time the Revolution has survived, the phases it has passed through, and the passions it has aroused.

The initial responses after 1959 tended to focus either positively on the social changes (defining the process as some form of socialism) or negatively on the emerging evidence of a perceived totalitarianism. This latter perspective tended to be couched either in terms of Stalinism and Communism (as experienced and studied in its Socialist bloc forms)—especially from American liberals or from Cuban exiles—or in terms of Castro's personalist dictatorship. There were also attempts to place "Castroism" into a perceived Latin American model of *caudillismo*, albeit that such a phenomenon really belonged to patterns and thinking of a century earlier. While all of these interpretations may well have had some light to shed on the evolving phenomenon, they all tended to suffer from two underlying problems. The first was the assumption that all Communist systems were de facto similar if not identical (in structure, in process, and in their inherently undemocratic nature) and therefore that what happened in Cuba could be properly understood through a lens shaped by Russia after 1917 or Poland after 1945. The second was that Cuba's particularities defied easy categorization according to terms essentially coined for a North Atlantic or European context; without repeating sterile arguments of the 1960s about Cuba's supposed exceptionalism (which assumed that all or most other countries did fit a common pattern and did not possess their own particularities), it is sufficient that we remind ourselves of the critical features that shaped modern Cuba in order to realize how inapplicable such models might be. For example, we should not forget the unusual, if not unique, combination of a late adherence to slavery and a late abolition of it, a prolonged and distorting Spanish colonialism, a particularly onerous and influential (and licit) neocolonialism, and an unusually powerful and recent Spanish immigration (to name but a few of these determining factors) when seeking to place Cuba inside a model or pattern developed elsewhere.

Introduction: Responding to Crisis at the Grass Roots / 17

By the 1970s, of course, the concepts of socialism were being universally applied to Cuba, partly because of the clear evidence of the path that Cuba was openly following but also because, by then, political analysis had developed sufficiently for the term to mean any number of things without conjuring up automatically images and expectations of the Stalinism of the 1930s or the China of the 1950s. In fact, the Cuban analyses that emerged from that time onward (and particularly in the challenging 1990s and beyond) have tended to assume that a socialist model (however defined and clearly seen to be evolving) is the perspective within which to understand the system. The contours of this debate are detailed in the analysis provided by Michelle Marín-Dogan's essay.

One other caveat is also important: the need to be wary of, and precise about, terminology when examining and writing about politics in Cuba. This is not simply a matter of pedantry or semantics, but more about a necessary caution about the preconceptions that accompany conventional terms. We should remember that familiar terms have the capacity both to reflect and determine our interpretations, and also that terms do not simply translate from English to Spanish or vice versa without changing meaning. Hence, for example, the English word "revolution" needs to be used precisely rather than loosely, with an awareness of the question of process, while "la Revolución" can mean different things to different Cubans according to one's perspective and experience but has increasingly tended to be an all-encompassing term for the whole collective, cumulative, and evolving experience, or as an equivalent to "Patria." Equally "the state" implies a set of patterns, behaviors, and structures that may not necessarily be reflected in the Cuban case and has tended increasingly to mean, in northern political parlance, a somewhat impersonal or neutral actor at best and an interfering and controlling presence at worst; in Cuba, however, "*estado*" has either positive connotations (not unlike the usage in Britain after 1945, as a social benefactor and protective structure) or, for dissidents, the negative connotations of Orwell's Big Brother. Furthermore, the U.S. sanctions from 1960 onward are either the *bloqueo*, meaning "blockade" (for Cubans), reflecting and reinforcing the siege mentality and recalling the dark days of October 1962, the embargo (for more neutral observers), or sanctions (for advocates within the United States). Meanwhile *democracia* is, in common Cuban parlance, a broad definition of participation, involvement, and representation, while "democracy" tends increasingly, to the North, to mean pluralism, contested elections, and, above all, a free market. Put simply, language is part of the ideological battleground over Cuba, part of the inherent difficulty in understanding alternative perspectives, and part of the overriding need to be precise on terms, definitions, and analyses.

About This Book

Finally, this is the point to establish clearly what the purpose and aim of the book are, and, thus, which questions it is addressing and also not addressing. It is first and foremost a compilation of analyses of, and perspectives about, the changes and challenges of the 1990s as they affected something called Cuban civil society and its relationship with the Cuban state and also with something still called "the Revolution." Therefore, it essentially offers a focus on the micro-level processes and practices rather than the macro-level theories or models.

However, it is as well here to introduce one caveat. Because in this book this micro-level focus is on Havana, partly by accident and partly by design (for consistency of analysis and perspective), it is important to remember that it is fundamental to any full understanding of Cuba to recognize that Havana is not Cuba and that the rest of the island often offers very different experiences, levels of involvement, attitudes, and support. Indeed, one can go further: Havana is occasionally the point where both support for, and dissent from, the Revolution are exaggerated, where the majority of committed activists are concentrated, and where mass rallies take place with enormous and not simply regimented participation, but it is also where the island's fragmented opposition activists are most numerous and, with access to the foreign press and to the U.S. Interests Section, tend to be the most vociferous and evident. Havana is also where the daily grumbling is loudest and most persistent and where the informality is most rampant and even the best organized, where tourists are most concentrated and accessible and therefore where *jineterismo* is most obvious and active.

The second aim of the book, therefore, is to present a study of the dynamics of Cuban civil society's relationship with the state in the midst of the profound and destabilizing changes produced by the challenges of the 1990s and beyond. Discussion and debate surrounding the topic of civil society in Cuba were virtually absent from Cuban public forums throughout the Cold War. However, following Castro's introduction of the topic during a speech at the Rio summit in 1992, academics turned their attention to the topic, for example Haroldo Dilla and others in and around the Centro de Estudios sobre América (Center for American Studies, CEA). This increased attention arose from the particular combination of the contraction of the state, social change, the growth of individual and group organization to meet changing needs, and the arrival for the first time of international donor agencies and Western NGOs. In the face of these changes, foreign actors, including academics and other observers of Cuba, also turned their attention toward civil society. Some were prompted by the notion that civil society may provide the space for dramatic social and political changes; others, as is the case with this book, were intrigued by the changing patterns of the relationship between the overtly political system and the ways in which ordinary Cubans lead their lives.

This work, therefore, aims to provide information on, and thus illuminate this relationship. By bringing together several micro-studies, based on primary research, and by offering different perspectives that challenge conventional wisdom, this collection of essays introduces a fresh and innovative approach to the question of something called "civil society" in Cuba.

Notes

1. The Special Period remained in force for most of the decade; its end has never officially been declared, but it is assumed to have ended with the Elián González affair of 1999–2000, which then generated the next "phase," namely the "Battle of Ideas." Hence, throughout this book, the term "Special Period" will be used to refer to the whole period after 1990.

2. In October 2004, responding to a series of U.S. measures to tighten the embargo, the Cuban government changed the currency system, eliminating the free use of the dollar in the domestic economy (but not recriminalizing it) and replacing it with the existing *peso convertible*, to be used henceforth in all tourism-oriented areas and enterprises, and so forth. Because, during the period being discussed in this book, the dollar was relevant in 1993–2004, and the *peso convertible* was relevant after that date, we have used the global term "hard currency" or *divisas* to refer to the non-peso economy.

References

Eckstein, S. E. 1994. *Back from the Future: Cuba under Castro*. Princeton, N.J.: Princeton University Press.

Kapcia, A. 2000. *Cuba: Island of Dreams*. New York: Berg.

Kirk, John. 1989. *Between God and the Party: Religion and Politics in Revolutionary Cuba*. Tampa: University of South Florida Press.

Lumsden, I. 1996. *Machos, Gays, and Maricones: Cuba and Homosexuality*. Philadelphia: Temple University Press.

1

Setting the Stage for a Discussion of Cuban Civil Society

The Nature of Cuban "Communism" and of the Revolution's Political Culture

ANTONI KAPCIA

When assessing the nature of the Cuban political system since 1959, any attempt to apply notions of civil society (and certainly of the state and civil society) should be treated with caution. This is because the term "civil society" is now highly contested (Tester 1992). Although the concept has evolved, often beyond recognition, since its genesis, its focus has always essentially been European or North American. As such, it has arisen from specific historical experiences and periods that may not always be useful for defining and understanding experiences arising from postcolonial societies and especially ones born from processes of revolutionary change.

Caution especially arises, however, from the ideology that has been underpinning the concept since the 1980s. With the onset of the last phase of the Cold War and the ascendancy of Hayekian and Friedmanite orthodoxy, bolstered by the hegemony of Reaganism, Thatcherism, and eventually neoconservatism, the concept was successfully appropriated to support an increasingly "anti-state" discourse, "state and civil society" being increasingly taken to mean "civil society *against* the state." This was what especially shaped much of the ideological rationalization of political change among intellectual circles in Eastern Europe in the late 1980s (and certainly, subsequently, helped explain events in an almost teleological fashion). This was particularly true for the Polish activist Adam Michnik, who turned his previous Marxism on its head by arguing that as the Polish state entered a deep crisis beginning in 1981 Polish civil society should act as though it were free and thus strengthen itself against a weakening state. Since 1989, there has been an often unhelpful tendency to apply universally a paradigm that arose from a specific set of events in Eastern Europe and the Soviet Union, especially to societies with a seemingly totalitarian state or an avowedly Communist one such as Cuba. This domino tendency

Setting the Stage for a Discussion of Cuban Civil Society / 21

has led both to expectations of inevitable state collapse, in an unstoppable process of history (curiously paralleling Marxism's deterministic historicism), and also to sustained policies (chiefly by U.S. administrations, policymakers, and conservative think tanks) aimed at strengthening civil society in those systems and creating the desirable and inevitable state collapse. One can certainly see such a thought process at work over Cuba, where internal dissidence—and especially, since 2003, the rise of the more uncompromising Asamblea para la Promoción de una Sociedad Civil (Assembly to Promote Civil Society—has provided the link and justification for a sustained strategy to undermine the state by strengthening civil society; this is the "twin-track" policy followed by the Clinton administration beginning in 1992, "constructed as a scene of destabilization of the system" (Hernández 2003, 28).

However, *pace* ideology and claims for exceptionalism, the application to the Cuban case of the paradigm ought to be questionable simply on the grounds of certain fundamental patterns and historical experiences. One such pattern is the fact that between independence in 1902 and the revolution in 1959, Cuba was characterized by a demonstrably "weak" state structure, arising from the effects of the Platt Amendment and the Reciprocity Treaty of 1903,[2] and then by the processes of dependence and neocolonialism. Even the revolution of 1933 did not create in the "Second Republic" (1934–58) the powerful state that it intended, but, rather, a state that was in effect more interventionist and regulatory because the new economic relationship with the United States allowed it to be so.[3] Hence, with Batista's coup of 1952, by the time the Revolution succeeded, the Cuban state was already falling apart again. However, Cuban "civil society" was by no means necessarily any stronger; indeed, Cuba's social weaknesses can justifiably be seen as a prime factor behind the republic's collapse and the drift toward radicalization and revolution, with civil institutions such as the Catholic Church, the judiciary, and the bureaucracy being visibly undermined by their partiality or limited social base or endemic corruption. Hence, the new revolutionary vanguard's limited base found the task of constructing both a new state and a new civil society made all the more difficult by the lack of a nationwide organization with expertise (to achieve the former) and the departure of the middle class (for the latter), at a time, moreover, when social mobility reached bewildering proportions because of dramatic changes in residential location.[4] Hence, by the end of the 1960s, both the revolutionary state and a new civil society were far from fully formed.

The second factor questioning the use of the paradigm in the Cuban case follows from this: namely that the 1960s were characterized by an extraordinarily complex and fluid process wherein the political mechanisms that had been created, some deliberately and others empirically, tended to militate against the notion of a separation of state and civil society. The participatory mechanisms (notably the Committees for the Defense of the Revolution [CDRs], the militias, and the 1961 Literacy Campaign) kept the boundaries of the state constantly in a condition of flux and redefinition, while the changes in the Revolution's nature and direction, especially in the first six years, could not but act against the consolidation of a clear-cut new state.

The third challenging factor refers to these changes. Especially as the process redirected itself again after 1965, it became increasingly useful to understand the process less in terms of "Communism" (with all that the term meant in the mid-1960s) than in terms of "revolution." The question is not simply semantic; as the Revolution formally defined itself as socialist (beginning in April 1961) and then Marxist (after December 1961), it arrived at this definition not from a familiarity with, or influence by, existing models but, rather, from a radicalized nationalism that had driven the insurrection, shaped the early nature, and continued to affect the patterns of representation, participation, and action. Hence, when the rebel leaders (apart perhaps from the ex-PSP activists who brought their own, more orthodox, ideas to the process) spoke of "socialism" or "Communism" they envisaged less the systems prevailing in Warsaw, Beijing, or even Hanoi (although sympathies were decidedly with the latter),[5] and more the socialists of Cuban history, of Mella, of Martínez Villena,[6] and, in the case of Guevara, of the act of creating an objective revolution out of the subjective conditions (Gerassi 1968, 136–37). Indeed only Guevara and perhaps Raúl Castro of the ex-guerrillas thought of a recognizable socialism, with Che challenging Soviet orthodoxy in so many ways.

Yet, once the Revolution was under way, the demands of the "siege" created their own imperatives for the vanguard, who then articulated their belief in the unity and integration inherent in *cubanía* and in the inheritance from Martí (Kapcia 2000) to shape a resistant consensus out of a process of change.[7] Hence the evolving revolutionary state was one with a constantly shifting society at its core, where all organizations had political connotations and purposes and all political structures had, by definition, social implications. The well of commitment and simple peer pressure that drove the mobilizations of the 1960s was every bit as significant as any coercive power of a still inchoate state, continuing to blur and fuse the boundaries between the state and civil society. Indeed, so intent was the Revolution on its characteristic patterns of mobilization that any attempt to construct a monolithic state was resisted and undermined by the processes of involvement (Karol 1970).

In the 1970s and 1980s, however, a separation between state and civil society became slightly discernible. While the process of institutionalization after 1975 (Mesa-Lago 1978), under a more powerful Communist Party led by people who had been activists in the PSP prior to 1959 and Soviet-trained

Setting the Stage for a Discussion of Cuban Civil Society / 23

"technocrats," tried to construct a stable and strong state, the deceleration of the process, coupled with the effects of the earlier educational and social changes, began to create a more stable social fabric, with strengths in education but without the constant recourse to mobilization. It was, indeed, these changes that ultimately shaped the drive for rectification after 1986.[8] At that time, the perception became clear that a stronger state had also created new problems—privilege, a lack of accountability, and a new inertia (Habel 1991, 79–115)—while the only real resistance to these problems came from below through individual "foot-dragging" (Eckstein 1994, 10 passim), or from collective grumbling through weakened institutions such as the CDRs, or from political groups associated with the momentum of the process of the 1960s.

Given that Rectification, led by those groups and stimulated by a familiar desire to open up the closed areas to a fuller debate, looked back to the 1960s for inspiration, it is valid here to address the critical questions of participation, ideology, and debate that had characterized the early political system in Cuba and that were now seen by the "rectifiers" as elements to be recovered. Moreover, given also that the subsequent drive (after the crisis of 1989–91) to reassert the "essence" of the Revolution also sought inspiration in the 1960s, and that some of the changes after 1993 were based on that process, we clearly need to understand the essential nature of that early system.

A starting point for that understanding is the role of ideology, the Revolution's ideological underpinning being fundamental to its success and eventual path (Kapcia 1989). Here, of course, the focus is less about Marxism and more about nationalism and *cubanía* (Kapcia 2000), although there was little visible antagonism to the United States. Instead, the rebel movement's discourse focused on concepts such as *tiranía* (tyranny) and corruption, concepts that were as essentially nationalist as any anti-Americanism, striking at the heart of the Cuban-U.S. relationship, which in turn defined the Cuban state.

These concepts were nationalist, first, because the *Batistato* (Batista dictatorship) of the 1950s was the corrupt and repressive reincarnation of the once legitimate leader, and, second, because endemic corruption had, from the outset of the questionably independent state, grown out of the instabilities created by the Platt Amendment and the opportunities created by the relationship with the United States. Hence, *tiranía* and corruption became signifiers for the notion that something was essentially wrong within Cuba.

Thus, beginning in 1959, the growing national sense of shame and desire for renewal were accelerated by developments: U.S. opposition to popular reforms, the growing sense of national unity, the movements toward involvement and defense, the departure of a U.S.-bound largely white middle class, and above all the increasing isolation that the "siege" induced from late 1960. In this context, nationalism meant several things: greater unity (and conformity) to create the Revolution despite austerity, siege, and shortage; a sense of national pride as Cuba challenged both superpowers and then, after 1975, launched its campaign for "internationalism;"[9] and a sense of belonging to an embattled enclave whose righteous claims to independence and revolution were a fulfillment of a historic destiny.

Participation was therefore fundamental. Starting with the largely unplanned mechanisms of 1959–61, the manifestations were developed with more deliberation, as with the mass organizations such as those for women (Federación de Mujeres Cubanas [Federation of Cuban Women], FMC), private farmers (Asociación Nacional de Agricultores Pequeños [National Association of Small Farmers], ANAP), and youth (Unión de Jóvenes Comunistas [Union of Communist Youth], UJC); and the Federación de Estudiantes Universitarios [University Students' Federation], FEU). Hence, by the time the Cuban Communist Party emerged in 1965 and even for some time thereafter (as the party remained small, with fifty thousand members at best [Domínguez 1978, 321; Azicri 1988, 79]), and also remained without a clear national forum until 1975), the majority of the Cuban population was being regularly mobilized in a range of both structured and ad hoc organizations, geared to defense, work, and political campaigning. The motivations behind this participation were mixed and evolving but were essentially rooted in a number of critical factors.

The first was the simple fact that the early days were decidedly participatory, with strikes, occupations, rallies, and a general mobilization. In the initial institutional vacuum (as the old state collapsed), habits of involvement were created that many wished to continue, not least to maintain the momentum of empowerment. Second, participation was generally seen as integral to the Revolution's drive to rebuild the nation, consciously trying to achieve the historically elusive Cuba Libre.[10] Hence, participation also enabled the leadership to define the Revolution as something essentially different from the preceding system, which had been characterized by divisions, inequalities, and disintegration. Third, the leadership saw participation as essential to gathering, cementing, and then activating popular support for the collective project, especially as the embargo and the exodus of the middle class deprived the Revolution of vital skilled expertise in the task of building a new system and economy. In this sense, therefore, participation also ensured a constant mobilization for defense; as the "siege" descended and the invasion was realized, embedding itself in the collective memory, it became increasingly important to organize the Cuban citizenry into the collective task of defending gains. Here, the mechanisms of participation were important less for their defensive effectiveness than for their political benefits, giving ordinary Cubans a role and a stake in the emerging system. Finally, of course, participation enabled

Setting the Stage for a Discussion of Cuban Civil Society / 25

the ex-guerrilla leaders to translate the struggle in the Sierra into a model that saw the whole nation both as one gigantic *foco* (guerrilla unit) and as the context for the creation of the New Man, the myth that both emerged from and shaped the political structures and culture, above all as articulated by Che Guevara (Guevara 1987).

The third characteristic of the early Revolution was its patterns of debate. However beguiling the image of the Cuban system as monolithic and coercive, this description is a simplification, ignoring the patterns of evolution, the tensions within the activist structures, and the reality of discussion and dissent. Instead, we should see a revolutionary process that has operated in accordance with a repeated pattern of evolution: of certainty, crisis, debate. Hence, instead of reading the bewildering policy changes since 1959 as a zigzag process, with a focus on factions (Mesa-Lago 1978, 7 passim) or on the temperamental nature of leadership (Gonzalez 1974), we should see an essential continuity in a cycle resulting from Cuba's economic weakness as a small dependent primary-producing country. According to this interpretation, the Revolution, between 1959 and 1990, followed a trajectory in which evolution continued until a point of crisis (resulting from policies followed during that evolutionary period or from external factors), after which reassessment and "debate" (in search of possible alternatives and explanations) then led to a period of certainty and further evolution, until the next crisis.

While the periods of radical change or consolidation are recognized by most observers, and while the crises were familiar to all, the intervening debates are mostly ignored, apart from the more public ones (notably the "Great Debate" of 1963–65, or the 1985–87 debates of Rectification). One reason for this neglect is, of course, the underlying expectation that Communist systems, and Cuba in particular, do not tolerate debate, dissent, or differences. Here, therefore, one must both reiterate the caveat against applying Eastern European paradigms to the Cuban case and recommend a more nuanced analysis than the appealingly simple focus on Castro as *caudillo*, despot, or Saddam-like controller.

Another reason for this neglect, however, is that debates are rarely obvious to the outsider, being always held *within* the system. In addition, they are enclosed (and often behind closed doors, metaphorically and literally) rather than open, private rather than public, and rarely as decisive or as total as one would expect. Essentially they follow Castro's much misunderstood dictum, in June 1961, in his "Palabras a los Intelectuales": "dentro de la Revolución, todo, contra la Revolución, nada" [within the Revolution, everything; against the Revolution, nothing] (Castro Ruz 1980, 14). This position, which was from the outset often interpreted as ambiguous, sinister, and threatening (Cabrera Infante 1994, 70), conceding nothing real, was not simply a mollifying sop to troubled intellectuals (in the wake of the bitter wrangles around the film *PM* and the magazine *Lunes de Revolución*). It was a recognition of an underlying reality of an existing process at all levels, by which, within the enclosed confines of loyalty to the Revolution, several points of view could be expressed, especially when requested in the face of crisis. At the same time, any attempt to take the debate outside those confines, to a public position, ran the risk of weakening the process; certainly open opposition, criticism, and dissent were unacceptable as long as the Revolution was seen as threatened from without. In a real sense, that principle had, indeed, operated in the debates of the leadership meetings in Tarará of early 1959, when a small group of ex-guerrillas, ex-urban rebels, PSP members, and others gathered regularly to plan radicalization in a range of areas (Szulc 1986, 381), not least the land reform law of May 1959 and an overall strategy for revolution.

Similarly, the tenor of the more open discussions around *Lunes* and the other poles of the cultural revolution (Casa de las Américas and the Instituto Cubano de Arte e Industria Cinematográficos [Cuban Film Institute], ICAIC) fitted this description. Until the circumstances changed with external conflict, growing radicalization, and the rise within the cultural authorities of those associated with the old PSP, the debates were indeed open and wide ranging, seeking to define the role of culture within the Revolution and the role of the Revolution within culture.

The subsequent periods of debate have also fitted this pattern. The most closed was possibly that arising from the attempt by Aníbal Escalante and others to shift the Revolution in a more orthodox direction in 1961–62 by stacking the new directorate of the Organizaciones Revolucionarias Integradas (ORI, or Integrated Revolutionary Organizations) with former activists in the PSP.[11] It was closed principally because of sensitivities about U.S. pressure and Soviet interest. However, this was followed by the most open debate, which was waged in 1962–65 at the behest of the leaders in the pages of the ideological and economic journals about the future and nature of a Cuban socialist economic development strategy. The nature of that debate was astonishing; Trotskyists, pro-Soviet economists, eastern European reformists, ex-leaders of the PSP, and above all Che Guevara debated openly until the discussion was formally settled in 1965 by Castro's decision on the economic path to be followed.

The next significant period of debate, following the disastrous *zafra* (sugar harvest) of 1970, was less open, again because of Soviet sensitivities and the sense of disillusion that affected those who had enlisted in the mobilizations to achieve the elusive ten-million ton goal. Hence, although the debate did indeed rage within the political vanguard, resulting in the process of institutionalization, that same freedom did not extend to the cultural vanguard, which,

Setting the Stage for a Discussion of Cuban Civil Society / 27

beginning in 1971, began to feel the pressure of orthodoxy in the *quinquenio gris* (five gray years), which effectively brought down a veil over the more adventurous aspects of Cuban culture.[12] The last debate before the Special Period set in was that associated with the Rectification drive from 1986. This time the pattern of 1970–75 was reversed. The political debate (but decidedly not its effects) took place behind closed doors, notably at the two sessions of the Third Congress and at the hundreds of grass-roots party *núcleo* (branch) meetings that preceded both sessions (Kapcia 1987). Meanwhile the cultural world found itself invited by the new minister of culture, Armando Hart, to reassess all aspects of previous cultural policy and criticize itself rigorously and openly.

Throughout, two features of the debates were consistent. The first was that the "losers" in any one debate rarely found themselves excluded politically, condemned to humiliating obscurity or imprisoned, unless, like Escalante, they had transgressed enough to challenge the authority of the vanguard and the leaders. Even he, in 1962, was simply expelled to Eastern Europe, although his second transgression in 1968 (with the so-called *microfacción* affair) did lead to his long-term imprisonment.[13] Instead, the pattern was largely that those on the defeated "side" were kept within the system, without access to power and authority but not disgraced or marginalized completely; hence, when the next debate or crisis came along, they could be called into service again, their opinion sought and perhaps even rehabilitated effectively. Certainly, those defeated in 1961 and 1962–65 returned after 1975 to direct the economic strategy and dominate the political structure. Also, those intellectuals who were associated with Guevarist ideas in the late 1960s and marginalized after 1975 were restored to positions of academic and political authority after 1986. Indeed, one significant characteristic of the Revolution has always been the absence of major splits in the leadership (comparable to Soviet Russia or China); instead, the inner core of the Cuban leadership has maintained a remarkable unity since 1959, the only departures coming through age, death, or the changes of the 1990s. Supposedly high-level and high-publicity defections have generally tended to be by activists who were much lower down in the system; usually, in fact, they were defecting precisely because of their exclusion or marginalization. While this pattern obviously reflects loyalties within a small group of leaders who have shared struggles since 1953, it also reflects a deeper set of principles and values.

This indeed is the second consistent feature of the debates: their motivation. The desire to maintain a necessary balance between open and closed discussions has been driven by various motives: by a need for constant unity (to prevent damaging splits, shore up defenses, and reflect the underlying ideological imperative), by the underlying belief that Cuba's solutions to crisis can best be found from within the nation's own human resources, by the pragmatic need not to alienate those whose support is necessary and whose contribution may well be later essential, and by the increasing faith in the principle of "democratic centralism," which, for all its Marxist-Leninist origins, reflected a strong current of thinking within the *cubanía* prior to 1959.

The 1990s, however, presented the Cuban leadership with a totally new set of challenges. First, the crisis immediately weakened the Cuban state, as shortages undermined its ability to manage and protect. This meant an inevitable process of even more fundamental reassessment, readjustment, and even retreat from earlier positions, and an accompanying redefinition not just of ideological underpinnings and economic priorities but also of the boundaries of the state and the system. Simultaneously, however, rather than strengthening an alternative "civil society," the same crisis and the subsequent reforms saw social unity and cohesiveness begin to disintegrate in the face of multiple individual battles to survive, an atomization of perspectives, and a growth of individualism rather than collectivism and solidarity. However, by the late 1990s, a new phenomenon was beginning to emerge from the ashes: a new concept of *solidarismo* (practice of, or belief in, solidarity), which had political connotations (in the revived willingness to rally in support of campaigns) and social connotations, in an awareness of the responsibility to solve social problems and support those left out of the partial recovery and the new dollar-based economy. It was *solidarismo* rather than collectivism because it came not from a notion of equality (which was under threat from the changes) but of social responsibility, and thus it was related to older (and *martiano*) concepts of moral and social duty, and even religious values. Indeed, it was this concept of *solidarismo* that began to provide a social cement as the country pulled out of the worst of the recession, counterbalancing the discontent, the individualizing tendencies and pressures, and the disillusionment with the previously beneficent state. Hence, alongside the clearly atomized tendencies in the run-down parts of Centro Habana (the site of the most serious disturbances in August 1994), one could see a *solidario* effort to rebuild and refurbish housing, driven by an alliance of the state (without the manpower to rebuild but willing to provide the resources), the cultural world (in the form of architects), and local residents.

This is important because, if *solidarismo* exists, it challenges assumptions about the supposed emergence of a civil society in the vacuum of the 1990s as something new and essentially opposed to the state. Indeed, what seems to be happening in the Cuba of 2000–2007 may well be more a revision of the old forms of participation than a new form of self-expression against the state.

This is because studies of the apparently state-imposed mobilization systems of the 1960s and 1970s have perhaps ignored two important features of the

Cuban system. The first is that mechanisms introduced from above have often been gradually appropriated from below; this has certainly been the case with the CDRs and the People's Councils, both of whose functions have evolved organically and empirically beyond their original purposes. The second is that all new mechanisms of participation and representation have tended not to replace previous mechanisms but, rather, to accompany them, with the exception of the Poder Local (Local Power) of the 1960s. The result has been confusion at times, with ordinary Cubans being unclear on the differences between, and hierarchy of, the various structures. But, more importantly, the "layers" of mechanisms led to the creation of gaps in the interstices between the different structures and mechanisms, gaps wherein Cubans have either resisted (Eckstein 1994, 199 passim) or negotiated political space. Hence, it seems likely that the new forms and *solidarismo* are not simply another flexible adaptation to the new circumstances, but are essentially a renegotiation of those spaces and thus a new arrangement between an existing (and not new) civil society and a still legitimate (rather than challenged) state.

The new challenges of the 1990s, however, presented the Cuban leadership and the Revolution's loyal activists with an urgent need to redefine everything, including the Revolution itself. This was necessary because the new threats from Washington and from the dollar and the new social demands of a less actively loyal population had to be met by "saving the Revolution's soul" (as it was often expressed), which meant first of all discovering, defining, and then redefining what that "soul" actually was. Hence, between 1991 and 1996, the Revolution was pared down to its basics not only economically, but also politically and ideologically. This meant reducing the characteristic mobilization to a minimum, a decision enforced by the grass-roots reality that, given the daily demands of survival, ordinary Cubans were anyway unable and unwilling to participate in rallies and the usual rituals of participation and belonging. Therefore, the revolutionary leaders faced a dilemma: if they insisted on mobilization on the old scale, they risked alienation (of even fully committed Cubans) and visible discredit, as once million-strong rallies would be replaced by pale shadows of their former glory; yet, if they neglected the old rallying mechanisms, they would have no weapons to resist the momentum of individualization or, with the reforms after 1993, of a creeping capitalism. What therefore tended to happen was a recourse to the minimum, using mobilization only in times of real stress or threat or asking the committed to rally as and when they could.

The former was most clearly seen in August 1994, when the days after the street disturbances saw thousands of citizens pour onto the Malecón (Havana's sea-front esplanade) in response to Castro's demands for expressions of support. While, as ever, this display was undoubtedly the result of pressure, exhortation, and the efforts of the mass organizations and the party itself (although the display itself was not an insignificant achievement in the light of the apparent stagnation of, and pressure on, the political system), it also evidently reflected a deeper unease among those Cubans, both the committed and the passively supportive, who, for all their complaints, stresses, and demoralization, saw the disturbances as posing an even greater threat to "the Revolution" (whatever that meant by 1994) than the economic crisis. The fact that the unrest was unprecedented was a concern in itself, posing all sorts of unanswered questions about the system's vulnerability and credibility, but this was compounded by the international reality. The disturbances occurred only two years after the passage of the Torricelli-Graham law, which tightened the embargo even more in a deliberate attempt to destabilize the political system and to bring about the Revolution's demise, and at a time when U.S. military intervention seemed imminent in Haiti to end unrest there and to stem the flow of boat-people to Florida. Hence, without the protection of a Soviet Union and with the Revolution demonstrably on its economic knees, the prospect of U.S. intervention and all that that implied (mass resistance, widespread violence, civic unrest, and the return of the émigrés to reclaim now shared property), and the feared end of the valued guarantees of social provision (fueled by the horror stories of Cubans returning from Eastern Europe after 1989), seemed real and frightening enough for ordinary Cubans to respond viscerally and emotionally to appeals for manifest support and for one last mass ritualization of belonging, even those highly critical of the leaders' failure to respond adequately to the crisis and those longing for some sort of economic opening to ease the pressure. Certainly, those demonstrations played their part in calming nerves, as did the decision to allow the disaffected to leave over the next two months and the emergency U.S.-Cuban migration agreements that guaranteed a safety valve of increased and orderly emigration. It was almost as though, having seen the scale of underlying support for the system, many Cubans (apart from the deeply disaffected, alienated, or dissident) were relieved to see how many of their fellow citizens shared their concern and their commitment, making their struggle and commitment less individual and lonely than they had begun to imagine.

This of course highlights another reality of the political system by 1994, namely that the concept "Revolución" had anyway begun to acquire dimensions that went beyond its original meaning. In the 1960s, it had meant the experiences of participation, social change, mobilization, and empowerment, as well as the collective sense of belonging to an exciting if frightening project of social transformation, enhanced by the "siege mentality" after 1961–62 but also by the reality of dramatic social improvement, especially in education and housing, both transforming the thinking and involvement of whole groups of Cubans hitherto unaffected directly by political life. In the 1970s and 1980s, however, Revolución had tended to become a concept that was somewhat more ritualized, amorphous, and perhaps even distant as an affective experience, but more present as a "system"; for the experience of the 1960s could rarely be defined as a "system" given the scale, speed, and destabilizing nature of the constant changes. Now, however, a clear system evolved with "institutionalization," transforming Revolución into something synonymous with "the state," on the one hand, and the political class, on the other.

The crisis of 1990–94, however, transformed Revolución again, tapping into the reserves of commitment, nationalism, and collective struggle from the early days but also building on the collective need to redefine in the face of threat. Now the term became increasingly synonymous not with "change" or collective struggle (as in the 1960s), since change was now frightening and the struggle individual, nor with "system" (as in the 1970s), since that was severely under threat and barely capable of organizing more than the minimum. Instead it became synonymous with *Patria*, "community," and "solidarity," given that the threats after 1990 were interpreted by many, if not most, Cubans as threats to a way of life that guaranteed certain basics of civilization and community and a certain freedom from crime and poverty, and as the end of a whole world of achievements (social, cultural, sporting, and even political) that had previously constituted something of which to be proud. Hence as the Revolution's leaders (and, curiously, even the erstwhile dissenting Catholic Church) began to see the new crisis as a worrying threat to social cohesion and unity and began to use a discourse of community, social responsibility, and solidarity, many Cubans began to respond to the crisis in nationalistic rather than Communist terms: the Revolución that people were being asked to defend was not necessarily a Communist system but a collective experience of nation building that had empowered many, created a new sense of belonging, and brought a sense of community.

Therefore, the U.S. administration's responses, in the Cuba Democracy Act (the Torricelli-Graham law) of 1992 and then the Cuban Liberty and Democratic Solidarity Act (the Helms-Burton law) of 1996, together with the strategies adopted by those Cuban-American émigrés who, eagerly expecting the system's collapse at any moment, engineered the Hermanos al Rescate incident of February 1996 and those incidents linked to the Havana hotel bombings in 1997, all played into the hands of this renewed nationalism. By attacking the Revolución, these émigrés could be portrayed as attacking the Patria and by supporting the embargo they could be seen as engaging in anti-patriotic activities. Hence, dissidents who increasingly came out into the open and, expecting U.S. support (especially after George W. Bush's election in November 2000), became more active in supporting Cuba's isolation, also succeeded in provoking a nationalist reaction among those very Cubans who might otherwise sympathize with some of their concrete demands and proposals, Cubans who might not wish to defend and preserve the political and economic system but who were clearly willing to protect the Revolución as Patria.

In the meantime, the demands on the committed activists went on at a low level. The *guardia nocturna* (night guard-duty) of the CDR continued, however ritualized this might be and however abused. Regular calls for *trabajo voluntario* (voluntary work) at weekends and during the summer were repeated with varying degrees of enthusiasm and success, and debate and mobilization were encouraged within the union confederation (Central de Trabajadores de Cuba, CTC), the Communist Party, and the UJC.

However, if mobilization was reduced, what became of the state during this period? Fundamentally, the state had three political functions: defense, regulation, and beneficence. Defense, of course, ranged from mobilization of military and reserve forces against real or imagined external threats (as in February 1996) to action against the growing, if still small, threat of petty crime that was engendered by the crisis and the subsequent reforms. This action took the form, among other things, of the enhancement of the CDRs (as the veterans of the new Asociación de Combatientes de la Revolución Cubana were enrolled in local *barrio* activity), and clampdowns on *jineterismo* (hustling) in January 1997 and then again in 2003–4. It also, however, extended to civil defense operations mobilized to great effect against tropical storms, most notably in November 2001 when, after an astonishingly effective evacuation, only three Cubans were killed by a storm that swept devastatingly across the island. Regulation referred above all to the economy, to the protection of the remaining significant public sector areas, to the provision of food and other supplies (via the freer but still regulated markets), and to the mitigation of the effects of the increasing economic opening from 1993. Beneficence, of course, referred to the guarantees of social provision, especially healthcare, education, employment, and welfare, all evident priorities in the "dark days" of 1990–94 in a campaign that played a fundamental part in ensuring continuing tolerance of if not support for the system. The latter became most visible in the remarkable campaign started in August 2001 to initiate what promised to become something of a second education revolution through a nationwide network of training schools designed to mop up potentially disaffected and delinquent youth by enrolling them as "stake-holders" in the system, working as teachers, social workers, nurses, and cultural educators.

By 1998, the effects of social provision and economic reform were sufficient to generate a visible recovery not only in economic performance (evident beginning in 1995) but also in political attitudes and confidence. In part this had been glimpsed as early as 1993, when electoral reforms seemed to produce a

Setting the Stage for a Discussion of Cuban Civil Society / 33

perhaps revealing increase in participation rates from the embarrassing and worrying lows of December 1992,[14] and then again after August 1994; however, the continuing external threats of 1996–97 helped postpone both political relaxation and confidence, those years being characterized again by a mood of vigilance, paranoia, and therefore restriction. January 1998, however, saw the political gamble of the pope's visit pay off with dramatic effect, as thousands of Cubans rallied in a moment of broadly based national celebration. There were committed revolutionaries who by no means shared the anti-Communist religious leader's worldviews but who saw his visit as external recognition and legitimization and welcomed his criticisms of the embargo; there were devout and orthodox believers who either opposed the system or managed to fuse passive support for the system with a loyalty to the Catholic Church; and also of course there were the thousands of *creyentes*, whose formal Catholicism belied an adherence to syncretic variants that acknowledged the pope but were in turn roundly disapproved of by him.

Between November 1999 and June 2000, that success was followed by the seminal campaign for the return of Elián González to Cuba from Florida, a campaign that transformed the nature, tone, and mechanisms of Cuban political life. In particular, the whole campaign struck a public chord among most Cubans, who responded organically and with little pressure to the appeals to notions of family and childhood, and among the many who shared histories of divided families and lost children from the early days of separation and exodus. This was enhanced by the fact that the majority of the campaign was led and carried out by young Cubans, chiefly through the three youth organizations (the UJC, the FEU, and the Federación de Estudiantes de la Enseñanza Media [Federation of Secondary School Students]) and their high-profile leaders, notably the UJC's Otto Rivero and the FEU's Hassan Pérez. Not only did this experience bring young Cubans back into the Revolution's political structures in ways and to an extent not seen since the 1960s, it also brought youth to the forefront of the political agenda, generating in particular the educational campaign beginning in August 2001. Moreover, the experience restored mobilization again as a characteristic mechanism of political involvement and socialization, generating a new culture of rallies and marches that both revived regular events such as the annual May Day rally and saw a return of the system's ability to "call out the troops" quickly and massively when faced with perceived threats, such as the public pressure with regard to the dissident Proyecto Varela in June 2002 and the Bush measures in May 2004 to tighten the embargo before the presidential elections in November.

It was, indeed, the campaign for Elián González that suddenly gave the Cuban political system a much-needed revival by focusing on youth and visibly incorporating youth organizations and leaders into the active political stage. This revival proved necessary in 2003 when two pressures combined to create a more unmanageable problem of dissidence. These pressures came principally from the Bush administration, which, taking advantage of the authority and momentum generated by the "war against terrorism," the rapid success of the invasion of Afghanistan, and the seemingly free hand in Iraq, began to use the U.S. Interests Section in Havana, under the new Bush appointee James Cason, as a base for disseminating funds, supplies, and written materials to dissident groups, officially to encourage civil society (against a supposedly repressive and weakened state). More importantly, this was done to engender sufficient unrest to provoke the Cuban authorities to react forcefully and thus play into Washington's hands in its new strategy of isolating Cuba for its repression of human rights, persuading its new and more pliant European allies to follow suit. This strategy was aided by the new discourse of the "axis of evil," which, implicitly and occasionally explicitly, was broadened to include Cuba, and by a sustained "black propaganda" campaign to portray Cuba as a potential manufacturer of (biological) "weapons of mass destruction." Meanwhile, domestic opposition in Cuba seized the opportunity offered by the new administration in Washington and the new discourse to come out into the open much more than before and challenge the system, especially through four activities: the anti-dialogue Asamblea, the various miniscule "human rights" organizations, and the two associated "movements" of "independent librarians" and "independent journalists." The latter two successfully presented themselves as a movement (rather than the reality of an array of individuals, not all of whom were professional journalists or librarians) and also attracted support from professional activist organizations in the United States and Europe. The combination of these two strategies, external and internal, was ultimately what provoked the Cuban government to clamp down on dissident activity in March and April 2003, leading to seventy-five long sentences and Cuba's condemnation in many world forums and capitals.

Yet this was, of course, as much about Cuban-U.S. relations and the ongoing war of words, propaganda, and annoyance between Havana and Washington as it was about any fractures in, or challenges to, the Cuban political system. That is to say that there was no real evidence in 2003 that the Cuban system was any more vulnerable to internal dissent and any more in a crisis of legitimacy than it had been in 1993. What had changed was the U.S. government.

This does, however, raise the question of dissidence and dissent in the Cuban system, a vexed question and one that is usually difficult to divorce from a priori positions and political expectations. The starting point for such a discussion must, however, be the fact that the Cuban system, as it has evolved, reacted, and adapted to changing circumstances, has managed dissent in dif-

Setting the Stage for a Discussion of Cuban Civil Society / 35

ferent ways, according to the degree of disagreement and the nature of the circumstances. Fundamentally, what is suggested is that one might better understand the treatment of dissent by seeing the system as a series of concentric circles, all defined by Castro's dictum of 1961 about all things being "within the Revolution."

The Cuban political culture has, from 1959 onward, been an essentially, and often surprisingly, inclusive culture; this inclusivity has been fundamental to its definition, survival, and legitimacy. This is, of course, surprising, because of its periodic recourse to coercion; because of outside, eastern European-oriented preconceptions about "Communist" systems; and because of its generally militant tone. Yet it is important to understand that its inclusiveness comes not from a liberal definition of pluralism (although this may well have been partly true in 1959–60, even among some of the leaders) or from a populist state (one of the occasional explanations of the nature of the system), but rather from an essentially historicist perspective of a "Cuban nation" as an "imagined community" (Anderson 1991). This notion was clearly rooted in those traditions, pressures, and sentiments that existed prior to 1953 but was reinforced from 1961 onward by the collective experience of shared struggle (through such seminal moments as Playa Girón [the Bay of Pigs invasion] and the Missile Crisis), by the "siege mentality" after 1961 that did so much to petrify as well as unite the system, and by the growing sense of embattlement, isolation, and shared growth after 1972. As essential part of that "imagining" has been the need to define the "community." In 1960–71 the definition tended to exclude those who chose to leave Cuba for the United States (and then, in official and popular eyes, conspire with the United States against the Revolution). In 1962–68 it excluded, or marginalized, those who "conspired" with the Soviet Union to shift the Revolution onto a more orthodox and controllable path. After 1985, it excluded those who now sided with Gorbachev but were generally seen as guilty of association with practices and perspectives that had constituted the "errors and negative tendencies" of 1975–85. Yet, in fact, these "exclusions" were not equal. Only the émigrés of 1960–71 were seen as beyond the pale, as not subsequently includable within a definition of community (at least until they too were allowed back, as *gusanos* become *mariposas* in 1979).[15] The "heretics" of 1962–68 or 1975–85 were in fact never excluded totally but, as with all "debates," were shunted aside and kept for future reference and use. For, while the émigrés of the 1960s were, for some time at least, outside the outer circle of the "community," the ex-PSP activists or the pro-Soviet sympathizers actually belonged to circles within the "community" but outside the trusted inner core.

Throughout the Revolution, "community" has effectively been defined by these circles. At times of external threat, exaggerated fear, or internal crisis, the definition has necessarily been restricted to the innermost circle or circles, occasionally only trusting those who, for example, shared the struggle in the Sierra, or, increasingly, considering as "the nation" those who chose to remain, who participated in the regular rituals of belonging and support. However, at other times, usually of relative calm, détente, and economic success, this inclusiveness has been broadened, even including the hitherto excluded émigrés. Only with the 1990s was that pattern broken as the newly engendered visceral and popular identification between Revolución and Patria allowed the Cuban government to extend the definition of "nation" and "community" beyond the narrow confines of the inner circles that previously would have been the case at times of crisis to encompass even the Catholic Church and other churches, including *santería*, and the émigré community (and with the 1994–95 Nación y Emigración conferences). Indeed, it was this definition that made the pope's visit logical and even necessary to cement national unity and redefine the "community" at a time when the sense of crisis was declining and when the emerging "feel-good factor" could be used to good effect; in a clear sense, what was being done here was to define as "nation" and "community" all those who, in the phrase used in 1961, were not *contra*.

The point here is that, within this variable definition of "community," dissent has been treated variably, with the genuine opposition's capacity to challenge being attenuated by a range of structural factors: the system's ready recourse to mass emigration at moments of stress (notably during the Mariel exodus of 1980 and again in August 1994); the pervasive efficacy of the CDR system; the government's use of infiltrators within opposition groups; and, most fatally of all, the recurrent tendency for all opposition groups to fragment continually, not least in the face of opportunities that arise to "come in from the cold" and be reintegrated through some understanding or dialogue. Hence, the Cuban government's claim that opposition has been minimal over the years and linked to the United States or to political activists in Miami has often not been without foundation, since the active and relatively united opposition has frequently been found in Miami rather than in Havana, a status that immediately presents the opposition with problems of legitimacy inside Cuba, where its standard depiction as counterrevolutionary and therefore anti-patriotic has often struck a greater chord than one might expect.

In 2003, however, the delicate balancing act of community defining was unbalanced by external factors, and the dissident activists overstepped the boundaries of tolerance, not least by becoming so directly associated with a U.S. administration that was seen by many Cubans as openly aggressive and as threatening domestic social peace. This reaction of the Cubans not only allowed the government to act against the dissidents with a higher than normal degree of popular credibility, citing national security at a time of crisis and threat, but also acknowledged the dissidents' transgression of the normal rules

Setting the Stage for a Discussion of Cuban Civil Society / 37

of the game, according to which dissident activity is either tolerated broadly but harassed in the particular or is restricted for long periods until circumstances change.

This then finally returns us to the question of the state, the other side of the state–civil society coin, the side that in debates on Cuban civil society tends occasionally to be ignored or to be subject to preconceptions. What is suggested here is that, in the light of the evidence of a less monolithic and more complex structure, the "state" be reconsidered, less in terms of a strong-weak dichotomy or a repressive-permissive paradigm and more in terms of its efficacy and its legitimacy. Efficacy, of course, refers primarily to the state's principal functions in Cuba, namely in getting social provision adequately and more or less equally to the people for most of the time and in affording protection against external threat or internal disorder. In this sense, the Cuban state has broadly, since 1959 and even after 1990, been successful, less perhaps because of its formal structures and Leviathan nature than through its subtle linkages between the formal and the informal. The Cuban state, like many but perhaps more so than most, uses its informal resources as well as its formal ones (just as the formal economy uses the informal to cover those areas that the formal economy cannot cover adequately). These informal resources consist of family networks (often overlooked by external observers), émigrés, local and broader solidarities, local survival networks, and even semi-legal informal supply mechanisms, not necessarily replacing the state, as many after 1993 seemed to believe and even desire, but reinforcing and legitimizing the state, reflecting the state's hidden and underlying legitimacy.

That legitimacy is not a simple matter of open support, loyalty, or belief. Often for most Cubans it is a question of a willingness not to challenge the state or rebel and to ritualize adherence through elections (however predictable the outcome), celebrations, or *trabajo voluntario*. Hence, appropriation of state mechanisms (as we have seen, a constant feature of the Cuban system) should also perhaps be interpreted as a strength of the Cuban state as well as a weakness, and the efficacy of civil defense at critical moments may actually tell us much about the underlying legitimacy of a state that performs when needed, unlike, for example, the Mexican state in 1985 or the Nicaraguan state in 1972, wherein the inadequate and blatantly unequal treatment meted out highlighted and provoked a serious loss of credibility in the system and thence in the governments.

Notes

1. This loose organization of a large number of small dissident groupings was created in 2003 as a deliberate challenge to the more pro-dialogue groups gathered around the so-called Varela Project, led by Osvaldo Payá; it was led above all by the former

economist Martha Beatriz Roque and closely linked from the outset with both the U.S. diplomatic corps in Havana and Miami-based Cuban-American activists.

2. The Platt Amendment was the source of the wording inserted by pressure from the occupation authorities onto the Cuban Constitutional Convention and into the forthcoming republic's embryonic Constitution, effectively legitimizing the post-1902 neocolonial control of Cuba by the United States; the 1903 treaty (the republic's first) tied Cuba into a relationship with the U.S. economy, exporting raw sugar and importing manufactured goods, thus providing the economic counterpart to the amendment.

3. The 1934 Reciprocity Treaty effectively updated the 1903 version; although the terms of the Platt Amendment were abrogated in 1934, the U.S.-Cuban link was now cemented by the new U.S. sugar quota system, which allocated shares of the U.S. market to preferred producers, including Cuba.

4. These dramatic changes came about because of the urban reform laws of 1959–60 and the process of replacing the fleeing middle class by poorer residents of Havana, who moved into the vacated properties of the middle class and changed the residential patterns of former bourgeois areas.

5. The PSP was the Partido Socialista Popular, the name taken by the Communist Party after 1944. In 1958 it formally joined the rebel alliance under the 26 July Movement.

6. Julio Antonio Mella was a former radical student leader who co-founded the Communist Party in 1925, opposed President Machado, and was killed (probably by Machado's agents) in Mexico in 1929; the poet Rubén Martínez Villena led the party beginning in 1927.

7. José Martí was the leader of the rebellion against Spain in 1895; he died in battle within weeks of the uprising's start. After his death, he rapidly became raised to the status of "national hero," influencing subsequent generations of Cuban radicals and leaving a vast body of writings and ideas, as well as an example.

8. In 1986, the Third Congress of the Communist Party formalized the process of "Rectification of Past Errors and Negative Tendencies," a thorough reassessment of the party's membership and policies.

9. "Internationalism" was the policy, from the mid-1970s onward, of sending material and personnel on aid missions to dozens of Third World countries.

10. *Cuba Libre* was the slogan and ideal of the rebels in Cuba's two wars of independence (1868–78 and 1895–98), which was taken up as the symbol of a frustrated independence after 1902.

11. The ORI was the umbrella organization set up in 1960 for the three rebel groups that came to power, the 26 July Movement, the PSP, and the Directorio Revolucionario 13 de Marzo; Escalante was given the task of establishing its structures.

12. This period of cultural restriction followed the notorious Padilla case of 1968–71 (and the fierce debates about intellectuals that it generated) and the Congress on Education and Culture of 1971.

13. The *microfacción* affair occurred when Escalante, having returned to Cuba from Moscow, was accused of leading a faction seeking to change Cuba's political, economic, and ideological direction to one more amenable to Moscow.

14. In the municipal elections that month the lowest turnout since 1976 was recorded.

15. A change in rhetoric occurred, whereby, after years of being disparaged in public discourse as *gusanos* (worms, or grubs), those émigrés who took advantage of the improved relations after 1977 to return to Cuba on family visits in 1979 were referred to as *mariposas* (butterflies).

References

Anderson, B. 1991. *Imagined Communities: Reflection on the Origin and Spread of Nationalism*. London and New York: Verso.

Azicri, M. 1988. *Cuba: Politics, Economics, and Society*. London and New York: Pinter Publishers.

Cabrera Infante, G. 1994. *Mea Cuba*. London: Faber and Faber.

Castro Ruz, F. 1980. "Palabras a los Intelectuales." In *Revolución, Letras, Arte*, edited by Varios, 7–30. Havana: Editorial Letras Cubanas.

Dominguez, J. I. 1978. *Cuba: Order and Revolution*. Cambridge, Mass., and London: Harvard University Press, Belknap Press.

Eckstein, S. E. 1994. *Back from the Future: Cuba under Castro*. Princeton, N.J.: Princeton University Press.

Gerassi, J. (ed.) 1968. *Venceremos. The Speeches and Writings of Ernesto Che Guevara*. London: Weidenfeld & Nicolson.

Gonzalez, E. 1974. *Cuba under Castro: The Limits of Charisma*. Boston and London: Houghton Mifflin.

Guevara, E. 1987. "Socialism and Man in Cuba." In *Che Guevara and the Cuban Revolution: Writings and Speeches of Ernesto Che Guevara*, edited by David Deutschmann, 246–61. Sydney: Pathfinder.

Habel, J. 1991. *Cuba: The Revolution in Peril*. New York and London: Verso.

Hernández, R. 2003. *Looking at Cuba: Essays on Culture and Civil Society*. Gainesville: University Press of Florida.

Kapcia, A. 1987. "Back to Basics: The Deferred Session of the Third Congress of the Cuban Communist Party." *Journal of Communist Studies* 3, no. 3 (September): 311–13.

———. 1989. "Martí, Marxism, and Morality: The Evolution of an Ideology of Revolution." In *Cuba after Thirty Years: Rectification and the Revolution*, edited by Richard Gillespie, 161–83. London: Frank Cass.

———. 2000. *Cuba: Island of Dreams*. Oxford: Berg.

Karol, K. S. 1970. *Guerrillas in Power: The Course of the Cuban Revolution*. New York: Hill and Wang.

Mesa-Lago, C. 1978. *Cuba in the 1970s: Pragmatism and Institutionalization*. Albuquerque: University of New Mexico Press.

Szulc, T. 1986. *Fidel: A Critical Portrait*. London, Melbourne, Auckland, and Johannesburg: Hutchinson.

Tester, K. 1992. *Civil Society*. London and New York: Routledge.

2

Civil Society

The Cuban Debate

MICHELLE MARÍN-DOGAN

It is widely accepted in Cuba that the debate about civil society was one of the great debates of the 1990s. During this decade there was a boom in interest in civil society and an explosion in the use and study of the term within Cuban intellectual circles (Monal 1999; Acanda 1996). According to one Cuban analyst, such reflection represented the conceptual renovation of a term that was in need of critical rescue, having been "continually distorted" within socialist thought during the last quarter of the twentieth century (Alonso Tejada 1996, 119–20). By the end of the decade, the political scientist Miguel Limia David argued that interest in the theme was little short of "an intoxication," which, he perceived, could not last much longer. In his view, people were quite simply "drunk on civil society" (Limia David 1999, 175). Speaking in 2003, another key figure in the Cuban intellectual world, Fernando Martínez Heredia, claimed that the debate on civil society had become "an adornment" and was no longer "profound."[1] Martínez suggested that there were other more important questions to be discussed in Cuba that had been pushed to one side or overshadowed by the interest in civil society.[2] However, on 4 April 2003 and amid much publicity, a new book by the Cuban philosopher Jorge Luis Acanda was launched. It was entitled *Civil Society and Hegemony* (2002). With its arrival, Acanda deftly moved the theme of civil society back toward the center of debate in Cuba. Over a decade after it first began to intoxicate its Cuban audience, civil society was back on the agenda.

The Contours of the Debate

The fertile debate that evolved in Cuba around the theme of civil society can be traced within publications and through discussions held on the subject by research centers and Cuban NGOs whose findings were later disseminated publicly via journals and cultural magazines.[3] Like their counterparts elsewhere, Cuban analysts concentrated on the philosophical controversies surrounding civil society and on issues of conceptual definition. The provenance of the idea was an important matter for many, particularly those socialist thinkers who were accustomed to regarding civil society as a liberal term. Most contributors traced the intellectual lineage of the concept from the early contributions of Hobbes and Locke—at times making reference to Rousseau en route—to Hegel and then on to Marx and Gramsci (see Valdés Hernández and Estrella Márquez 1994; Acanda 1996, 2002; Limia David 1997; Recio Silva 1997, 1999; Fung Riverón 2000). Others examined the relevance of the concept for what they called the "concrete" or "actually existing" internal situation of contemporary and, more occasionally, historical Cuba (Alonso Tejada 2000; López Vigil 1997), while still others balanced the two approaches, offering fascinating insights into both (Hernández 1994, 1999a; Azcuy Henríquez 1995; Alonso Tejada 1996; Dilla Alfonso and Oxhorn 1998). All, through their contributions to the debate, enriched the very dynamic that was both their focus and their impetus for reflection: the reactivation of a vibrant public space, populated by an ever more diverse range of actors and groups, provoked by the economic, political, and social changes of the Special Period.

The debate was by no means confined to academic circles, nor was it heard solely within the ambit of the social sciences. Rather it spilled over and was taken up by other actors within Cuban civil society, most notably by the new development NGOs that had emerged during the late 1980s, the Cuban Catholic Church, and the *políticos* of the party (the Partido Comunista de Cuba [PCC], or the Cuban Communist Party [CCP]) and state. In addition, key cultural figures increasingly began to use and analyze the concept in public spaces. In a more general sense, the theme of civil society moved toward the center of public opinion as the 1990s progressed, a fact borne out by the sheer number and range of publications that began to run articles taking civil society as their focus, including *La Gaceta de Cuba, Temas, Granma, Envío, Marx Ahora*, and *Revista Casa de las Américas*, to name just a handful.

Although academics, bureaucrats, politicians, and activists were all talking about "civil society," they by no means shared the same opinion of the concept, nor were they all convinced of its suitability or relevance for Cuba's experiences during the last decade of the twentieth century. Hence, although civil society provided a shared language with which to enter the debate, it did not bring with it a shared understanding of desirable outcomes or how these were to be achieved.

The primary cause of controversy among scholars engaged in the debate was the degree of ambiguity surrounding the term itself (see Azcuy Henríquez 1995; Dilla Alfonso and Oxhorn 1998; Monal 1999; Acanda 2002). Monal (1999) argues that since its birth in early liberal thought, civil society has been an ambiguous concept. Likewise, Acanda (2002) talks of "the heterogeneity of the dissimilar processes" that have been labeled as civil society and the "diversity of meanings" and "breadth, ambiguity, and imprecise utilization" that the concept started to have in the 1990s, as much in the social sciences as in political discourse, "after being forgotten for almost 120 years" (Acanda 2002, 317). In Marxist theory the term had not been merely "forgotten" but had, for decades, been fiercely anathematized (Dilla Alfonso 1999). Added to this, the reinvention of civil society as the rallying call of those struggling against Soviet-style regimes in Eastern Europe in the 1980s and its adoption in the 1990s by the U.S. government as part of an overt strategy aimed at subverting the Cuban Revolution, made the concept a difficult one for Cuban analysts to use. However, for many in Cuba, the key debate regarding the role of civil society has revolved around the issues of how to restructure the hegemony of revolutionary socialist power on the island and how to continue legitimizing it. As such, civil society has been identified as an important space for "the rearticulation of consensus" (Dilla Alfonso 1999, 161). Those who adopt this perspective suggest that strengthening civil society would not imply weakening the Communist Party or government as the United States would have us believe.

The ambiguities, contradictions, and disorientating array of interpretations from both liberal and Marxist sources, not to mention the general lack of familiarity with the term among Cuban scholars, added to the confusion surrounding "civil society" both as an idea and a social phenomenon in Cuba. It is ironic that at a time of great uncertainty as to the future direction of the country, an idea charged with similar ambiguities and uncertainties was the subject of such close attention and, moreover, that for some the phenomenon of Cuban civil society was considered to offer the key to rebuilding Cuba's political consensus in the midst of a deep economic crisis.

Can we identify any general tendencies that have characterized the Cuban debate? First, in contrast to the eastern European debate of the late 1980s, there was a broad rejection by Cuban analysts of those neoliberal interpretations of civil society that came to dominance following the revolutions of 1989 (see Kaldor 2003). Though acknowledging that civil society can be differentiated from the state, most Cuban analysts argued that this difference need not necessarily represent an antagonism. In fact, the majority of those who participated in the debate discussed the problem of the dichotomy between the state and civil society by pointing out that the portrayal of state and civil society as two independent spheres in polar opposition to each other raised particular problems for socialist interpretations. Many Cuban analysts considered the clear separation of public and private spaces to be false. Public space, with its maximum representation in the state as the only bearer of political relations and interests, was seen to be a conceptually flawed interpretation, in the same way that a vision of civil society as the ambit of the private sphere where such relations are not established was also dismissed. Most analysts agreed that civil society is an area that is internally contradictory, as it is in civil society that differences and confrontations of diverse types, including those of class, race, ethnicity, generations, gender, culture, and politics, are produced and reproduced. As such, civil society is perceived to be an area permanently in multiple and complex relations with the state.

Those interested in the philosophical aspects of the debate examined how civil society was originally conceptualized in classical texts, emphasizing that in the work of Hobbes and Locke civil society and the state are not conceived as separate realms. Second, and in much the same way as elsewhere, the debate in Cuba was characterized by contradictions and disputes in the interpretation of fundamental texts. While most claimed that it was Hegel who first introduced a harsh distinction between state and civil society, this position was by no means universally accepted, and Alonso Tejada (1996) for one was at pains to point out that the Hegelian vision was not exactly a dichotomy. Unsurprisingly, Marx and Gramsci were the two theorists most often referred to within the Cuban literature dealing with this theme, and, in particular, the work of Gramsci has been critical in orienting socialist interpretations of the concept. This rediscovery of the concept's Marxist lineage has legitimized its use within the Cuban context. The debate did not, however, produce consensus with respect to a single interpretation of the concept of civil society, nor regarding the utility of the term for the Cuban context. Despite the significant amount of academic work that has taken place in Cuba on the theme, Limia David represents many who remain unconvinced that Marxist theory can benefit from a concept that remains "gnostically very poor" and suffers from "imprecision" and that is, as a result, of "limited scientific value" (Limia David 1999, 172).

López articulated the view put forward by those who were critical of this preoccupation with theory, arguing that within Cuba questions regarding civil society could become little more than an opportunity for polemic and theorizing that might end up being a "blind alley" (López Vigil 1997, 17). Concerned not to become embroiled in a series of abstruse and abstract conceptual debates, she suggests that theoretical considerations should be left to one side. Instead analysts should start from the concrete, thereby enabling an understanding to be reached regarding the coordinates of "actually existing" Cuban civil society. This suggestion was largely taken on by analysts, including those primarily concerned with theoretical issues, such as Acanda who describes contemporary Cuban civil society in the following terms:

Cuban civil society is not only the Félix Varela Center, or the Dr. Martin Luther King Jr. Memorial Center or the Catholic Church. It is the film on Saturday night. It is also the ICRT [Instituto Cubano de Radio y Televisión], which broadcasts televised messages with an ideological content that does not always correspond fully with our project. . . . It is also expressed in a march for the first of May. . . . The Communist Party is within civil society, not only as a political party, but as a structure that creates and diffuses values, principles, norms. (Acanda 1999, 161–162)

Clearly, the manner in which civil society is understood, and how its relationship with the state is conceptualized, has had an impact in Cuba that has been far greater than these intellectual discussions might at first suggest. For if civil society is understood as a site in opposition to the state, as an arena in which dissent can form and from which it can be mobilized, then the existence of such a realm could not be tolerated by a political leadership ever on the alert for evidence of counterrevolutionary sabotage. As we shall see below, such issues have characterized what has at times been a tense dialogue between intellectuals and the state.

A New Debate in Cuba?

Pinpointing the precise start of any debate is always problematic and the case of the debate about civil society in Cuba is no exception. Recio Silva (1997) claims that the debate that evolved in Cuba during the 1990s was to a large extent characterized by a "revisiting" of those debates that were at the heart of the Rectification Process (from 1986 to 1990) and also those raised by the Fourth Party Congress of 1991. Hence, although there is a direct correlation between interest in the idea of civil society and the economic transformations that were taking place in the early 1990s, the debate about civil society should be understood as part of a trend that predates the economic crisis and the introduction of the reforms. The debates at the end of the 1980s had at their center the demand to perfect the Cuban economic and political scheme, to accept the growing and increasingly evident heterogeneity of the social fabric, and to rectify the errors committed as a result of the application of a Soviet-style model that had a tendency to be verticalist and homogeneous and was, in many respects, unsuitable for the Cuban context.

More significantly, Rectification was a policy that set out to change the dynamic of the relationship that had developed between the state and civil society prior to that point and precipitate a fundamental re-composition of the economy, politics, and society, which would lead Cuba back toward an authentic Cuban form of socialism. The Third and Fourth Party Congresses, celebrated in 1986 and 1991 respectively, involved critical debate about the problems of the model. In particular, the public discussion throughout 1989–

90 of the document *Call to the IV Congress* has been hailed as an example of one of the most democratic and broad-based discussions known to Cuba in the last decades (Hernández 1998). It was from the discussions that took place across the island that a number of national problems were identified. The importance and role of these open and public debates cannot be underestimated. They offered a clear encouragement to academics and activists to go beyond orthodoxies in search of new answers to the problems facing the system.

It is no coincidence that it was during a moment when Soviet-style socialism had "failed" that there was a renewed interest in the political thought of the Italian Marxist Antonio Gramsci. The ideological crisis of the late 1980s and early 1990s within Cuban socialist thought prepared the conditions for the revival of interest in socialist alternatives as intellectuals searched to make sense of the new realities confronting them. Within this context, it was Gramsci's ideas of the state, hegemony, and civil society that inspired particular interest among intellectual circles. The movement toward more unorthodox interpretations linked the debate about civil society to the more fundamental debate within which it was embedded: the debate about socialism in Cuba. What socialism "is," how it is built, and the ways in which it can be maintained and perfected were, of course, not new issues. However, the debate about socialism has been and remains to this day the primary debate in Cuba. This debate has been given urgency since the collapse of socialism in Eastern Europe and the Soviet Union. In a recent conversation Limia David reflected on the crisis in Cuban socialism and described the loss of the Soviet paradigm in the following terms:

> All of a sudden we were left without stereotypes. We were not only facing a crisis in the economy but an ideological crisis in the definition of socialist ideals. Suddenly we didn't know what an efficient socialist economy was. What, we asked ourselves, was a socialist state? What was socialist culture? These uncertainties arose because what we had considered to be our paradigm, the U.S.S.R., had fallen. Suddenly we didn't know how to construct the socialist mode of production.[4]

Far, then, from being seen as a parallel discussion, the debate about civil society that took place in Cuba must be set within the matrix of a range of debates that emerged in the context of a crisis in all of its manifestations, but particularly the ideological crisis in mechanistic interpretations of Marxism and the economic crisis of the Special Period. In contrast to the tendency among outside observers, the key discussion for many Cubans has been whether to maintain the existing model of socialism or transform it, where "transformation" does not imply the abandonment of socialism but rather its reform and perfection.

Why Was Civil Society on the Agenda in the 1990s?

The trajectory of the debate on civil society in Cuba during the 1990s was influenced by the interplay of political strategies and events both within Cuba and without. It is possible to identify a combination of exogenous and endogenous influences that together conditioned the emergence and course of the debate. As well as affecting the parameters and nature of the debate, these influences represented the context within which the debate was articulated.

What then were the key factors precipitating interest in the theme? Observing that the discussion in Cuba took greater force and began to establish itself in academic and political spaces around the years 1993 and 1994, when Cuba was in the middle of the harshest phase of the economic crisis, Recio Silva (1997) is one among many Cuban analysts who argues that the economic and political transformations introduced by the state in an attempt to combat the economic decline precipitated by the crisis conditioned the rise and development of the debate about civil society. The growth in those spaces available for the market and the greater presence of its laws, together with the development of diverse forms of property, the emergence of new social and economic actors, increased levels of social differentiation, the introduction of foreign investment, and the arrival of international NGOs, were all factors that contributed to activating the discussion about civil society. As such, it was a debate inspired both by the innovative actions of the state in the political as well as economic ambits, and their consequences: namely, the reconstitution of Cuban civil society.

The activation of civil society in Cuba was manifested in its appropriation, however partial and incomplete, of those spaces and processes that had previously been the exclusive preserve of the state. Since the late 1980s the Cuban state had been unable to undertake with the same efficiency the role that it had previously carried out in securing the social needs of the population (Basail Rodríquez 1999; Dilla Alfonso 1999). During the Special Period the state was forced to hand over spaces to competing actors within the social structure, the most important being the market, which began to make its entrance with the development of tourism, the liberalization of the dollar, the aperture in the agricultural and industrial markets, introduction of self-employed workers, and other consequences of the economic reforms. In parallel, the community began to assume new roles, and different associative modalities appeared, as was the case with the community movements that in many instances were encouraged by the state. There is a high degree of consensus among Cuban analysts that the most important factor conditioning the development of the debate was the new relationship between the state and civil society, which had been precipitated by a combination of the economic crisis and the reforms and subsequent transformations within the economic and political order.

In the main, the protagonists of the debate were members of the academic community, but community movements and NGOs operating on the island also had a key role in initiating debate on the subject (see Habitat-Cuba 2000). There is evidence to suggest that the debate about civil society was closely linked to discussions concerning the entry and role of international NGOs, some of which—as the state had feared—brought with them a "discourse of opposition" (Dilla Alfonso and Oxhorn 1998).

Although many Cubans stress endogenous forces as the catalyst for the start of the debate, domestic issues were intimately connected to exogenous events and processes, demonstrating the inescapable intertwinings of national level developments with changing world historical contexts. Cuban analysts note that the debate in Cuba followed a global trend in the use of the concept, both in the academic world and within the developmental field (particularly concerning NGOs) where, since the late 1980s, the term had enjoyed a renaissance. Although literature from Eastern Europe, the former Soviet Union, and Latin America influenced and contributed to the debate on the island (Dilla Alfonso and Oxhorn 1998; Azcuy Henríquez 1995; Recio Silva 1997), the use of the term to describe events and processes emerging in contexts as dissimilar as Europe and Latin America, and in relation to an assortment of social movements, NGOs, human rights advocates, religious communities, and indigenous organizations, to name but a few, added to the confusion of those seeking to identify the elements that constituted civil society in order to define the category.

Almost without exception, Cuban analysts refer to the influence of the disappearance of the socialist camp in Eastern Europe and the Soviet Union as the key factor stimulating the revival of the discussion about civil society on the island. However, Alonso Tejada (1996) argues that the idea of civil society that appeared in relation to Eastern Europe was one that was closely tied to processes of dissidence and political opposition. In this context, civil society was understood as a program of resistance against Communism, appearing first in Poland with the Solidarity movement. This pattern was not repeated in Cuba. Commenting on the differences between Latin American and eastern European understandings and the Cuban experience, Hernández writes: "Unlike in Latin America where they want to gestate a parallel power with no articulations to the state or in Europe where the 'song' of civil society is a song of the crisis of real socialism, of privatization and of neo-liberalism, the Cuban experience of civil society provides the key to re-thinking socialism as an alternative" (Hernández 1999c, 166).

48 / Michelle Marín-Dogan

Another factor influencing the emergence of the Cuban debate in the 1990s was the impact of the international right's political discourse and program of democracy promotion and transition. The new interpretations generated by this group regarding the need to roll back the state were coupled with a renewed interest in the use of civil society to weaken the state and fight against socialism. Limia David (1999) maintains that the domestic polemic on civil society was to a very large degree induced in response to this neoliberal offensive.

Influencing the domestic debate and heightening the political controversy surrounding it was the introduction in the 1990s of Track II of the U.S. policy to promote regime change in Cuba. Spelled out in the text of the Cuban Democracy Act of 1992 (the Torricelli-Graham law), which hardened and extended the sanctions against the island, it was proposed more openly in 1994 and then strengthened in 1996 with the introduction of the Cuban Liberty and Democratic Solidarity Act (the Helms-Burton law) (see Hoffman 1997; Diaz 2002). Track II was a policy designed to use cultural, professional, and personal exchanges between Cuba and the United States as the vehicle through which the U.S. administration's objective of promoting a civil society that would destabilize and ultimately overthrow the Cuban government could be achieved. The aim was to contaminate ideologically a nascent civil society that would then be a key element in the defeat of the Revolution. Consequently, the aim of the U.S. administration was the promotion of a civil society in Cuba that would be populated not merely by *non*-government organizations but by *anti*-government organizations that would eventually precipitate the fall of Cuban socialism. It was this intensification in U.S. hostility toward Cuba and in particular the emphasis placed on Cuban civil society's potential for making dynamic proposals for capitalist transformations within the country that Raúl Valdés Vivo (1999) regards as the point of departure for the civil society debate in Cuba.

Although the debate about civil society in Cuba may well have been stimulated in part as a reaction to U.S. policy, it was also constrained by it. The hostile mediations of the U.S. administration, which was intent upon using Cuban civil society for subversive and counterrevolutionary ends, added to the caution and reticence with which many Cubans viewed it as an analytical category and as a tool for rebuilding political consensus in the midst of an intense crisis.

Landmarks in the Cuban Debate

In the initial stages of the Cuban debate, civil society was used by the Catholic Church as a theoretical instrument with which to criticize the past, present

Civil Society: The Cuban Debate / 49

strategies of the Revolution, and suggest ways out of the situation of crisis that had nothing to do with socialist alternatives. Valdés Hernández's and Estrella Márquez's work of 1994, "Reconstruir la sociedad civil: Un proyecto para Cuba" (Reconstructing Civil Society: A Project for Cuba) was presented during the Catholic Church's Second Social Week in November 1994 and was undoubtedly a landmark text in the civil society debate. In this document the church presented a classical liberal interpretation of civil society that enabled it to be identified as "independent voluntary associations" and "a sphere to be contrasted with the state." According to these authors, in Cuba civil society did not exist because there was "a total lack of organizations" that generated their own ideas as opposed to those of the state (Valdés Hernández and Estrella Márquez 1994, 2). Within this context, the only spaces for "true" participation were those provided by the organizations of the Catholic Church. According to the church, what was needed was a radical change of system, with the introduction of a pluralistic multi-party democracy and a system of private property guided by the laws of the free market. Unsurprisingly, it was proposed that the traditional values of the church would provide the normative foundation for Cuban civil society. The form in which civil society would be reconstructed implied the elimination of the main achievements of the Revolution. As such, the majority of Cubans viewed the Catholic Church's project as an essentially retrogressive step.

The second landmark in the debate was the publication of Rafael Hernández's "Mirar a Cuba" (1993), which was closely followed by his article "La sociedad civil y sus alrededores" (1994), which appeared in the cultural magazine La Gaceta.[5] As well as taking a new path in the analysis of the political and social reality in Cuba, Hernández's texts were regarded by many Cuban analysts as the proper point of departure for the Cuban debate. They appeared at a time when many works were published that presented different positions on the theme and when, particularly in the cultural camp, civil society became a popular theme for reflection. Although Hernández had first spoken of the importance of civil society in the early 1980s, Dilla Alfonso (2003) suggests that the positive allusion to the role of civil society in Latin America made by Fidel Castro in a speech at the Rio Summit was interpreted by Cuban intellectuals and social activists as a signal that the subject was now "safe" to talk about after having been harshly proscribed by Soviet Marxism.

Like many participants in the debate, Hernández was interested in the conceptual dimensions of civil society, but he was also concerned to correct the impression given by some analysts that Cuban civil society is dormant or, as he puts it, "sleeping," which, he argued, is tantamount to saying that civil society practically does not exist in Cuba (Hernández 1994, 17). This, he claims, is an extension of the opinion that exists outside the island that in Cuba there is, on the one hand, the party-state and, on the other, the mass of passive subjects. The "abuse" that the concept of civil society has suffered, both at the hands of foreign analysts who study Cuba from the outside, but also by some Cuban analysts who regard it as a conservative concept, is highlighted by Hernández as a problem that needs to be resolved if Cuban civil society is to be adequately understood. For Hernández, Cuban socialism has its roots in civil society, a civil society that since 1959 has become ever more complex and heterogeneous.

Hernández's articles reoriented debate in Cuba toward socialist interpretations of civil society. Stressing the Marxist provenance of the idea, the work of Gramsci was a key point of reference for Hernández. Like Alonso Tejada (2000), he objected to the "demonization" that the concept had suffered at the hands of dogmatic Marxists, but he also rejected the then-fashionable liberal ideas that civil society was either a neutral ideological sphere separate from the political one or else an expression of opposition to the state and support of civil disobedience, which, in the Cuban context, meant that only dissident groups and the Catholic Church would merit the title "civil society." Through his treatment of the concept, Hernández effectively rescued the term from its imprisonment within the liberal and neoliberal vernacular and its exclusion from the Marxist. Civil society was to be converted into an instrument with which to perfect, as opposed to destroy, Cuban socialism.

Other analysts recognized the importance of Hernández's pioneering work. Alonso Tejada (2000), for example, argued that Hernández was, without doubt, one of those who consistently and rigorously introduced the difficult theme of civil society for analysis, enabling a middle path to be found between *oficialistas* and those who dissent from the official line. This middle way was adopted by those "critical Marxists," as Acanda calls them, who saw that civil society might, potentially, be a space in which the Revolutionary project could be strengthened.[6] These individuals did not represent a homogenous group, but they did share a vision to consolidate the Cuban revolutionary process. It is not surprising that their position was reminiscent of that of the small group of intellectuals who in the 1960s had sought to find socialist alternatives to the "only thought" advocated by those in power, for in many cases they were the same people.

Spaces for the Debate

One of the principal spaces in which the debate about civil society took place was within the pages of the journal *Temas*. Established in 1994, in the midst of the economic crisis, *Temas* was, and remains to this day, a journal dedicated to the social sciences and humanities. Since its founding, the director of the editorial board has been Rafael Hernández. The "Initial Words" of the editorial team, included in the first edition, set out the journal's vision, which was essentially to stimulate an open and lively exchange of ideas and opinions in order to promote reflection, dialogue, and debate within contemporary cultural circles in Cuba and Latin America more widely. The journal's ethos was one of inclusivity. It was hoped that, by presenting a diverse range of perspectives, the plurality of opinion that existed within Cuba could be represented. As well as this, *Temas* had a strategic objective: to fight the challenges of the Special Period by offering a space in which new directions could be articulated and alternative solutions discussed.

Although the quarterly publication is not the official mouthpiece of any state organism, the journal has close links to the Ministry of Culture and, since 1998, the minister of culture, Abel Prieto, has held a position on its editorial board. Since the launch of the first issue in 1995 to the present day, *Temas* has been funded by contributions from a range of sources including the Cuban Ministry of Culture's Fund for the Development of Culture and Education, Oxfam-Canada, UNESCO, Oxfam-América, Ayuda Popular Noruega, and, more recently (and arguably more surprisingly), Harvard University's David Rockefeller Center for Latin American Studies.

Although other journals such as *Contracorriente* and *Debates Americanos* also appeared in the 1990s, it was *Temas* that was most successful in establishing itself as the central forum for discussion in the social sciences in Cuba. Arturo Arango (2002, 12) describes the appearance of these cultural magazines as "an expression of a renovated polemic" that regained space on the island after a period of silence during the 1970s and 1980s. For the first time, Cubans found in them reflections that centered on problems that had long been hidden by the press. The catalyst for such reflections and the backdrop against which they were set was the crisis in the economy. According to Arango, it was the crisis that had generated a wide debate about the destiny of the country, not just externally but also in Cuba. In her analysis of politics and culture in Cuba after 1990, Davies (2000) identifies other spheres within which important debates were being played out, for example, in the performance arts, such as film and theater, but also in the fine arts and, to a lesser extent, in literature. However, like Arango, she notes that it was in the glossy cultural journals that proliferated at the time, rather than in books, that the key debates took place (see Davies 2000, 112–14).

By the time that the fourth issue of *Temas* was being prepared for press in late 1995, other developments were about to influence the debate on civil society. In *Temas* an article by Hugo Azcuy took up the debate initiated by Hernández in *La Gaceta*. In "State and Civil Society in Cuba," Azcuy Henríquez (1995) argued that given the diversity and plurality of interests emerging within Cuban society, it was no longer appropriate to organize society solely through the six mass organizations. He suggested, furthermore, that civil society should not only be used as an instrument of analysis but also as a project. Azcuy Henríquez went on to argue:

> It would seem desirable and necessary that the debate over this important theme is broadened and deepened in a positive way, allowing a better appreciation of its place in the processes through which this country is currently living. . . . There are aspects that should be discussed more in Cuba. . . . It is not right to defensively fence-in or self-limit our responses, neither [is it right] that we should leave it to others to think for us about our own national reality. (Azcuy Henríquez 1995, 112–13).

This was not the sort of talk that the more conservative sectors of the Communist Party wanted to hear. They became concerned that the discussion about civil society had enabled alternative discourses to gain space, which had the potential to challenge their hegemony. Recognizing the danger, the party-state responded.

The Response of the Party-State

On 4 January 1996 the daily newspaper and official organ of the Cuban Communist Party, *Granma*, ran an article entitled "La sociedad civil o gato por liebre?" (Civil society or confidence trick?) by Raúl Valdés Vivó, the rector of the Ñico López Party School. In it, Valdés Vivó denounced civil society as a "neoliberal excrescence" and NGOs as its "institutional expression, designed to undermine from within socialist society" (Valdés Vivó 1996). Civil society was condemned as an instrument to cause internal fracture and undermine the progressive role of the state in social development. Somewhat paradoxically, Valdés Vivó was describing precisely the kind of civil society that the U.S. administration wished to foster in Cuba. He negated any role for civil society other than as a force antagonistic to the Cuban state. Having identified civil society as a site for dissent and opposition, Valdés Vivó, along with the most conservative elements of the state and party apparatus, began an offensive against Cuban civil society. This offensive gained momentum after the introduction of the U.S. administration's Helms-Burton legislation in March of the same year. Azcuy Henríquez (1995) had argued that it was entirely logical for the Cuban state to take measures to protect national independence and to prevent U.S. influence on the island, even if this meant a curtailment of liberties and rights for Cuban citizens, given the fact that the U.S. administration was using a series of policies that focused on an emergent civil society as a possible space for the subversion that, it hoped, would enable it to become an internal actor in Cuba. His words were to prove prophetic. In addition to the Torricelli-Graham and Helms-Burton legislation of 1992 and 1996 respectively, the U.S. administration approved financing, through USAID, to stimulate the activities of small groups of radical opposition on the island. A former minister of culture, Armando Hart, described U.S strategy in the following terms: "Now [Washington] is attempting to provoke chaos in our society by establishing direct relationships with some individuals and promoting organizational models outside of our political system that seek to destabilize the democratic order of our society" (Hart 1996, 3).

Acanda has called the position adopted by Valdés Vivó as one of a "Marxism of suspicion" (Acanda 2002, 323). Those who took up such a position regarded civil society both as a weapon for the United States to deploy against Cuba and as a cynical maneuver on the part of the enemies of the Revolution within the island. For these individuals, only one interpretation of the term was accepted, one that was in essence the same as the liberal position that counterposed the state against autonomous associative spaces in civil society.

It was in March 1996 that the Cuban state produced an official version of what it understood by the term "civil society." On 23 March Raúl Castro, the head of the armed forces and vice president of the Council of State, read an official pronouncement by the Central Committee of the Cuban Communist Party at its Fifth Congress.[7] In this discourse the party mounted an attack on various Cuban NGOs, calling them a "Trojan horse" used by the United States to "ferment division and subversion" within Cuba (Castro Ruz 1996, 5). The book *Cuba: Crisis and Transition* (1992), published by the University of Miami, was specifically mentioned, and those intellectuals contributing to it were accused of being "in the service of the U.S. government" (Castro Ruz 1996, 5). Apparently, this book was itself an example of a new counterrevolutionary strategy at a time when the Soviet Union was dissolving and when, in Miami, there were "shouts to prepare the suitcases for a return to Cuba" (Castro Ruz 1996, 5).

According to Raúl Castro, the book characterized Cuban civil society as having "nothing to do with the state," but rather as something that could "oppose and destroy" it (Castro Ruz 1996, 5). In contrast, the party offered the following definition of civil society:

> For us, civil society is not that to which the U.S. refers. . . . Cuban socialist civil society is composed of our powerful mass organizations—the CTC, CDRs, FMC, ANAP, FEU, FEEM and even the Pioneers—as well as social organizations that group together, among others, the veterans of the Revolution, economists, lawyers, journalists, artists and writers, and those NGOs that act within the law and do not try to undermine the

economic, political, and social system that has been freely selected by our *pueblo* [and which] together with the Cuban state pursue the common objective of building socialism. (Castro Ruz 1996, 5)

As Dilla Alfonso and Oxhorn (1998) were later to reflect, Raúl Castro's "Informe" offered a utilitarian definition of "socialist civil society," whose elements included the traditional social and mass organizations and those NGOs that were considered acceptable. It appeared that, despite sweeping changes in the structure of Cuban society, many of which had been precipitated by the state, the state and the party adhered to an outdated model of civil society. Moreover, it was one that enabled the bureaucracy to control civil society by defining what did and did not belong to it as a category. What was, however, a dramatic change, was that the term "civil society" was being used by high-ranking officials from within the political class.

The Campaign against Ideological Subversion

Through the discourse presented by Raúl Castro, the party launched an attack on some of Cuba's social science community, with the Centro de Estudios de América (CEA) and to a lesser extent the Centro de Estudios Europeos (CEE) as its main targets. The accusations were harsh. The following extract provides an example of the tone of the discourse:

> Of course we need to make a distinction—and we have done so in relation to said Center (the CEA) and elsewhere—between the Cuban investigator who might think in ways that are different from the accepted position regarding a particular subject—yet from a socialist standpoint and using an appropriate framework—from the investigator who is a Cuban citizen, and even holds a party card, but who has turned into a Cubanologist, disseminating his views with the complacency of our enemies (Castro Ruz 1996, 5).

The CEA was by no means the only target for attack. Other academic centers and publications were criticized as "a variant of Glasnost," as having "an annexationist orientation," and as representing "the growth of fifth columnists" functioning at the behest of U.S. interests within Cuban society (Castro Ruz 1996; for an analysis, see Dilla Alfonso and Oxhorn 1998). The attack on intellectuals and the battle between the organic intellectuals of the party-state and alternative "independent" intellectuals from within Cuban civil society was broadened: "Within the universal environments of the cinema, radio, television—of culture in general—two types of conduct are discernible: that which is linked to the fidelity of our revolutionary *pueblo*, and then that of the small minority whose conduct, with its annexationist orientation that is completely alien to patriotism, characterizes the behavior of the majority of our intellectuals" (Castro Ruz 1996, 5).

Raúl Castro's speech was little less than an "ideological crusade" by the politburo. What was interesting about this particular attack was that it was aimed primarily at the social sciences, although it was broadened to include the cultural sphere more widely. This was a departure from past strategy, for up until this point it had been largely from the cultural sphere that examples were taken and denunciations made in order to define the limits of what was acceptable and unacceptable.

In practice, the party's "crusade" led to the virtual dismantling of the CEA. Right after the discourse, Luis Suárez Salazar, the director of the CEA, lost his position. Although members of the CEA were dispersed, none were expelled from the party and many continued to work on the same research themes in other organizations. In his account of the affair, Giuliano (1998) argues that although this was clearly not a victory for democracy or civil rights neither was it a victory for the party orthodoxy.

The CEA, like its sister organization the CEE, had been created in the 1970s by the Central Committee of the Party as an "autonomous institute" that was intended to function as a state-sponsored yet independent think tank (Edelstein 2002). During the 1980s, some scholars with the CEA had begun to study domestic affairs and, by 1996, the center had been reinvented as an NGO, receiving funding from external sources as well as the party. It was at this time that the thinking at the CEA had become so "independent" that it had begun to think "the unthinkable," as Chanan (2001, 401) put it, and come up with proposals that looked to hard-liners in the Central Committee like economic reformism.

It was in the CEA that the "veteran Gramscians" of the 1960s had found a home, alongside a team of younger researchers who owed their intellectual formation to the Revolution. Many of those who had been involved on the "losing side," so to speak, in the closure of the journal *Pensamiento Crítico* in the 1970s found themselves once again at the center of a confrontation between dogmatists and Gramscians within the party.

More and tighter controls over NGOs, the dissolution of some associations in the process of being formed, and a reluctance to accept new organizations for legal registration followed the denunciation of the CEA. The official definition of civil society implied an intention on the part of the state to introduce a series of administrative controls over civil society in a bid to curb its dynamic, but the uncertainty left as a result of the attack meant that, although no one knew who would receive the next blow, "everyone lowered their head[s]" (Hoffmann 1998, 81).

56 / Michelle Marín-Dogan

Though not specifically mentioned, the journal *Temas* could consider itself one of the accused. Tragically, Hugo Azcuy died of a heart attack soon after Raúl Castro's discourse, and although the fourth issue, which featured his article, was presented to the public as normal, it was under difficult circumstances. While *Temas* continued to be published, the impact on the journal of Raúl Castro's speech was evident. One only has to compare the themes covered by the journal, both before and after the discourse, to note the dramatic change in their tone and content after the fourth issue. Less controversial issues dominated later editions and gone were the frank discussions that had set the journal apart from its rivals. It appeared that the editorial board's vision was out of step with the realities of the new political environment.

Raúl Castro's discourse was an important text in the history of the debate about civil society. With it, the idea of "socialist civil society" and the need for its perfection became part of the theoretical arsenal of the party. In his analysis of the impact of the "Informe," Armando Hart, the former minister of culture, argued that the document presented to the Central Committee in 1996 did not "shy away" from the expression "civil society" but rather characterized it as "*socialist* civil society" (Hart 1999, 156). For Hart, this distinction was critical, for he was of the opinion that the key to the use of the idea of civil society in the Cuban context was that the types of organizations labeled "civil society" were of a socialist character. Principal among them were the unions, what Hart called civil society's "motors," followed by the social and mass organizations. Hart explained that there was no longer any need to fear either the existence of different organizations in society—so long as they were in line with the Constitution of the republic—or the term "civil society" itself (Hart 1999, 156). In a collection of articles published during 1996 in *Granma* and *Habanera*, two periodicals with huge circulations within Cuba, Hart consistently used the concept and stressed the importance of its deployment in the consolidation of the Cuban revolutionary process. Unity could be secured, he argued, "only through the strengthening of both socialist civil society and the authority of the state," without which there would be chaos (Hart 1999, 158). From this it would appear that one way in which the authority of the state could be strengthened was through the use of a discourse that legitimized different types of exclusion. Those academics who had worked at the CEA were to be excluded on grounds that would receive the unequivocal support of the majority of the population: the charge of aiding and abetting the United States in its efforts to undermine both the socialist system and national sovereignty in Cuba. By becoming what was effectively a non-party alternative, which did not speak the official language of the political class, the CEA had laid itself open to misuse as an instrument for enemy propaganda.[8]

It is important at this point to contextualize the attack on the CEA. Although conditions had been facilitated by the U.S. administration's decades-long program of hostility against the island, the incident in February 1996 when two small aircraft flown by Brothers to the Rescue, an organization of exiles based in Miami, were shot down after violating Cuban air space has been identified by many as the immediate precipitant (see, for example, Edelstein 2002). For those who uphold this view, it was no coincidence that it was immediately afterward that President Clinton responded by signing the Helms-Burton law.

In a move to strengthen the hegemonic discourse of the leadership, in 1996 the party's journal *Cuba Socialista* was relaunched by the PCC under the editorial leadership of José Ramón Balaguer, the man who had been asked to investigate the CEA. This journal was to be the mouthpiece for "politically correct" official political discourse. A few months later, a study by the party's school was published in which participants talked of civil society in Cuba as a legitimate space for action. Although no attempt was made to conceptualize the term, the study's authors stressed that they were against the bourgeois use of civil society to destabilize the Revolution (CEE 1997). Again, the state had closed the debate within civil society and about civil society, using arguments qualitatively similar to those that have since been used against its opponents. By so doing, Dilla Alfonso (2003) argues, the state effectively displaced critical debate toward the right. What can therefore be possibly said of the response of the "critical Marxists"?

The Debate after 1996

Acanda (2002, 324) claims that, after the fixed positions in the Fifth Congress of the Central Committee of the PCC and the pronouncements of Armando Hart, the possibilities of rejecting the use of the concept of civil society or for considering it anti-Marxist and anti-socialist have been delegitimized and are now "views that hardly anyone maintains." Further, he notes that some Cuban Marxists who originally rejected the term now use it but "tend to accept, in an a-critical way, the liberal interpretation" and think of civil society as little more than a group of NGOs, reducing the discussion to a question of what type of organizations are acceptable, or not, in Cuba (Acanda 2002, 324). Those who take a Gramscian perspective interpret civil society as the sphere of ideological production, organically interconnected with and tied to the state. These theorists center their reflection on the need to perfect Cuban civil society through the development of structures and institutions for ideological-cultural production within the framework of socialism.

By 2001 the political climate in Cuba was sufficiently open to enable a group of authors to publish a book that took as its theme Rosa Luxemburg's ideas about liberty. Luxemburg's assertion that "liberty can never be anything other than the liberty to think in another way" (quoted in Acanda 2001, 67) was the focal point of the discussion. In the book (which contains articles by members of the Cátedra de Estudios Antonio Gramsci who, in collaboration with the Dr. Martin Luther King Jr. Memorial Center, met in February 1999 to discuss the application of Luxemburg's ideas for contemporary Cuba), Acanda argues: "Without the liberty to produce new thought, to express it and discuss the conceptions generated from diverse points of view . . . without the liberty to think "in another way," which allows the disruptive and libertarian components of socialism to flower and germinate, there is no possible guarantee of the continuity of the Revolution" (Acanda 2001, 76). He goes on to quote Abel Prieto's observation that the Revolution has before it the task of creating a culture that is both "affirmative and critical at the same time" (Acanda 2001, 76). In contrast to the official perspective, for Acanda the discussion and development of "heretical" positions within the Revolution is essential: "The thought of the Revolution needs to be affirmative of its moments of subversion and critical of the persistence of old ways of thinking" (Acanda 2001, 76). From this it would appear that Acanda, together with other critical Marxists, is continuing the Cuban tradition that the journal *Pensamiento Crítico* had so briefly begun in the late 1960s and early 1970s: that of offering socialist alternatives to the "official" socialist perspective.

The principal spaces in which reflection has continued over these questions are the journal *Temas*[9] and its monthly open discussion meetings called Último Jueves (Last Thursday), as well as the seminars organized by the Cátedra de Estudios Antonio Gramsci at the Juan Marinello Center for Research and Development of Cuban Culture, in Havana. This center describes itself as an NGO, yet like *Temas* it comes under the wing of the Ministry of Culture. The Antonio Gramsci Group was founded in 1997 and, according to Acanda, demonstrated "the Ministry of Culture's commitment . . . to the renovation of reflection on the cultural dimension of the Revolution" (Acanda 2002, 337). This group of intellectuals, which has included Fernando Martínez Heredia, Jorge Luis Acanda, Juan Valdés Paz, Aurelio Alonso Tejada, and Néstor Kohan, among others, also receives the sponsorship of the Protestant NGO Centro Memorial Dr. Martin Luther King Jr.[10] Miller (2003) observes that despite the obstacles facing academics working in the shadow of "an increasingly authoritarian state" and with the practical difficulties of the Special Period, some remarkable work has been carried out by Cuban intellectuals. For Miller, "The [recent] opening of a series of small windows, like those in an Advent Calendar, suggests that academics in the humanities are positioning themselves to take their place in a potential civil society that is gradually assembling its cumulative force for when it can emerge from the shadow" (Miller 2003, 157).

Civil Society: The Cuban Debate / 59

Despite the openings, shadows remain. In 2003 one Cuban academic recounted the difficulties faced by those who wish to run open courses that the general public can attend. Discussions are "closed" not by direct imposition by the state but through more subtle means. For example, the presence of personnel from the Central Committee who sit in on the debates has proved to be more than enough to limit their scope. "Either no one would talk," this individual reflected, "or else certain themes could not be raised, effectively closing down the discussion."[11]

The "Problem" of Alternatives

In the early 1990s, elements within Cuban civil society tried either to occupy those spaces abandoned by the state or simply share social action in the economic realm. This was replicated in the cultural sphere and corresponded to a rearticulation of civil society in both theory and practice. In the same way that the state had hardened its position toward emerging community associations and extended over them greater control as the decade wore on, a similar process was repeated in the academic sphere. Despite the party's claims, those academics whom it denounced had not articulated liberal positions regarding civil society; it was quite the contrary, but in many ways this presented a greater danger. As in the early 1970s, any discussion of socialist "alternatives" frightened the already nervous party-state leadership, which recognized that within the context of the Special Period alternative socialist discourses had the potential to emerge, coalesce, and challenge the dominant hegemonic discourse that underpinned its political dominance. The existence of multiple discourses could not be tolerated, for the emergence of heterodoxy, self-reflection, and dispersion was fundamentally at odds with the state's aim to assimilate differences where possible. The official Marxist narrative had been legitimate in Cuba for three decades (1960–90) and although it had been losing its attraction since the 1980s (Davies 2000), it was not until the economic collapse that alternative "stories" began to appear in public culture (Davies 2000, 105). By the mid-1990s, when economic recovery, though tentative, appeared more certain, the principal preoccupation of the Cuban state was not merely the existence of an organized opposition but the fear that this opposition could link itself to those growing spaces of disillusion, discontent, and demobilization that were manifesting themselves in Cuban society. Given this, the role of the social sciences in analyzing and labeling such spaces and processes took on an even greater significance.

At this time, a process began that has been described as the "re-birth" of social science in Cuba (Hoffmann 1999, 72), as the academic establishment started to debate the problems of the country in a form that had not been seen

60 / Michelle Marín-Dogan

in the previous twenty-five years, that is, with openness. During the crisis of the Special Period, Cubans sought to find out about and learn from alternatives. Their need to do so finds resonance with Kuhn's (1970) interpretation of crises as times characterized by a proliferation of competing articulations, the willingness to try anything, the expression of discontent, and the recourse to philosophy and to debate over fundamentals. As one academic put it: "The crisis that we have experienced reveals underlying tensions. It is during this moment of crisis that different currents of thought have surfaced in Cuba."[12]

The debate about civil society linked up struggles in the public sphere to those in the political sphere. The need for both a space in the public sphere for political deliberation and expression and a space within the political sphere for this expression to be incorporated and acknowledged highlighted an important change in state-civil society relations. The state reacted quickly to what it perceived as a threat to its hegemony and moved to regain its monopoly of both the agenda for debate and the space within which debate could take place. This involved the suppression of existing organizations (such as the CEA), the co-option of others (such as *Temas*), and the creation or revitalization of its own organizations (as occurred with the relaunch of the journal *Cuba Socialista*).

Hence, civil society was on the agenda during the 1990s precisely because the relationship between the state and civil society was changing. The debate over civil society in Cuba was itself a reflection of this process of readjustment between the state and society in a post-Soviet era. It cannot be regarded as coincidence that at a time when the relationship was changing on the ground it was also being rethought by social scientists at the conceptual level. Their contributions to the debate and their subsequent interpretations of it, affected civil society's new course. The response of the party's organic intellectuals— essentially to co-opt the concept of civil society that they recognized could be used as a metaphor for social change—was an attempt to influence the direction of that change, diluting the potency of the concept as an analytical tool in understanding what was actually happening.

Conclusion

The 1990s were a decade during which both the Cuban state and civil society struggled to find a tentative equilibrium in their relationship within the maelstrom of transformations that were taking place at the national and international levels. At this time, Cuban intellectuals were rethinking fundamental debates, questioning their guiding paradigms, and searching for stable ground amid the ideological quicksand that appeared to surround them. In the case of the debate about civil society, the contributions and interpretations of Cu-

Civil Society: The Cuban Debate / 61

ban intellectuals affected the very course of the processes that they studied: the new relationship that was being renegotiated between the state and civil society. The site of this struggle, as Gramsci would have predicted, was civil society itself. The debate about civil society in Cuba, at least that which has been made public, has overwhelmingly been between distinct voices from *within* the Revolution itself, that is, between those respecting and wishing to preserve the Revolution's interests and achievements. This does not mean, however, that there has been consensus. Within the parameters of socialist debate there have been fierce critiques, and equally fierce defenses, of both traditional and alternative views (see Arango 2002, 87). Of those voices outside the socialist fraternity, those of the organic intellectuals of the Catholic Church have arguably been the most significant.

This chapter has mapped the contours of this debate, the pathways along which it has traveled, its characteristics, and some of the controversies that have surrounded it. An attempt has been made to set the debate within its historical and contemporary context. It has been argued that the interplay between external and internal politics in Cuba, together with changes in social relations on the island during the 1990s, influenced the nature of the debate, those who participated in it, and the spaces that they were able to use for their discussions.

The very fact that the idea of civil society was on the public agenda in Cuba during the 1990s, that a debate emerged spontaneously and found for itself a space within public forums, points to an important change in the relationship between state and society during the decade, which in itself is worthy of analysis. It would seem that civil society was enjoying a renaissance both as an idea and as a process at this time, a dynamic that has not continued with the same vibrancy and openness today.

Notes

1. Fernando Martínez Heredia, interview, Havana, 21 April 2003.

2. Both Miguel Limia David and Fernando Martínez Heredia point to the need for greater emphasis to be placed on the issue of participation, which both claim to be insufficient (Martínez Heredia, interview, Havana, 21 April 2003; Limia David, interview, Havana, 12 May 2003).

3. Discussions were held, for example, by the Cátedra de Estudios Marxistas Julio A. Mella of the Institute of Philosophy from 1994 under the direction of Dr. Isabel Monal. Other workshops included "Reflections on Civil Society" run by the Escuela Superior del Partido "Ñico López" from 14–15 March 1996 (see Limia David 1997 for other examples).

4. Miguel Limia David, interview, Havana, 12 May 2003.

5. Hernández's 1994 article was itself a response to a letter by the writer Armando

Cristóbal Pérez, which was sent to the editor of *La Gaceta* and reproduced in the magazine (see *La Gaceta*, January 1994, 28). For a discussion of Cristóbal Pérez's letter and Hernández's reply see Fernández (2000).

6. In his article in the collection *Rosa Luxemburg: Una Rosa roja para el siglo XXI* Acanda discusses the importance of Luxemburg's thought (along with that of Marx, Gramsci, and Foucault) for a "critical Marxism" that reinterprets and stands against the "dogmatic" position of many Marxists. This internal struggle within Marxism to construct the conditions that will make possible another alternative mode of thought is identified by Acanda as essential (see Acanda 2001, 67–77).

7. See Castro Ruz 1996 for the full text.

8. Seven years later, during data collection for the study on which this analysis is based, sentiments still ran high among the intellectual community regarding the "caso CEA," and although some showed sympathy for the position of those academics who had been involved, others still regarded them as "traitors." See Marín-Dogan (2004).

9. This was especially true of volume 16–17 of 1999, with its round-table debate on civil society in the regularly featured "Controversia" section of the journal. Participants included Milena Recio, Jorge Luis Acanda, Berta Alvarez, Haroldo Dilla, Armando Hart, Rafael Hernández, Miguel Limia David, Isabel Monal, and Raúl Valdés Vivó.

10. They have recently held international sessions on the following themes: "Rosa Luxemburg and Contemporary Problems" (11–12 February 1999) and "The Work of Michel Foucault" (2000). From each conference a book has been produced, again, as with many editions of *Temas*, with funding from the Ministry of Culture's Fund for the Development of Education and Culture.

11. Anonymous respondent, interview, Havana, 22 February 2003.

12. Anonymous respondent, interview, Havana, 19 February 2003.

References

Acanda, J. L. 1996. "Sociedad civil y hegemonía." *Temas* 6: 87–93.

———. 1999. "Controversia: Sociedad civil en los 90: El debate cubano." *Temas* 16–17: 159–62.

———. 2001. "Aprender a pensar de otro modo." In *Rosa Luxemburg: Una Rosa roja para el siglo XXI*, edited by Cátedra de Estudios Antonio Gramsci. Havana: Centro de Investigación y Desarrollo de la Cultura Cubana Juan Marinello.

———. 2002. *Sociedad civil y hegemonía*. Havana: Centro de Investigación y Desarrollo de la Cultura Cubana Juan Marinello.

Alonso Tejada, A. 1996. "El concepto de sociedad civil en el debate contemporáneo: Los contextos." *Marx Ahora* 2: 119–35.

———. 2000. "Cuba: Tres miradas a los 90 desde los 90." *Casa de las Américas* 220 (July–September): 171–78.

Arango, A. 2002. *Segundas reincidencias (escribir en Cuba ayer)*. Santa Clara, Cuba: Editorial Capiro.

Azcuy Henríquez, H. 1995. "Estado y sociedad civil en Cuba." *Temas* 4: 105–11.

Civil Society: The Cuban Debate / 63

Basail Rodríguez, A. 1999. "Legitimidad y eficacia del sistema político Cubano: Ensayo sobre las políticas públicas en los 90." Unpublished paper, Department of Sociology, University of Havana.

Castro Ruz, R. 1996. "Informe del Buró Político." *Granma* (27 March): 2–6.

CEE. 1997. "Reflexiones sobre la sociedad civil." *Mensaje de Cuba* 36.

Chanan, M. 2001. "Cuba and Civil Society, or Why Cuban Intellectuals Are Talking about Gramsci." *Nepantla: Views from the South* 2, no. 2: 387–406.

Davies, C. 2000. "Surviving (on) the Soup of Signs: Postmodernism, Politics, and Culture in Cuba." *Latin American Perspectives* 27, no. 4: 103–21.

Diaz, J. A. 2002. "The Helms Burton Act and the EU-US Transatlantic Relationship." Ph.D. diss., University of Kent.

Dilla Alfonso, H. 1999. "Controversia: Sociedad civil en los 90: El debate cubano." *Temas* 16–17: 162–65.

———. 2003. "Civil Society." In *The Cuba Reader: History, Culture, Politics*, edited by A. Chomsky, B. Carr, and P. M. Smorkaloff, 650–59. London: Duke University Press.

Dilla Alfonso, H., and P. Oxhorn. 1998. "Cuba: Virtudes e infortunios de la sociedad civil." Mimeograph. Havana (November): 1–18. Later published as Dilla, H., and P. Oxhorn. 2001. "Virtudes e infortunios de la sociedad civil en Cuba." *Nueva Sociedad* 171: 157–75. Also published later as Dilla, H., and P. Oxhorn. 2002. "The Virtues and Misfortunes of Civil Society in Cuba." *Latin American Perspectives*, issue 125, vol. 29, no. 4: 11–30.

Edelstein, J. 2002. "The Centro de Estudios sobre América: An account of a regrettable loss." *Latin American Perspectives* 29, no. 4: 80–82.

Fernández, M. 2000. "Pensar la sociedad civil." *Encuentro de la Cultura Cubana*, Winter 2000/2001, 129–133.

Fung Riverón, T. M. 2000. "Aproximándonos a la noción 'sociedad civil.'" In *Democracia, derecho y sociedad civil*, edited by C. R. Delgado, J. Rosales, T. Fung, H. A. Aroas, and J. E. Tapia, 57–92. Havana: Editorial Ciencias Sociales.

Giuliano, M. 1998. *El "caso" CEA. Intelectuales e Inquisidores en Cuba. ¿Perestroika en la Isla?* Miami: Ediciones Universal.

Habitat-Cuba. 2000. *Sociedad civil y ONGs en Cuba: Una recopilación de textos para una primera aproximación a estos temas.* Havana: Habitat-Cuba.

Hart, A. 1996. "Sociedad civil y organizaciones no gubernamentales." *Granma Internacional* (18 September): 3

———. 1999. "Controversia: Sociedad civil en los 90: El debate cubano." *Temas* 16–17: 155–57.

Hernández, R. 1993. "Mirar a Cuba." *La Gaceta de Cuba* (September-October): 2–7.

———. 1994. "La sociedad civil y sus alrededores." *La Gaceta de Cuba* (January): 28–31.

———. 1998. "¿Hacia una nueva sociedad socialista?" *Nueva Sociedad* 157 (September-October): 137–53.

———. 1999a. "Mirar a Cuba: Notas para una discusión." In *Mirar a Cuba: Ensayos sobre cultura y sociedad civil*, edited by R. Hernández, 9–30. Havana: Editorial Letras Cubanas.

—, ed. 1999b. *Mirar a Cuba: Ensayos sobre cultura y sociedad civil.* Havana: Editorial Letras Cubanas.

—, 1999c, in M. Recio, "Controversia: Sociedad civil en los 90: el debate cubano," *Temas* 16–17: 165–167.

Hoffmann, B. 1997. "¿Helms-Burton a perpetuidad? Repercusiones y perspectivas para Cuba, Estados Unidos y Europa." *Nueva Sociedad* 151: 57–72.

—. 1998. "La reforma que no fue: El resurgimiento de las ciencias sociales en Cuba y la reacción del estado: Un panorama de las recientes publicaciones sobre la crisis económica, política y social de la isla." *Encuentro de la Cultura Cubana* 10: 71–82.

Kaldor, M. 2003. *Global Civil Society: An Answer to War.* Cambridge: Polity.

Kuhn, T. 1970. *The Structure of Scientific Revolutions.* Chicago: University of Chicago Press.

Limia David, M. 1999. "Controversia: Sociedad civil en los 90: El debate cubano." *Temas* 16–17: 171–75.

—. 1997. "Sociedad Civil y Participación en Cuba." Unpublished document, Havana, Instituto de Filosofía.

López Vigil, M. 1997. "Sociedad civil en Cuba." *Envío* 184: 17–40.

Marín-Dogan, M. A. 2004. "A Space in Which to Breathe: Civil Society and the State in Cuba: The Transformation of a Relationship?" Ph.D. diss., University of East Anglia.

Miller, N. 2003. "The Absolution of History: Uses of the Past in Castro's Cuba." *Journal of Contemporary History* 38, no. 1: 147–62.

Monal, I. 1999. "Controversia: Sociedad civil en los 90: El debate cubano." *Temas* 16–17: 170–71.

Recio Silva, M. 1997. "Sociedad civil en los 90: El debate cubano." B.A. thesis, Faculty of Communication, University of Havana.

—. 1999. "Controversia: Sociedad civil en los 90: El debate cubano." *Temas* 16–17: 155–76.

Valdés Hernández, D., and L. E. Estrella Márquez. 1994. "Reconstruir la sociedad civil: Un proyecto para Cuba." Ponencia a la II Semana Social Católica, Havana, 17–20 November.

Valdés Vivó, R. 1996. "¿La sociedad civil o gato por liebre?" *Granma Internacional* (24 January): 3

—. 1999. "Controversia: Sociedad civil en los 90: El debate cubano." *Temas* 16–17: 167–69.

3

The Rise of the Private Sector in Cuba

FRANCISCO DOMÍNGUEZ

It has been seventeen years since the collapse of the Soviet bloc, which led to both the loss of 80 percent of Cuba's foreign trade and a tightening of the U.S. blockade, forcing the Cuban government to adopt an unprecedented set of economic measures known as the Special Period. At one level the Special Period involved the reinsertion of Cuba into the world economy and the adoption of certain market mechanisms in the national economy. In this regard, significant changes in the national economy have been the introduction of markets for agricultural goods, the growth of the self-employed sector, and the liberalization of norms regarding the holding of dollars by Cuban nationals (and since 2004 its replacement by the convertible peso).

As a result, a layer of petty entrepreneurs has emerged in an otherwise state-led economy. On the one hand, this layer plays a necessary role in the production and distribution of goods and services in post-Soviet Cuba; on the other hand, its activities, economic dynamics, social objectives, and very existence contradict important aspects of the socialist direction toward which the Cuban economy is still firmly steered. That is, whereas most of the economy is organized around the principle of social solidarity—especially with regard to universal free education, free healthcare, equality of opportunities, and social equality—the economic universe of this layer is, objectively, organized around personal gain, capital accumulation, the desirability and legitimacy of social inequality, and the expansion of mercantilist relations to the whole economy.

By some accounts, its socioeconomic significance is much greater than the mere statistical weight of the self-employed. Janette Habel, a French specialist on Cuba, has suggested recently that on the island there might have already emerged a new social class of entrepreneurs, associated with the foreign investment sector in the form of "comrade investors," and directors of mixed or state enterprises linked to the market (Habel 2004, 20–21). According to official statistics, by the end of 2006 there was still a substantial number of people in the private sector. When we take their dependents into account, Cuba may have about 1.5 million people who derive their incomes from market-related economic activities. In a country of 11 million that is under the intense hostil-

66 / Francisco Domínguez

ity of the United States and economically blockaded the size of this "private" sector makes it potentially a potent factor in Cuban society and politics. This chapter examines the intricacies of this new, potentially threatening phenomenon of Cuban socialist contemporary reality.[1]

The Size of the Crisis: The Collapse of the Soviet Union

The collapse of the Soviet Union in 1991 had nearly catastrophic consequences for the Cuban economy and society. The most widely accepted view is that almost overnight Cuba lost about 85 percent of its foreign trade, which, among other things, meant the drastic decline of Soviet oil supplies from 12 million tons in 1989 to about 2 million tons in 1992–93, a severe decline of food imports from the socialist bloc, and a decline in spare parts, transport, fertilizers (agriculture), raw and intermediate materials (industry), and education. Overall, GDP declined abruptly by about 35–40 percent. The severity of the crisis was such that Cuba adopted the Período Especial en Tiempo de Paz (Special Period in Peacetime), a variant of the Período Especial en Tiempos de Guerra (Special Period in Wartime), which was originally designed for the eventuality of a U.S. military invasion of the island. The situation deteriorated so rapidly and so profoundly that Cubans, to this day, refer to the crisis that hit rock bottom in 1993–94, as "Armageddon." Predictably, the mainstream press, especially the mouthpieces of world financial capital, such as the *Financial Times*, *The Economist*, and the *Wall Street Journal*, wrote editorial after editorial as though Cuba's economic collapse was a "chronicle of a death foretold."[2]

The disappearance of Cuba's trade with the Eastern bloc was not the end of the country's woes. The administration of George Bush Sr. saw Cuba's troubles as the longed-for opportunity to deal with the "Cuba problem" once and for all and proceeded to tighten drastically the U.S. embargo against the socialist island by supporting measures such as the Torricelli-Graham law. Known officially as the Cuban Democracy Act, the act stipulated that "ships registered in any nation that touched port in Cuba or transported goods to or on behalf of Cuba were prohibited from entering U.S. ports for a period of 180 days and threatened with inclusion on a 'blacklist,' in open violation of the basic norms of freedom of trade and navigation enshrined in international law, international agreements, and United Nations provisions on this matter" (Republic of Cuba 2002). The objective of the Torricelli-Graham law was to strangle Cuba economically by punishing individuals, companies, and countries that traded with the Caribbean island.

The tightening of the U.S. economic blockade against Cuba commenced with the Torricelli-Graham law, "which aimed to restrain the development of the Cuban economy's new driving forces by hitting the inflow of funds and goods by: i) the strict limitations of the transfers of foreign currencies by the families in exile, ii) the six-month ban to enter U.S. harbors of all ships that had anchored in a Cuban port, iii) sanctions against firms doing commerce with the island even though under the jurisdiction of a third state" (Herrera 2003). The tightening of the U.S. blockade continued with alacrity after that, especially when Cuba's economic strategy began to produce positive dividends by attracting foreign investment to the island:

> The embargo was systematized by the Cuban Liberty and Democratic Solidarity Act (the Helms-Burton law) of March 1996, aimed to harden the "international" sanctions against Cuba. Its Title I generalizes the ban to import Cuban goods, demanding, for example, that exporters give proof that no Cuban sugar has been integrated in their products, as was already the case with nickel. It conditions the authorization of currency transfers to the creation on the island of a private sector including employment of salaried staff. Still more enterprising, Title II fixes the modalities of a transition to a "post-Castro" power, as well as the nature of the relationship to have with the United States. Title III grants the U.S. tribunals the right to judge demands for damage and interest made by a civil and moral person of U.S. nationality that considers having been injured by the loss of property in Cuba due to nationalization, and claims compensation from the users or beneficiaries of this property. At the request of the old owners, any national (and family) of a third state, having made transactions with these users or beneficiaries, can be sued in the United States. The sanctions incurred are set out in Title IV, which provides, *inter alia*, the refusal of the State Department to give U.S. entrance visas to these individuals and their families. (Herrera 2003)

Furthermore, the whole of the Western Hemisphere was at that time overwhelmingly dominated by neoliberalism, most governments in the region being right-wingers heavily committed to the idea and with none of them in the slightest sympathetic to Cuba's plight. To many of these governments, Cuba's crisis came as ideological manna from heaven, since many of their most prominent figures in the preceding period had performed extraordinary somersaults in metamorphosing themselves from Marxist intellectuals into enthusiastic neoliberal politicians.[3] Additionally, in 1991 the United States had announced that it was embarking on the Initiative for the Americas, which aimed at creating a free trade area from Canada to Tierra del Fuego and whose first installment would be NAFTA, a free trade area that aimed to integrate the economies of Canada, Mexico, and the United States itself. The U.S. authorities have in fact made it absolutely clear that this continental objective specifically excludes socialist Cuba.

Although since the beginning of the crisis Cuba has been able to develop positive and growing commercial relations with most countries of the European Union (EU), it now had to face systematic hostility and interference in its internal affairs by the increasingly aggressive and pro-U.S. José María Aznar, the prime minister of Spain until 2004, through whom the United States sought to align the European Union on an anti-Castro stance, with some considerable degree of success.

Cuba's Reinsertion in the World Economy: Foreign Direct Investment and Its Significance

Cuba has largely been able to come out of its desperate economic situation thanks to the influx, in the critical period, of foreign direct investment (FDI). Attracting growing amounts of FDI to the country was not only necessary but inevitable. Cuba had to substitute, with a diversity of new commercial partners, the 85 percent of foreign trade lost as a result of the collapse of the Soviet bloc. Unlike other Third World countries, however, the Cuban state insists on being directly involved as a partner with foreign capital in the form of *asociaciones económicas* (AEs, joint ventures), where normally the venture is established on a 50–50 basis. The number of AEs grew steadily from the beginning of the crisis up to 2003, when Cuba adopted a strict vetting process on entering into AEs with foreign partners, monitoring the benefits they bring to the economy in terms of new capital, technology, markets, or management expertise, with an additional emphasis on larger companies as joint ventures. Thus, by the end of 2003, the total had declined to 342 (Economist Intelligence Unit 2004, 28), and in 2005 the figure was 258. The AEs do remain, however, a central plank of Cuba's strategy to deal with the crisis (see table 3.1).

It is clear that FDI is a novel development in post-Soviet Cuba and will remain one of the country's structural features for a long time to come. Cuba's FDI policies are aimed at resolving specific economic problems, such as the diversification of exports, the obtaining of raw materials and fresh capital, its own insertion in new markets, the acquisition of new and advanced tech-

Table 3.1. Number of associations with foreign capital in Cuba, 1990–2005

1990	1991	1992	1993	1994	1995	1996	1997	1998	1999	2000	2001	2002	2003	2004	2005
20	50	80	112	176	226	260	317	340	374	392	400	403	342	313	258

Source: http://www.uscuba.org/02Spadoni_presentation.ppt#9

Table 3.2. Economic associations by economic sector

Basic industry	85
Tourism	76
Construction	48
Light industry	26
Agriculture	24
SIME[1]	17
Food	18
Transport	15
Communications	15
Sugar	12
Science and technology	5
Public health	4
Fishing	6
Biotechnology	6
Finances	3
Other	53

Source: Data are from the statistics of the Ministry of Investment, October 2002
1. Ministerio de la Industria Sideromecánica (Ministry of Iron & Steel and Mechanical Industry).

nologies, and the introduction of modern economic management techniques (Pérez Villanueva 2002).

Despite the generalized belief that FDI goes to the tourist sector, in fact most of it has been invested in the national manufacturing industry. Out the total 403 AEs in 2002, 111 were in both basic and light industry, with construction being a close second, having attracted foreign capital into 48 *asociaciones*. Only 76 were established in the area of tourism. This can be seen in table 3.2.

What is of note in table 3.2 is that FDI has gone to almost every area of the Cuban economy, including agriculture (24 AEs), food (18), and communications (15), as well as diverse fields such as sugar, transport, science and technology, fishing, and biotechnology. So the idea that Cuba is becoming a sensual paradise for tourists in search of entertainment and exciting personal experiences is exaggerated, although plenty of tourists do visit the island for those very reasons. The spread and diversity of FDI also shows that Cuba's economic recovery is comprehensive, since it includes the most important areas of the economy whose individual recovery is not the result of fiscal transfers of

70 / Francisco Domínguez

Table 3.3. Number of economic associations by country of origin

Spain	87
Canada	72
Italy	57
France	18
Mexico	13
United Kingdom	13
Venezuela	12
Germany	7
Israel	5
Rest of Latin America	58
Rest of the world	34

Source: Data is from the statistics of the Estadísticas del Ministerio de Inversión Extranjera y Colaboración (Statistics Ministry of Foreign Investment and Collaboration), February 2000.

resources but rather of real economic activity and hard economic calculations made by investors, whose output has real demand both in the domestic and international spheres. Although Cuba is still far from having resolved all of its national economic needs, the gross formation of fixed capital, at FDI current prices, was 8.2 percent by the end of 2002 (and it has remained roughly at that level up to 2004), comparable to world average figures (Pérez Villanueva 2002). Additionally, the contribution of AEs to the export of Cuban commodities, goods, and services has been highly positive, indicating a clear, sustained, and solid reinsertion into the world economy. The commercial partners of Cuba's AEs come primarily from Europe, since European capital has an overwhelming presence in these enterprises, with AEs from Latin America and Canada also being numerous; Asia and Africa come third and last. The biggest absence, for well-known reasons, is the United States.

By the end of 2003, Spain was the leading foreign investor in Cuba, followed by Canada, Italy, France, Mexico, the United Kingdom, and others in descending order. This spread shows the government's determination never again to depend on a single source for its connections with the world economy, as had happened from 1961 until 1991 with the Soviet bloc, or as had been the case from about 1850 until 1959 with the United States (see table 3.3).

As a result, Cuba currently enjoys a diversified portfolio of trading partners from the four corners of the earth. Taken in blocs, however, Europe and then the Americas are the two main sources of FDI, capital, and imports and are the destination for Cuba's exports. Table 3.4 shows the magnitude of economic links with Venezuela, China, Spain, and other countries.

The Rise of the Private Sector in Cuba / 71

Table 3.4. Origin and destination of foreign direct investment (FDI) in Cuba

Country of origin	Number of foreign associations	Destination of investment	Number of Cuban associations
Spain	77	Basic industry	55
Canada	41	Tourism	44
Italy	40	Construction	21
France	14	Light industry	19
China	10	Agriculture	14
U.K.	9	Food	14
Mexico	7	Steel-metal	12
Panama	6	Transport	11
Germany	6	Defense Ministry	7
Venezuela	5	Sugar	6
Other	43	Other	55

Note: Figures represent number of Asociaciones Económicas (economic associations/joint ventures) with foreign capital.
Source: Conrado Hernández García, "La inversión extranjera en Cuba. Actualidades y perspectivas," www.spri.es/Web/ponencias/intergune/cuba.pdf.

Cuba's approach to FDI, unlike that of the rest of the world, is conceived as integral to the overall policy of economic reactivation and employment generation, but it is also designed so as to fulfill the double function of protecting national sovereignty and preventing the rise of foreign economic enclaves that have characterized FDI in tourism elsewhere. In this connection, restrictions placed on FDI in places such as Havana, Varadero, and Cayo Largo are stipulations that make the signing of *asociaciones económicas* conditional on the foreign partner either having previously invested in or simultaneously investing in other regions of the country (Pérez Villanueva 2002).

Furthermore, a key aspect of the integral nature of Cuba's approach to FDI is that the country has competitive enterprises that produce goods and services with international standards of productivity and quality so as to be able to supply domestically the demand generated by tourism and thus avoid an explosion of imports of those inputs. This is why a part of FDI has been directed toward the beverages and food industries, as can be seen in table 3.5.

Furthermore, the changes that Cuba has undergone in just over a decade are indeed staggering, since in 1989, just before "Armageddon," over 85 percent of Cuba's trade was with Europe, almost exclusively with Eastern Europe and primarily with the Soviet Union. At that time Cuba had commercial exchanges with Asia of around 3–4 percent, approximately 4–5 percent with

Table 3.5. Associations with foreign capital in the food and beverage industry

	Investor	Production and sales	Retailer	Industry
Bravo S.A.		X		Meats
Campo Florido S.A.		X		Meats and by-products
Tasajo Uruguay S.A.	X			Meats
Mercosur S.A.			X	Meats
Bucanero S.A.	X			Beer
Biotek S.A.		X		Soybean research
Río Zaza Ingelco	X			Dairy
CORALAC S.A.		X		Dairy
Francesa del Pan	X			Bakery
Haricari S.A.			X	Grain
Procesadora de Soya S.A.	X			Soybean research
Stella S.A.			X	Candy
Meztler S.A.		X		Candy
Cubagua S.A.	X			Water and soft drinks
Vinos Fantinel S.A.		X		Wine
Los Portales S.A.		X		Water and soft drinks

Data for this table are from Dirección de Planificación (Directorate of Planning). MINAL, citado en Omar Pérez Villanueva, Estabilidad macroeconomica y financiamiento externo: la inversion extranjera directa en Cuba, http://www.nodo50.org/cubasigloXXI/economia/villanueva3_300902.htm (web page visited 29 July 2007).

the Americas, and about 1 percent with the rest of the world. As early as 1995, when its GDP was 35 percent smaller than in 1989, Cuba did 42 percent of its foreign trade with Europe. At the same time, its trade with Asia had increased to more than 10 percent, while its trade with the Americas had increased to about 40 percent. It must be stressed that Cuba's European trade was not only drastically smaller but qualitatively different in that, as is well known, a minute and declining proportion was with Eastern Europe and the Soviet Union/Russia, while a greater and growing proportion was with Western Europe.[4] Table 3.6 below shows the current structure of Cuba's foreign trade.

Thus, if we take into account the fact that the Soviet Union, which was by far Cuba's biggest eastern European trading partner, collapsed at the end of 1991, leading to a sharp decline in commercial exchanges between the two countries in 1992–93, the reinsertion of Cuba into the world economy took place in two to three years. The Cuban authorities have displayed an extraordinary agility in responding to a highly difficult, if not impossible, challenge. By any standards they have been pretty successful.

Table 3.6. Foreign trade, in millions of pesos

2003	2004	
6,280,9	7,710.1	Total trade
1,662.0	2,169.9	Exports of goods
917.8	1,151.7	Europe
141.4	140.4	Asia
16.8	7.6	Africa
584.9	869.6	America
1.1	0.6	Oceania
4,618.8	5,540.1	Imports of goods
1,539.9	1,530.5	Europe
921.5	1,090.5	Asia
85.6	69.9	Africa
2,022.6	2,794.7	America
49.2	54.5	Oceania
-2,956.8	-3,370.2	Trade balance

Source: Anuario Estadístico de Cuba (Cuba National Statistics Yearbook), 2004.

The "Co-operativization" of the Agricultural Sector

It is in Cuban agriculture where the deepest and the largest structural transformations have taken place with the creation in 1993 of agricultural cooperatives known as Unidades Básicas de Producción Cooperativa (UBPCs, Basic Units of Cooperative Production). Although different sources give slightly different figures, between September 1993 and the end of 1995 2,804 UBPCs, encompassing 42 percent of total agricultural land, had been created. These UBPCs aimed to address the acute problems faced by Cuba's agriculture, and, since all of the land came from state farms previously devoted to sugar cultivation, these cooperatives were created to foster a much needed diversification of the sector for both domestic consumption and exports, which can be seen in table 3.7.

The efficiency and profitability of many of these UBPCs have not been as good as expected, leading to a significant reduction in their number. By the end of 2003, there were 885 UBPCs in total; 707 of them were devoted to sugar cane and 178 to other crops. In addition, there were 1,116 Cooperativas de Producción Agrícola (CPAs, Agricultural Production Cooperatives), of which 347 were devoted to the cultivation of sugar cane. Finally, there were 2,556 Cooperativas de Crédito y Servicios (CCSs, Credit and Service Cooperatives) (Nova González 2004; Sinclair and Thompson 2001, 14).

74 / Francisco Domínguez

Table 3.7. Number of UBPCs in 1996

Type	Number
Sugar cane	1,288
Livestock	735
Fruit crops	26
Citrus	115
Tobacco	51
Rice	15
Coffee and cacao	232
Various crops	342

Source: William A. Messina, Jr., "Agricultural
Reform in Cuba: Implications for Agricultural
Production, Markets and Trade," in Cuba in
Transition 9, ASCE 1999, p. 433.

The establishment of the UBPCs is a step toward privatization or, at the very least, a step away from absolute state ownership. The regime under which they operate makes their categorization difficult because they can be defined either as part of the rising private sector or as part of the public sector, given the state's ownership of the land and the restrictions the state places on them. Nevertheless, the change in land tenure is dramatic. Before the reform, in 1989, state farms represented 82 percent of the arable land of the country with the remaining 18 percent basically in the private sector. By 1999 the state farms had dropped to barely 24 percent, while the nonstate sector grew to a formidable 76 percent, with the newly formed UBPCs representing 47 percent of that total. No doubt this is one of the most profound economic transformations of a previously heavily socialized economy. The regime under which the UBPCs operate is given succinctly as follows:

> The UBPCs allow collectives of workers to lease state farmlands rent-free, in perpetuity. Members elect management teams that determine the division of jobs, what crops will be planted on which parcels, and how much credit will be taken out to pay for the purchase of inputs. Property rights remain in the hands of the state, and the UBPCs must still meet production quotas for their key crops, but the collectives are owners of what they produce. Perhaps most importantly, what they produce in excess of their quotas can now be freely sold on the newly reopened farmers markets. This last reform, made in 1994, offered a price incentive to farmers both to sell their produce through legal channels rather than the black market, and also to make effective use of the new technologies. (Rosset 1998)

Sugar-cane UBPCs have found it difficult to survive and become competitive, compared to the trends visible in most other economic activities. No doubt, the disappearance of preferential prices and markets in the Eastern bloc countries accounts for the steady contraction of this sector.

These UBPCs face a fundamental problem of inefficiency that is likely to originate in heavy overstaffing, which can be deduced from a comparison with the performance of the private sector. In 1981 the state employed 91.8 percent of all workers in the country; in 2003, on the basis of official data, the state employed 76.6 percent in what for many people appeared to be a gradually declining trend. However, in order to correctly judge both the quantitative and particularly qualitative significance of the "private sector" it is necessary to observe that the bulk of the increase comes from the cooperative sector, which needs to be examined.

The agricultural workers involved in UBPCs make a decisive contribution to Cuba's economy: "The staff in these collectives . . . guarantees 72 percent of the sugar cane, 21 percent of the total production of various cultivations, 52 percent of the citrus, 36 percent of the cocoa, 20 percent of the coffee, and 24 percent of the milk. Hence the importance of a close relationship that enterprises and ministries must maintain with the management [of these collectives] in order to assess the reasons for insufficient progress in specific areas" (Varela 2003). However, the contribution that UBPCs make to agricultural production as a whole is indeed substantial. As can be seen from table 3.8, they make a considerable contribution to the output of cattle, coffee, citrus fruits, potatoes, bananas, cocoa, milk, beef, and so forth.

CPAs, meanwhile, have been characterized by a relative higher level of efficiency and profitability when compared to UBPCs. Table 3.9 gives the details.

Furthermore, not only is the private sector overwhelmingly more efficient than the UBPCs (and the state sector proper), but also its presence in the market is hugely more significant, as can be seen in table 3.10.

The private sector is responsible for over 30 percent of the sales of vegetables in the open market and of over 60 percent of the sales of beef-related products (*productos cárnicos*). The difference from the situation before the Special Period is the growing presence in the market place of the state/cooperative sector, whereas historically these sales were mostly monopolized by privateers of every description, through parallel markets, gray markets, or simply black market transactions. Despite these complexities, output in the agricultural sector as a whole has steadily increased in most key categories for consumption, as can be seen in table 3.11.

According to data from the Oficina Nacional de Estadísticas (ONE), at the end of 2004 membership in the cooperative sector was over 280,000, which

Table 3.8. Contribution of UBPCs and CPAs in cattle and agricultural production

	2000 MINAG						2001 MINAG					
	Nation (metric ton)[1]	Total (metric ton)	UBPC %	CPA %	Total Coop%	State	Nation (metric ton)	Total (metric ton)	UBPC %	CPA %	Total Coop%	State
Potatoes	1,230.9	967.9	22	12	34	47	1,380.6	1,059.8	25	12	37	47
Bananas	844.9	571.9	25	8	33	59	968.0	664.2	25	12	37	47
Vegetables	2,372.7	1,557.9	6	5	11	43	2,676.5	1,691.3	4	5	9	44
Green leaf vegetables	—	653.2	3	3	6	22	—	802.5	3	3	6	45
Rice consumption	276.4	64.7	24	4	28	63	300.5	75.1	25	4	29	40
Maize	273.2	197.7	10	8	18	27	298.8	231.7	8	7	15	25
Beans	106.3	58.3	6	8	14	22	99.1	53.8	6	8	14	20
Fruits	600.9	296.5	10	5	15	34	683.7	347.7	8	6	14	27
Citrus	958.6	892.6	31	2	33	60	957.1	858.2	34	2	36	57
Tobacco	38.0	38.8	7	13	20	2	37.9	37.9	6	14	20	15
Coffee	12.1	12.1	26	22	48	46	12.7	12.7	3	22	25	43
Milk (mml)[2]	517.5	403.7	36	10	46	23	523.1	415.7	36	9	45	22
Beef	151.5	142.8	6	—	6	94	149.9	135.9	6	—	6	94

Source: Oficina Nacional de Estadísticas, Principal Indicators, 2002, cited in Armando Nova González, "La UBPC y el cooperativismo en la agricultura cubana 1993–2001," paper presented to LASA 2003 XXIV International Congress, Dallas, Texas.

1. Nation (metric ton) includes the output of CCS (Cooperativas de Crédito y Servicio—Service and Credit Cooperatives) and the private sector, while Total (metric ton) refers to the categories "State," "CPA," and "UBPC."

2. Milk (mml) is in millions of liters.

Table 3.9. Selected production indicators of CPAs, 1996–2001

National	Unit of measure	1996	1997	1998	1999	2000	2001
Quantity	uno	758	750	741	732	721	707
Profitable	uno	649	603	621	635	663	655
Not profitable	uno	109	147	120	97	58	52
Quantity of members	uno	35,031	32,371	30,863	30,731	29,524	30,435
Profitable	uno	28,632	27,363	26,483	27,680	26,744	28,649
Not profitable	uno	6,399	5,008	4,380	3,051	2,780	1,786
Income/average/member/month	uno	187	175	191	202	228	237
Profitable	uno	200	182	199	208	234	241
Not profitable	uno	129	136	143	145	165	172
Profits/average/member/year	peso	851	545	674	756	832	826
Profitable	peso	0.65	0.75	0.72	0.68	0.71	0.68
Not profitable	peso	1.36	1.31	1.27	1.37	1.37	1.34

Source: Resumen Nacional de los Balances Económicos MINAG 1999–2001, cited in Armando Nova González, "La UBPC y el cooperativismo en la agricultura cubana 1993–2001," paper presented to LASA 2003 XXIV International Congress, Dallas, Texas.

78 / Francisco Domínguez

Table 3.10. Sales in agricultural markets per type of supplier, in percentage

	Agricultural produce					Meat byproducts				
	1997	1998	1999	2000	2001	1997	1998	1999	2000	2001
Total	100.0	100.0	100.0	100.0	100.0	100.0	100.0	100.0	100.0	100.0
State	41.5	53.8	75.1	65.7	63.6	39.1	32.1	32.1	31.3	36.2
UBPCs	4.8	2.3	1.5	2.5	3.2	0.2	0.2	0.2	1.2	2.8
CPAs	3.5	2.3	1.1	1.4	1.4	0.2	0.2	0.2	0.1	1.0
Private	50.2	41.6	22.3	30.4	31.8	60.5	67.5	67.5	67.4	60.0

Source: Ventas en Mercados Agropecuarios, Oficina Nacional de Estadísticas, 1997–2000, cited in Armando Nova González, "La UBPC y el cooperativismo en la agricultura cubana 1993–2001," paper presented to LASA 2003 XXIV International Congress, Dallas, Texas.

Table 3.11. Evolution of output in Cuban agriculture

2003	2004	Main productions (totals in tons)
2,956.2	3,162.0	Tubers, edible roots, and plantain
3,931.2	4,059.9	Vegetables
360.0	398.7	Corn
127.0	132.9	Beans
792.7	801.7	Citrus
807.2	908.0	Other fruits
		Delivery for slaughter
112.3	110.5	Cattle
142.4	148.9	Pork
43.2	45.7	Poultry
1,785.1	1,748.6	Eggs (MU)

Source: Oficina Nacional de Estadísticas (National Office for Statistics), 2004.

represents a decline from the 325,000 recorded in 1999. The total labor force for the two years was 4,359,400 in 1999 and 4,641,700 in 2004, thus making the cooperative sector a declining proportion of 7.5 percent and 6 percent respectively. With regard to the UBPCs, their contribution to the marketization of the Cuban economy is tenuous at best, since they must sell a fixed quota of production to the state and sell in the open market anything over and above it.

The Self-employed: *Cuentapropismo*

The structural changes experienced by the Cuban economy since the onset of the Special Period have not only transformed the relative weight of state,

The Rise of the Private Sector in Cuba / 79

mixed, private, and cooperative sectors, reducing the first and increasing all the others, but have also produced a layer of individuals whose livelihoods depend substantially or partially on the market or market-related activities. With Decree 192 of 1 December 1992, people involved in the handicraft and industrial products markets were authorized to register as self-employed and thus began this type of economic activity. For the period January–May 1996 the self-employed seller category represented 35 percent of all the sales in this sector (Financial Research Institute 1997, 28). Furthermore, with Decree-Law 141 of September 1993, self-employment was revitalized and expanded. The obvious reason behind this was the forcible shrinking of the economic role of the state by making large numbers of state employees redundant, for whom self-employment was to provide an alternative source of employment and income. With this first law, self-employment was authorized in 135 trades, and subsequent legislation has lifted restrictions on 19 other trades and activities, including the sales of refreshments, the opening of small restaurants, and the provision of catering services, with the legal restriction that the self-employed worker could not hire any staff except from his or her own family (Financial Research Institute 1997, 21).

Despite the intrinsically precarious nature of economic activities dominated by market fluctuations, the number of self-employed people at the end of 2004 was 166,700, an increase from 156,600 in 1999 (Oficina Nacional de Estadísticas 2004a). This might mean that a large proportion of the goods and services that they provide were previously absent, although the demand for them existed. The relative stability of their numbers must also mean that they earn relatively stable or rising incomes. Moreover, since a large proportion of the sales that they carry out were, up to 2004, conducted in dollars (whereas most of the inputs are largely obtained in pesos), the differential must have been highly beneficial. The number of *ayudantes* (assistants), especially in *paladares* (private restaurants), must be added to the figures, but, since nonalcoholic beverages and catering represented a bare 17 percent of the total category of *cuentapropistas* (self-employed), the total number of people in this category who depend on market-related activities for their income (but who do so as peso wage earners) is in the region of 28,000.

In addition to the *cuentapropistas*, there are two other categories of people in the private sector, namely those involved in transport (*transportistas*) and in house renting (*arrendadores*) in the following proportions (see table 3.12).

The tax payments of the *cuentapropistas* to the state have declined steadily (by over 26 million pesos between 1998 and 2001), indicating a deterioration in the income generated by some of their businesses and a general worsening of the economic performance of some of them. According to one study, between 1997 and 2002, 290,980 *cuentapropistas* ceased to be self-employed,

80 / Francisco Domínguez

Table 3.12. *Cuentapropistas* according to economic activity, in percentage

	1998	1999	2000	2001	2002
TCP[1]	80.93	72.46	69.96	68.39	67.65
Transport	15.56	20.17	22.17	22.14	22.61
Landlords	3.51	7.37	7.87	9.47	9.74

Source: Victoria Pérez Izquierdo, Fabian Oberto Calderón, and Mayelin González Rodríguez, "Los trabajadores por cuenta propia en Cuba," *Cuba Siglo XXI*, 47, October 2003, p. 10.
Note: TCP stands for *trabajo por cuenta propia* (self-employed).

Table 3.13. Proportion of licenses granted of the total requested

1995	1996	1997	1998	1999	2000	2001	2002	2003
55.39	80.77	52.44	35.21	29.67	25.54	23.37	22.45	22.31

Source: Victoria Pérez Izquierdo, Fabian Oberto Calderón and Mayelin González Rodríguez, "Los trabajadores por cuenta propia en Cuba," *Cuba Siglo XXI*, 47, October 2003, p. 10.

due mainly to a lack of demand for their services and/or a rise in the cost of inputs.[5] In contrast, *arrendadores* and *transportistas* kept their tax returns steady (Pérez Izquierdo, Oberto Calderón, and Gonzalez Rodríguez 2003, 8, 14–15). As a result, the authorities have grown increasingly reluctant to grant licenses to all those who request them. In fact, as can be seen in table 3.13, by 2003, of the total requested only about 22 percent were being granted. The overwhelming majority of these activities were concentrated in Havana, which in 2003 was responsible for 23 percent of the national total, that is, twenty-three thousand licenses.

Thus, overall, the phenomenon of *cuentapropismo* (including those in transport and house renting) is not a growing phenomenon, including at best about two hundred thousand workers. It is also much less significant economically and politically than previously thought.

However, there is yet another private entrepreneurship that must be discussed and included in our analysis: *jineterismo* (hustling). Although illegal but tolerated, *jineterismo* involves nonlicensed and/or outright illegal activities, such as working sporadically in domestic service, hustling of various types, engaging in unlicensed, illegal transport activities, and prostitution. It is impossible to quantify the number of people in this category; one well-known opponent of the Revolution, Carlos Alberto Montaner, suggests the figure of one hundred thousand, attributing the cause to "the stupid economic and social organization [of the country] imposed by the communists. . . ." (Montaner 2003). It is difficult to accept such a high figure, especially after the

The Rise of the Private Sector in Cuba / 81

Table 3.14. Approximate number of Cubans under mercantilist or
semi-mercantilist relations

Category	Numbers
UBPC, CPA, CCS	280,000
Cuentapropistas	167,000
Assistants	28,000
Jineteras/os	50,000
Tourism workers	13,000
Total	538,000

Source: Calculations are based on the data in this chapter.

severe crackdown on "antisocial behavior" in all of its manifestations, particularly prostitution, that was initiated by the regime as early as 1999 (Vicent
1999). However, for the purposes of calculation, we might assume fifty thousand in the broad category of jineterismo, including prostitution.

Finally, economic reform has created a marginalization of some sections of
youth, which, if the Western press is to be believed, manifests itself in the form
of a "crime wave" (The Economist 1999, 59). To all of this must be added the
corrosive effects that the "dollarization" of the economy had until 2004 when,
in response to U.S. sanctions, the government banned the dollar as a currency with which to conduct domestic transactions.[6] The introduction of the
convertible peso and the elimination of the dollar have de facto made part of
this problem evaporate, bringing about the "total monetary sovereignty of the
nation," to use the phrase of José Luis Rodríguez, the minister of economics
and planning, in his report to the National Assembly on 23 December 2004.
However, the circulation of the convertible peso, and the differential access
that people will have to it, will maintain some of the problematical socioeconomic inequalities that have emerged with economic reform. Nevertheless,
in the report, Rodríguez pointed out that the liquidity in pesos created by the
measure resulted in an increase in savings accounts, which would indicate
some confidence in the peso on the part of the population (Rodríguez 2004).

Thus, taking the private sector as a whole, the number of people employed
in or by the private sector was by the end of 2004 in the region of 20–25 percent of the total labor force (Oficina Nacional de Estadísticas 2004a). Adding
together all of the categories of workers in market or market-related activities, we find a total of over half a million (see table 3.14).[7] If we assume that
each of these has two dependents, then the number of Cubans whose income
partially depends on successful market transactions is about 1.5 million. This
conclusion must, however, be qualified by the fact that dependents in Cuba
(children, old people, and the disabled) are heavily protected by state welfare
provision.

The Private Sector: Base and Superstructure

Political power in Cuba is structured around three key institutional types of organizations: the Communist Party of Cuba (CCP) and the Union of Communist Youth (UJC), associations and mass organizations, and state organizations. The first category is self-explanatory. In the second category we find the Central de Trabajadores de Cuba (Cuban Workers' Confederation), the Federación de Estudiantes Universitarios (Federation of University Students), Asociación Nacional de Agricultores Pequeños (National Association of Small Farmers), the Comités de Defensa de la Revolución (Committees for the Defense of the Revolution), Federación de Mujeres Cubanas (Federation of Cuban Women), Federación de Estudiantes de la Enseñanza Media (Federation of Secondary School Students), and, recently, the Asociación Cubana de Combatientes de la Revolución (Cuban Association of Revolutionary Veterans). Finally, there is the National Assembly of the People's Power, with counterparts at municipal and provincial levels, above which comes the key state body, the Council of Ministers. The security forces (the Revolutionary Armed Forces, state security, and police) are subordinate to the Ministry of Interior. Similarly, the judicial system (the Supreme Court and the Tribunals) is subordinate to the National Assembly and Council of State, the latter being the highest organ of government in Cuba.

The social, political, and economic foundations of the Cuban state are stipulated in its Constitution: Cuba is a socialist republic of workers, peasants, and other manual and intellectual workers (Article 1). The people exert power through the provincial, municipal, and local Asambleas de Poder Popular (Assemblies of People's Power) and other state organs (Article 4). The Asambleas exert this power in close liaison and collaboration with social organizations in their geographical areas of jurisdiction; the local social organizations are in general the same as those found at the national level. In a nutshell, as far as the country's political institutional framework is concerned, Cuba is a republic of workers and peasants led by the Communist Party, with no constitutional provision for any other social layer, mainly because such layers just did not exist until recently.[8] Until 1989, that was the totality of Cuba's constitutional universe.

The collapse of the Soviet Union changed all of that. Cuba was then forced to adopt the Special Period, with all the attendant socioeconomic changes discussed above. In 1992, the Constitution was modified to take account of some of these changes. Essentially the amendments of 1992 involved making the election of representatives at the level of Provincial Assemblies of People's Power secret and direct. It also led to the establishment of an additional tier of new People's Councils at city, town, neighborhood, village, and rural zone levels (there are 14 provincial and 169 municipal assemblies). These amendments included the relaxation of the law concerning property relations as well as the management and control over some enterprises, in order to guarantee the operation of foreign capital, and the abolition of restrictions regarding simultaneous membership in the Communist Party and affiliation with a religion. The amendments emphasized the prohibition of religious discrimination and the application of sanctions for any form whatsoever of religious discrimination.

The constitutional amendments of 1992 did not make provisions for the expansion of the system in order to make political room for the "non-proletarian" social layer that has emerged since 1989. As we have seen above, there can be as many as half a million people (plus their dependents) who derive their income (or supplementary income) from mercantilized economic relations. In addition, there are marginalized sections of Cuban youth in the main cities,[9] although the percentage of such youth are smaller in Cuba than elsewhere in the world; it is likely that many of these also engage in *jineterismo*. The number of Cubans whose relatively better-off social situation is due to market-related activities, although substantial, is not very large. According to the Oficina Nacional de Estadísticas, at the end of 2004 Cuba's population in employment stood at 4,641,700, of which 4,194,900 worked in the state civil sector, 280,100 in cooperatives, and 166,700 in the private sector. The private sector proper (including workers in UBPCs) numbered about 500,000. The unemployment rate at the end of 2004 was officially 1.9 percent (Oficina Nacional de Estadísticas 2004a). For a society used to gainful and meaningful employment as well as to unparalleled levels of socioeconomic equality, the emergence of these new layers represents a formidable structural transformation. Peso-earning Cubans must envy the levels of income and particularly consumption of those Cubans working, and earning hard currency, in the private sector and are probably hostile to their evolving social outlook.

Despite the size and significance of these layers, the point should not be over-labored. A capitalist restoration is not about to break out in Cuba, and all Cuban citizens are part of the socialized health, education, housing, and state systems of social provision. Cubans, both state workers and marketeers, both those who earn pesos and those who earn convertible pesos, are overwhelmingly in favor of maintaining these "social gains of the Revolution." Furthermore, market-related activities are heavily restricted and subject to stern regulations. In short, they are not allowed to grow into large capitalist enterprises.

One approach to dealing with Cuba's growing social inequalities is taxation policy, confirming the regime's determination to prevent the rise of a fully fledged capitalist layer. The system of progressive taxation is, by Cuban standards, extremely harsh for high-income Cubans. Thus, for example, anybody earning up to 6,000 Cuban convertible pesos (or dollars) must pay 10–12 percent in taxes, while those earning 60,000 pesos or dollars must pay 50 percent in taxes. Income tax is also raised from the performance of intellectual, artistic, manual, and physical work, but not from state workers' salaries and wages (Financial Research Institute 1997, 35).

Nevertheless, these measures in themselves may not be sufficient to address the political problem that is emerging. After all, half a million people represent a substantial proportion of the economically active population, which, if we add their families, makes the phenomenon even larger. The constitutional incongruity here is conspicuous in that at least the members of the Asociación Nacional de Agricultores Pequeños (ANAP, National Association of Small Farmers)—a body that organizes Cuba's private farmers, the only non-proletarian social group that has been allowed to operate more or less on a market basis since 1959—enjoy the constitutional right to organize with the de jure right of representation at every level of the political system. From the onset of the Special Period, this incongruity has become more pronounced since similar rights have been granted to religious believers (this latter category has representation in the National Assembly), including the concessions made to the Catholic Church after the pope's visit. Granting Cuban private entrepreneurs the formal right to set up associations but constitutionally forbidding them to challenge the dominant socialist principles of society, which is the most consistent way they can pursue their economic interests, makes the problem potentially severe.

At a critical juncture these groups may raise the question of their specific socioeconomic interests that objectively fall outside the socialist parameters of the existing polity, and this questioning may lead them to contest the lack of political representation that they experience, when compared to the rights already enjoyed by every other social sector. The point here is not just their formal right to organize, which they do enjoy, but their political right to forward their specific socioeconomic interests, such as, for example, campaigning for alternative economic policies aimed at reducing regulation and taxation, the relaxation of the restrictions to employ labor and determine the size of their enterprises (*paladares* are allowed a maximum of twelve customers at a time), and even the right to trade directly with the world economy. The latter point, given that Florida is only ninety miles away, is objectively of strategic significance, both for the government and for this proto-capitalist layer, whose capital is likely to have originated in largish dollar remittances sent by relatives living in Florida. What all these restrictions amount to is the curtailing of the right of these proto-capitalist layers to develop into fully fledged capitalists. A possible relaxation of these restrictions might come about as

The Rise of the Private Sector in Cuba / 85

a result of a substantial improvement in Cuba's economic performance, an eventuality that may or may not materialize. The truth is that, although Cuba's economic recovery has indeed been impressive and solid, the world capitalist economy on which this recovery now depends is fragile and susceptible to sudden violent crises, as demonstrated by the South East Asian economic turmoil of 1999. Against this there is the generous largesse of Venezuela's commercial exchanges with Cuba, in the form of thousands of barrels of oil per day. However, the prospects of gradual normalization of trade relations with the United States, which looked possible under Clinton and which would furnish a substantial base from which to recover once and for all—despite the attendant dangers—is a somewhat unlikely eventuality under George W. Bush and the "war against terrorism," which is likely to dominate U.S. politics for a long time to come.

It is the geopolitical position of Cuba that dramatically reduces the options open to Cuba's political leadership. One can visualize the multiplier effect of the current U.S. aggression against Cuba if a substantial capitalist layer were allowed to develop and consolidate on Cuban soil. At present there are two political agents that can provide a coherent political and economic system for Cuba, namely, the Cuban Communist Party and the United States. For poor Cuba there is no Third Way available (if indeed such a thing is viable anywhere in this savagely neoliberal "New World Order"). Over the last forty-five years the United States has demonstrated its willingness to resort to any means to crush the Revolution.[10] It should be clear by now, after the failure of the Torricelli-Graham and Helms-Burton laws, that U.S.-inspired socioeconomic change in Cuba can come only from within the island itself. Hence it is important to prevent the newly created social layers from being alienated from socialist values or at least from the values of social solidarity. In specific circumstances, the objective interests of these new layers might undermine the social and political consensus on which the Revolution rests, a consensus that has been crucial in allowing Cuba to resist over forty-five years of unrelenting U.S. aggression. Were they to solidify as a fully fledged capitalist class, however small or weak, they could be a mass base that might serve the objectives of the United States against Cuba. This is no argument to advocate the disappearance or abolition of these layers, since they do fulfill an essential economic function in the Cuba of the Special Period, which is largely driven by the dynamism and expansion of tourism with the attendant expansion of the services sector of the economy to which they largely belong.

In this regard, it would appear that, given Cuba's predicament, if the Revolution is to survive and its social gains are to be maintained, the ruling position of the Cuban Communist Party must be maintained. This also necessitates the strengthening of the constitutional and political positions of Cuba's social organizations whose socioeconomic interests objectively coincide with the Revolution's political objectives of social solidarity, equality, and the preservation of the social, economic, and political gains. That is to say, the instances of participatory democracy must, as a matter of political and economic necessity, be enlarged and deepened. In short, for as long as Cuba remains in the geopolitical position in which it finds itself at present, party political pluralism would appear to be out of the question. This does not mean the dogmatization of the party, its policies, or its outlook; it means, in fact, quite the reverse. In the course of just over twelve years, Cuban society has changed dramatically. New, and necessary, socioeconomic actors have emerged and no administrative decision will wish them, or the socioeconomic interests that they have developed, away. Mechanisms are being found to integrate their concerns and interests in a harmonious manner within a carefully and gradually modified political system. In other words, the preservation of a socioeconomic consensus to ensure the Revolution's survival in the twenty-first century does not mean that changes in the economic base must have mechanical reflections in the superstructure.

Notes

1. There are variations in the sets of figures utilized throughout this paper; this is mainly due to their origination in different sources. However, they do not diverge widely and, since we are interested in trends, they have been used just as they appeared in the various sources consulted.

2. See, among many other references, *The Financial Times Survey* (26 September 1995) and *The Economist*. The latter, for instance, in its 14 August 1997 edition, ran an article with the suggestive title "Fidel, the Church, and Capitalism. Cuba's Leader Fights the Demonic Powers of Faith and Money. And Loses."

3. The list of Latin American intellectuals who fall into this category is long indeed, the most outstanding case being that of Fernando Henrique Cardoso, the former president of Brazil. For a detailed analysis of this ideological metamorphosis of truly continental proportions, see Petras 1992.

4. Since 2005 Venezuela and China have become Cuba's first and second trading partners respectively. However, trade with the EU continues to thrive, thus altering the structure but not the direction of Cuba's foreign trade strategy (for details, see Economist Intelligence Unit 2006, 28).

5. This initial explosion of *cuentapropismo* led many, including the author, to draw exaggerated conclusions about the rise of a powerful entrepreneurial private sector.

6. Over 50 percent of Cubans have access to dollars, through remittances from relatives in the United States or by working in the tourist sector or by engaging in various illegal activities (from the black market to *jineterismo*).

The Rise of the Private Sector in Cuba / 87

7. I have included workers in the tourism industry because they receive an important part of their income in the form of hard currency, in dollars until recently and in convertible pesos since the government's recent decision to eliminate the circulation of the U.S. currency in the domestic economy.

8. Professional and technical people, such as doctors, university lecturers, and the like, were deemed to be intellectual workers and were all organized through the CTC or similar organizations.

9. There is a degree of de facto discrimination in the tourist sector, where foreign managers are more likely to employ Aryan-looking Cubans than blacks.

10. James Cason, the officer in charge of the Office of U.S. Interests in Havana, and many of his staff were centrally involved in the recent events leading to the execution of three Cuban hijackers, which appeared to constitute a serious crisis, with a military dimension, between Cuba and the United States.

References

Central de Trabajadores de Cuba. http://www.cubasindical.cubaweb.cu/empleo_en_cuba/textos_y_fotos/algo_mas.htm, accessed 25 January 2005.

The Economist. 1997. "Fidel, the Church, and Capitalism. Cuba's Leader Fights the Demonic Powers of Faith and Money. And Loses." *The Economist*, vol. 344, issue 8030 (17 August): 27–28.

———. 1999. "Cuba Discovers Crime." *The Economist* (16 January): 33–35.

Economist Intelligence Unit. 2004. *Cuba Country Report* (May).

———. 2006. *Cuba Country Report* (May).

Financial Research Institute. 1997. *Cuba's Economic Reforms: Results and Future Prospects*. Havana: Financial Research Institute.

The Financial Times. 1995. "Cuba: Most Painful of Transitions." *Financial Times Survey* (26 September): 1–4.

Habel, J. 2004. "Cuba entre pressions externes et blocages internes." *Le Monde Diplomatique* (June): 20–21.

Hernández García, C. 2006. "La inversión extranjera en Cuba: Actualidades y perspectivas." http://www.spri.es/Web/ponencias/intergune/cuba.pdf, accessed 20 October 2006.

Herrera, R. 2003. "The Effects of the U.S. 'Embargo' against Cuba." In *Action and Communications Network for International Development: Alternatives for a Different World* (7 October). http://www.alternatives.ca/article876.html, accessed 17 March 2004.

Messina, W. A., Jr. 1999. "Agricultural Reform in Cuba: Implications for Agricultural Production, Markets, and Trade." In *Cuba in Transition 9* (papers and proceedings of the Ninth Annual Meeting of the Association for the Study of the Cuban Economy). http://lanic.utexas.edu/la/cb/cuba/asce/cuba9/messina.pdf, accessed 17 March 2004.

Ministerio de Azúcar. 2001. *Informe del MINAZ*. Centro Nacional de Capacitación Azucarera (CENCA).

88 / Francisco Domínguez

Ministerio de Inversión Extranjera y Colaboración. 2000. *Estadísticas*. Havana: Ministerio de Inversión Extranjera y Colaboración.

Ministerio Nacional de Agricultura. 1999–2001. *Resumen nacional de los balances económicos*. Havana: Ministerio Nacional de Agricultura.

———. 2002. *Resumen nacional de los balances económicos, 1996–2001*. Havana: Oficina Nacional de Estadísticas.

Montaner, C. A. 2003. "A las jineteras." http://www.firmaspress.com/247.htm, 9 March, accessed 17 March 2004.

Nova González, A. 2003. "La UBPC y el cooperativismo en la agricultura cubana, 1993–2001." Paper presented to the 24th International Congress of the LASA, Dallas, Texas, 27–29 March. http://www.clas.berkeley.edu:7001/Events/fall2004/10–11–04–cubasymposium/ELCOOPERATIVISMENCUBA1.pdf, accessed 25 January 2005.

———. 2004. "El cooperativismo línea de desarrollo en la agricultura cubana, 1993–2003." Paper presented to the 25th Internacional Congreso of the LASA, Las Vegas, Nevada, October 7–9.

Oficina Nacional de Estadísticas. 2001. *Anuario Estadístico de Cuba*. Havana: Oficina Nacional de Estadísticas.

———. 2002. *Anuario Estadístico de Cuba*. Havana: Oficina Nacional de Estadísticas.

———. 2003. *Anuario Estadístico de Cuba*. Havana: Oficina Nacional de Estadísticas.

———. 2004a. *Anuario Estadístico de Cuba*. Havana: Oficina Nacional de Estadísticas.

———. 2004b. *Estadísticas Seleccionadas*. Havana: Oficina Nacional de Estadísticas.

———. 2004c. *Panorama Económico y Social*. Havana: Oficina Nacional de Estadísticas.

———. 2004d. "Cuba en cifras 2004," http://www.cubagob.cu/otras_info/publicaciones/cubaencifras/contenido.pdf, accessed 25 January 2005.

———. 2006. "Panorama Económico y Social." Havana: Oficina Nacional de Estadísticas, www.one.cu/publicaciones/ultimas/panorama2006.pdf, accessed 22 June 2007.

Pérez Izquierdo, V., F. Oberto Calderón, and González. "Los trabajadores por cuenta propia en Cuba." *Cuba Siglo XXI* 47 (October 2003). http://www.nodo50.org/cubasigloXXI/economía/pizquierdo1_311004.pdf, accessed 17 March 2004.

Pérez Villanueva, O. 2002. "Estabilidad macroeconómica y financiamiento externo: La inversión extranjera directa en Cuba." *Cuba Siglo XXI* 22 (October 2003). http://www.nodo50.org/cubasigloXXI/economia.htm, accessed 17 March 2004.

Petras, J. 1992. "The Retreat of the Intellectuals." In *Latin America in the Time of the Cholera*, edited by J. Petras and M. Morley, 158–69. London: Routledge.

Republic of Cuba. 2002. *Cuba's Report to the UN Secretary General on General Assembly Resolution 57/11: Necessity of Ending the Economic, Commercial, and Financial Blockade Imposed by the United States of America against Cuba*. http://www.cubaminrex.cu/bloqueo/Eng/02_eng.htm, accessed 17 March 2004.

Rodríguez, J. L. 2004. *Informe sobre los resultados económicos del 2004 y el Plan Económico Social para el 2005*. Presented to the Asamblea Nacional del Poder Popular, 23 December. http://www.cubagob.cu/mapa.htm, accessed 25 January 2005.

Rodríguez, M. 2003. "Los trabajadores por cuenta propia en Cuba." *Cuba Siglo XXI* 47 (October). http://www.nodo50.org/cubasigloXXI/economia/pizquierdo1_311004.pdf, accessed 17 March 2004.

Rosset, P. 1998. "Alternative Agriculture Works: The Case of Cuba." *Monthly Review* 50, no. 3 (July–August): 137–46.

Sinclair, M., and M. Thompson. 2001. *Cuba Going against the Grain: Agricultural Crisis and Transformation*. Oxford: Oxfam America Report.

Varela, J. 2003. "Restructuración azucarera: El compromiso de dar uso a las tierras que pasan a otros cultivos." *Granma* (25 October). http://www.granma.cu, accessed 25 March 2004.

Vicent, M. 1999. "La Habana: Ciudad vigilada." *El País Internacional* (28 February). http://www.chez.com/jpquin/EP280299.html, accessed 17 March 2004.

4

Rediscovering *Lo Local*

The Potential and the Limits of Local Development in Havana

MIREN URIARTE

We work to develop the potential of the community itself, starting out from our own concerns, our own experiences, and our own initiatives. Now, because there are no resources because of the Special Period, we rely on our capacity to reach people, to get all of us to think about problems in a constructive way, to help come to solutions that will work for all of us.

Group interview, Taller de Transformación Integral de Atares, 1994

By the mid-1990s, garbage pickup in Pogolotti, a neighborhood in Havana's municipality of Marianao, had become very unreliable. At first, families hung their small plastic bags from trees and posts, but in time sidewalks, streets, and empty lots became dumping grounds for household wastes. The People's Council in Pogolotti collaborated with the Metropolitan Park of Havana, a major urban development project, in forming an environmental group made up of the Taller de Transformación Integral de Pogolotti (Pogolotti Transformation Workshop), staff of the Centro Memorial Martin Luther King (a Cuban nongovernmental organization, or NGO), and residents concerned about the environmental problems in the neighborhood. The group conducted an environmental diagnosis, documenting every dumping site and the areas where contamination was suspected. In community meetings, residents prioritized the elimination of the dumping sites but also raised the need for reforestation and spaces for recreation. The group designed a project that included all three: a pilot recycling program for 150 families, workshops on environmental education for the neighborhood, and the replacement of dumping sites by recreational sites for children or reforested areas. The Metropolitan Park of Havana obtained funds from the Canadian International Development Agency, which funded the project. Participation of the population was an integral part. "We involved the community from the start and they participated in the decision making on the project," said the project's social worker. "They . . . were helpful because they have great interest in the solution of their own problems. [Because of this] we had very concrete results" (La Hoz Padilla and Reyes Herrera 1999, 30).

The project in Pogolotti represents a new way of working in Havana's neighborhoods and is an exemplar of what Cuban sociologists have called the "neighborhood movement" (Dilla Alfonso, Fernández Soriano, and Castro Flores 1998, 65). It comprised dozens of local initiatives that sought to address local problems resulting from the economic hardships of the Special Period and the difficulties the state encountered in addressing local problems at that time. Not unlike similar efforts in Latin America, Cuba's community-based initiatives emerged from different sources (Campfens 1996; Oakley and Flores 1994; O'Gorman 1994). In Havana, some emerged from grass-roots efforts, for example, in the *huertos populares* (people's gardens)[1] that evolved into Cuba's urban agriculture movement (Cruz Hernández and Sánchez Medina 2003, 31) or from work at the local level by NGOs such as the Centro Memorial Martin Luther King, the Centro de Intercambio y Referencia sobre Iniciativas Comunitarias (CIERIC), and others. But by far the greatest number has emerged out of pilot initiatives sponsored by agencies such as the Grupo para el Desarrollo Integral de la Capital (GDIC), an urban policy think tank affiliated with the Provincial People's Power in the city of Havana, and the Ministry of Culture, and from the work of some People's Councils, the People's Power structure that is closest to the base.

Seeking complementarity rather than contradiction with the state, these neighborhood movements nevertheless succeeded in introducing a different practice at the local level that stepped away from both the highly centralized planning approaches and the massive mobilization practice that had prevailed. Local initiatives focus on neighborhood problems, promote collaboration among neighborhood entities, and encourage direct participation of those affected in the process of addressing local problems. Their processes are akin to those of micro-planning, but with a broader, more integrative perspective that spans the physical space, the social life, and the cultural manifestations and development of a neighborhood. Their experiences, although not applied universally, have influenced practice across the island.

The sustainability of the recycling project in Pogolotti involved the use of funds raised by the sale of the recycled wastes to pay for the salary of one worker to collect household wastes. Hard as they tried, the Taller de Transformación Integral del Pogolotti and the People's Council were unable to implement this financial plan: the project was not authorized by the municipality to open a bank account or pay the salary of the worker. Eventually a worker was hired by the municipality, but the project, now without Canadian support and without direct local oversight, runs more sporadically and in large measure has stopped involving community residents in an integral way. In this instance, Pogolotti is also an exemplar of the limits of the "neighborhood movement," since it demonstrates the effect of policies that discourage small-

92 / Miren Uriarte

scale local economic development and thereby create a barrier to the sustainability of the locally based initiatives.

This chapter, which is based on ongoing research on local governance in the City of Havana, argues that the "neighborhood movement" emerged in Havana in the 1990s in response to two situations: the changes taking place in the political economy of the city due to the economic crisis, and the weakening of the ability of the state (both central and local) to provide resources for local-level problems due to the crisis and to an incomplete process of decentralization and devolution. The chapter presents three stages for the evolution of community development practices as seen in the example of Pogolotti: early experimentation, the emergence of a new "local space" that brought together old and new actors and introduced new methodologies, and finally its current situation, one that shows the tremendous potential of this process as well as the institutional barriers that limit its development.

Old and New Challenges in the City's *Barrios*

The end of socialism in Europe in 1989 and the tightening of the U.S. economic embargo in the early 1990s resulted in the near collapse of the Cuban economy. With the disappearance of the socialist bloc, the country's principal trading partner, Cuba lost 80 percent of its export market and 75 percent of its imports. The GDP fell from 22,080 million pesos in 1988 to 12,868 million pesos in 1994, when the economy touched bottom (Oficina Nacional de Estadísticas 1997). By then, food production was 55 percent of what it had been in 1990 (Sinclair and Thompson 2001, 10), leading to a 33 percent drop in caloric intake between 1990 and 1995 in Havana (Cruz Hernández and Sánchez Medina 2003, 4). All of the industries that produced hard currency—sugar, tobacco, mining, cement—were strongly affected by the reduction in the imports of production materials, some grinding to a halt. Production of hard and soft goods for the domestic market stopped due to the lack of raw materials. *Apagones* (brownouts) were common, as the supply of electricity became closely rationed due to the lack of petroleum products, which also affected the availability of transportation throughout the island. Raw material for the production of medicines was suddenly unavailable as were imported medicines and medical supplies. Cuban economic indicators have not yet fully recovered from the "Special Period in Time of Peace" as the Cuban government labeled these difficult times.

Past problems interacted with the new ones as Havana and its *barrios* coped with the economic crisis. At the end of the 1980s, before the crisis, Havana showed the effect of forty years of policies meant to equalize its resources with those of the countryside. Prior to the Revolution, the City of Havana was privileged by the disproportionate presence of capital investment and economic, social, and educational activity in comparison to other areas of the country. In 1959, 20 percent of the country's population lived in Havana (Scarpacci, Segre, and Coyula 2002, 120), but 70 percent of non-sugar industries were located in the city, as were 64 percent of the country's doctors and 61 percent of its hospital beds. In addition, 80 percent of the students enrolled in higher education attended classes in Havana (Coyula and Hamberg 2003, 2).

Within Havana, development was also uneven. The present city evolved from a dense walled settlement on the western side of the bay, which expanded by successive movements of the upper classes to increasingly distant areas along the waterfront (Scarpacci, Segre, and Coyula 2002). The city grew in the wake of these movements, annexing smaller cities and creating low-density suburbs bordering the coastline to the west. The flight of the upper class through Havana's neighborhoods is evidenced by the elaborate buildings left behind in the first part of the twentieth century in Cerro and Vedado, as well as the luxurious chalets and modern homes of Miramar and the suburbs to the west, which were the areas where the upper class was moving just prior to the revolution (Coyula and Hamberg 2003, 4).

The presence of the poor and the working class, according to Coyula and Hamberg (2003), was well hidden in renters-only neighborhoods in the center of the city that had been abandoned by the rich, in those bordering the industrial areas by the bay, and in the growing marginal settlements in the peripheral areas to the south. The poor lived in *cuarterías* (rooming houses) or *ciudadelas* (tenements) that developed in the old mansions of the central city neighborhoods or in the marginal shantytowns in the periphery (Scarpacci, Segre, and Coyula 2002, 100). According to Scarpacci, Segre, and Coyula (2002, 101), those living in poor and marginal areas prior to the Revolution were employed in seasonal and part-time work, as domestics in the houses of the rich, or in the informal sector.

The policies of the early years of the Revolution sought to redress these inequities. The Revolution promoted policies that diminished the differences between urban and rural areas, encouraged the stability of the population of the countryside, and prevented the flight to the capital city that so characterizes the Latin American experience by supporting the stability of the population and providing economic, social, and cultural opportunities outside of Havana. These policies were largely successful. Although the city has grown, it is not an overpopulated metropolis; it retains its traditional pace and quality of life (Scarpacci, Segre, and Coyula 2002, 43). But this came at a cost to the city: lack of investment and delayed maintenance of the infrastructure, from water to telephones to roads and, especially, housing.

Other policies addressed the differences in opportunity within Havana.

The Urban Reform in 1959, for example, halved rents for tenants and provided opportunities for homeownership (Segre, Coyula, and Scarpacci 1997, 129). Housing construction for those living in marginal neighborhoods followed. With the implementation of measures to create jobs and reduce unemployment, conditions improved in the worst neighborhoods of Havana in a short period of time.

Be that as it may, living conditions still vary greatly in Havana, depending on quality of housing, access to transportation, and availability of services. Makeshift housing (shantytowns), large housing projects, and a dearth of services and transportation are characteristic of neighborhoods in the inner suburbs and in the periphery, such as Alamar (in the municipality of Habana del Este), La Guinera (in the municipality of Arroyo Naranjo), and some neighborhoods in Marianao, such as Pogolotti. The quality of the housing, the preponderance of tenements, the availability of water, and overcrowding are problems faced characteristically in central-city neighborhoods, such as Cayo Hueso (in Centro Habana) and Atarés (in Cerro).

Throughout the revolution, the tendency has been toward social and racial integration in Havana, which was highly segregated on both counts prior to 1959. This was eased, first, by the flight of large sectors of the upper and middle classes, a large percentage of which resided in Havana. This allowed for movement of the middle and working classes into the formerly upper-class neighborhoods. Integration was also made possible through the construction of public housing by workers' "microbrigades," which were interspersed through the city. Nevertheless, the populations of some neighborhoods retained historical characteristics of class and race, although full employment, social mobility, and social policies that guarantee universal access to all services have tended to diminish the social consequences not only of class and race but also of "place" in the lives of *habaneros*.

Local Governance

Cuba's governance relies on a very strong central government and comparatively weak provincial and municipal governments. At all levels there are legislative structures as well as administrative structures. At the national level, the National Assembly of People's Power is the highest legislative body, while the Council of Ministers is the highest level of the executive and administrative branch. There are 14 provincial assemblies and 169 municipal assemblies and their complementary provincial (CAP) and municipal (CAM) administrative councils replicate the central structure at these levels. In general, policy proposals and new policy directions are the purview of the central government and its ministries, but these share responsibility for administration with provincial and municipal administrative councils.

The Municipal Assembly of People's Power is the deliberative body closest to the base and the Municipal Administrative Council (CAM) is charged with administering most of the government services that Cubans encounter on a day-to-day basis. The population directly elects representatives to the municipal assembly from among its neighbors. These delegates in turn bring local problems to the attention of municipal authorities. The delegates report to the populace on the issues they were able to resolve through *asambleas de rendición de cuentas* (accountability assemblies). Roman (1999, 157) reports that about 70 percent of the problems raised in the assemblies are addressed, but there is evidence that most delegates do not raise complaints unless the problem is very serious and has a solution at hand. The effectiveness of the delegates and the municipal assembly is greatly constrained by the lack of resources and authority (Dilla Alfonso 1998).

This highly centralized structure has made it possible for the country to deploy resources quickly and focus them on national priorities, such as health and education, and has contributed to significant accomplishments in social policy. But this approach has not been effective in managing local problems. Although the intention is that central directives be adapted to local conditions, provinces and municipalities have had great difficulty in steering resources to their unique problems because of their lack of control over resources. Over time, a growing number of local problems have been left unresolved, particularly those that respond to specific characteristics not contemplated at the national level.

The "local level" in Cuba has traditionally meant the municipalities, but the Special Period underscored their weakness. Municipalities were too large and their populations' needs too diverse to be addressed by even municipal-level "one size fits all" solutions. The municipality of Plaza de la Revolución in Havana, for example, contains the famous Vedado neighborhood, the city's main cultural centers, most of the country's central government offices, key tourist areas along the Waterfront and Calle 23, and several marginal neighborhoods such as La Timba and El Fanguito. These areas face very different pressures: the social impact of the investment in the tourist areas on adjacent neighborhoods; the multiple demands of the marginal neighborhoods; the problems of housing that affect the whole municipality; and the specific priorities of different areas, such as the decline in the quality of services, the conflicts of daily life between youth and elders, and the needs of youth for recreation (García Ramos and González de la Hoz 1999, 20; González de la Hoz 2000, 30; Martínez Canals and García Brigos 2001). Responding differentially to the many demands was especially difficult during times of crisis.

96 / Miren Uriarte

The Special Period also demonstrated that, although the process of de-concentration of decision making and administration from the central government to the provinces and municipalities that began in the 1970s charged municipalities with the functioning of most of the services in their territory, municipalities have very little power. They oversee services that are commonly recognized as public services plus a host of services that are handled elsewhere by the private sector, such as grocery stores, bakeries, repair shops, and so forth—but they are not empowered to raise revenue, make budgetary decisions, or veer very far from established priorities (Dilla Alfonso 1998, 46).

The Effect of the Economic Crisis

The Special Period was harsh on the city and its neighborhoods. Initially, the most salient effect were the "lacks": the lack of food available through the ration card and the rise of the black market commerce in food; the lack of transportation (which was particularly hard for those in the inner suburbs and the peripheral areas, where getting to and from work became a serious challenge); and the lack of basic household goods, such as fuel for cooking and cleaning materials. Workers took to bicycles or walked long distances; many, particularly women and older workers, left their jobs (Uriarte 2003, 28). Then construction stopped throughout the city. There were no supplies for the upkeep of schools, hospitals, polyclinics, and other public service buildings. And as in the example of Pogolotti, which opens this chapter, garbage pickup became erratic as a result of the lack of fuel and parts.

Beginning in 1993, measures were introduced to address the economic crisis by creating conditions for foreign investment, including the legalization of the use of hard currency. Mixed enterprises consisting of partnerships between the Cuban government and foreign firms were developed, and ancillary firms were created to service this new sector. Key among the "new economy" sectors is tourism, which has grown exponentially over the last twelve years. Measures were also taken to allow small-scale private enterprise by Cubans citizens. These measures and subsequent ones succeeded in halting the economic decline and began a slow but steady recovery. But, as the Cuban leadership warned, these reforms also had the effect of creating a dual economy, which has transformed the structures of both the labor and commercial markets (Ferriol Murruaga 2001) and exacerbated social inequities (Espina Prieto 1998).

The changes touched all Cubans, but they changed the life of *habaneros* (residents of Havana) because it is here where the growing social differences were becoming evident (Espina Prieto 1998). The emerging social differences are intimately tied to the sector of the economy in which the individual works

Rediscovering Lo Local / 97

and the individual's access to hard currency. First, there has been a rise of unemployment among workers in state enterprises as these reduce the labor force in order to become more competitive. From 1990 to 1998, 155,000 workers became unemployed, a large percentage of them women (Centro de Investigaciones de la Economía Mundial 2000, 72, 93). In Havana, unemployment rose to 8.8 percent in 1994 from almost zero unemployment in the late 1980s; although it has improved, unemployment remains higher than it was in 1990 (Coyula and Hamberg 2003, 5). Second, new sectors of the economy have been created and these offer significantly better benefits and working conditions (Togores Gonzalez 2003, 2). Workers in the "new" economy receive a salary in Cuban pesos supplemented with "extras" that were hard to come by during the Special Period, such as clothes and toiletries; many either have access to hard currency through tips or are being paid a portion of their salary in hard currency. Third, access to hard currency is unequal in the new economic structure. With most goods (aside from rationed foods and foods sold in the farmers' markets) available only in hard currency, a household's access to such currency, be it from employment or remittances, is a determinant of its economic vulnerability.

In Havana, about 59 percent of the households have access to hard currency in some way (Pérez Villanueva 2002, 23). Many householders obtain it from their employment, be it tips in hotels and restaurants, partial salary payments for workers in strategic industries, or through formal and informal self-employment. In 1997, 37 percent of Cuban state workers received this type of payment (Togores Gonzalez 2002, 8), but opportunities for this type of work are not distributed evenly in Havana. One salient cleavage has to do with "place," in a marked departure from the recent past, and although not fueled completely by private enterprise as before, it does tend to favor similar areas (Oliveras and Núñez 2004). Havana is at the center of the tourism industry: more than half of the tourists who visit Cuba come to Havana (Pérez Villanueva 2002, 11). It is also the center of operations of mixed enterprises and the ancillary firms created to service the enterprises of the new economy. There has been a boom in tourism-oriented development concentrated in Old Havana, the beaches to the east of the city, and along the coastline through Vedado, Miramar, and points west (Dilla Alfonso, 1998, 49; Oliveras and Núñez 2004). Piggybacking on the tourism and trade boom, *habaneros* have also benefited from the possibilities of private enterprise and opened their homes for room rentals or for home restaurants. According to Oliveras and Núñez (2004), 30 percent of the country's accommodations of these types are located in Havana, many along the coastal fringe and on the beaches. This process of development fueled by the needs of the tourism industries has meant little investment outside of the coastal fringe and the Casco Histórico (Historic Cen-

98 / Miren Uriarte

ter). Historically disinvested areas—central city neighborhoods and peripheral areas—continue to show their deterioration, which is now exacerbated by the lack of materials for repairs. This has not only created differences in the physical appearance of these tourist areas as compared to areas less frequented by tourists, but, more importantly, it represents a clear gap in economic possibilities for households.

Remittances from families living abroad are another way in which Cubans gain access to hard currency. Estimates of remittances range between $400 and $800 million per year, now a major source of hard currency for the country and of income for many families (Snow 1998). Studies show that about one-third of the families in Havana receive remittances, but that these too are not distributed evenly. Espina Prieto (2003, 11) reports that remittances are most frequently going to families that already show high incomes due to the work they do and the ties they have to the new economy. Access to remittances, she concludes, represents marked social differences in the city.

Other studies reveal that 20.1 percent of households in Havana were determined to be "at risk" of not being able to meet basic needs (Ferriol Murruaga et al. 1998). Among the most economically vulnerable households are, first, those with unemployed workers and those that depend solely on the wages of low-paid state workers, on the fixed incomes of retirees, or on social assistance—that is, households wherein no member has the means to increase his or her income through private enterprise. The 41 percent of the households in Havana without access to hard currency through remittances or employment (Perez Villanueva 2002, 23) are also very vulnerable, primarily because they are excluded from participating in commerce in hard currency, which today provides access to most goods and services.

It is these very needy households that are also likely to be most vulnerable to the social disruptions that have accompanied the reinsertion of tourism in Cuba. An instance of this is the increase in the number of children working in the streets to earn hard currency from the tourists. Lutjens (2000, 63) reports, for example, that authorities had identified several thousand children working in the streets of the Casco Histórico, the renovated section of Old Havana, most of whom were five to eleven years old. Prostitution, petty crime, and other illicit street life has also returned to Havana (Segre et al. 2002, 229) after a forty-year absence, and the reappearance of these social problems is very troubling to a population that believed these social ills were problems of the past.

Effects at the Local Level

The economic crisis and the transformations reverberated at the community level. This happened, first, when the real conditions of life of people at the local level changed dramatically due to job losses, alterations in financial strategies for households (which now involved several jobs and/or a combination of formal and informal employment), and the deteriorating physical conditions of houses and institutions in the neighborhoods.

Second, people were now spending significantly more time in their communities: lack of work, difficulties in transportation, and the fact that any new independent economic initiative revolved around a person's home meant that people stayed in the neighborhood. Ulises Rosales del Toro, who chaired the Grupo Ministerial de Trabajo con las Comunidades (Ministerial Community Work Group), a multi-ministerial task force focused on the work at the community level, indicated that "over 5 million persons out of a total population of 10.9 million remain 'in the neighborhood' most of the time" (Grupo de Investigaciones Sociológicas 1996). This altered significantly the organization and rhythm of life of the neighborhoods, the demands on neighborhood services, and issues of public safety.

Third was the effect of the evolving stratification represented by growing differences within neighborhoods (related to source and type of income) as well as between neighborhoods (related to the new political economy of the urban space). Intra-neighborhood differences manifested themselves in part through the ways in which individuals and households interacted with the new economy and attained access to hard currency. Sometimes this happened legally through work; sometimes it happened through links with persons living abroad, up to then a situation not desirable in Cuban society; in still others, it happened through illegal activity, be it prostitution or the operation of the black market. All of these methods coexisted in the neighborhood, alongside households that had no access to hard currency at all, creating tensions and decreasing sociability.

Although at present there is no public data on the geographic distribution of poverty in Havana, qualitative assessments can be made about the differential impact upon neighborhoods. For example, physical differences were clearly visible by the late 1990s. Favored areas had remodeled spaces, cleaner streets, availability of food (in hard currency), all supported by investments of the state, while other areas struggled with their infrastructure problems and showed few visible effects of renovations. There were also clear distinctions in the opportunities available to residents in different neighborhoods: in the areas near tourism facilities there were increased possibilities for rentals, in-home restaurants, and other avenues of legal access to hard currency for households and individuals in the neighborhood. Other areas had few avenues to hard currency other than the few jobs in the new economy, remittances, or illegal activity.

Finally, the municipality, the first line of support for these communities, had no resources to give. With the great economic limits confronting the central government and with many local industries shuttered, provinces and municipalities had even fewer resources than before. Persons concerned about the neighborhoods felt left to their own devices, and in fact, for many, that was the case.

Neighborhoods in Havana are the site of intense community life. Populations are relatively stable, leading to the best and the worst results of intense familiarity. The main elements of social organization in Cuba are the mass organizations; in urban areas, the Committees for the Defense of the Revolution (CDRs) and the Federation of Cuban Women (FMC) are organized at the block level.[2] The FMC organizes vaccination campaigns and conducts public education in a variety of areas, while the CDRs, charged with the security of neighborhoods and with mobilization for activities and volunteer work, provide primary support for neighborhood residents. Family doctor-nurse teams, who live and work in the neighborhood, care for about 250 families, conducting regular home visits to the sick, the elderly, and newborn babies. Neighborhood schools are important actors at the local level and are used by neighborhood children all day. Depending on the resources available in the neighborhood, there may be a presence of staff of the Ministry of Culture or the National Sports Institute.

This strong community life served *habaneros* well during the economic crisis. Mass organizations proved to be a crucial element in the organization of support at the local level: when there was no transportation out of the neighborhood, the CDR could get a neighbor with gasoline to drive to the hospital in an emergency; the CDR provided recreation at the block level; the FMC distributed vitamins to every household and held meetings to talk about ways to cook meals with the limited choices available; in the darkest times of the crisis, the CDR would organize a neighborhood cleanup. Mass organizations also participated in the prevention of crime and delinquency, organizing neighborhood watches to prevent crime and organizing activities for youth. This consistent work at the local level, and the continuous accumulation of social capital, clearly was an important element of the way Havana weathered the crisis.

But the problems that surfaced during the economic crisis overwhelmed the resources of the mass organizations. Hampered by diminishing resources from their central organizations, local chapters of the FMC and the CDRs had little to offer but their own efforts, which were significant but clearly not enough to address the problems of unemployment and increasing economic hardship, of the lack of basic necessities, and of the rising temptation of drugs and illicit activities in the neighborhood. Mass organizations, whose activities are tightly controlled by their centralized structures, were often unable to respond to these problems because they were not yet recognized as such at the higher levels. Their proclivity to wait for *orientaciones* (directions) before stepping out of the usual line of work meant that the mass organizations were unable either to provide leadership or to respond to the specifics of the crisis facing individual communities (Grupo de Investigaciones Sociológicas 1996). Although an important element in the fabric of Cuban society, mass organizations proved not to be the best vehicles for more proactive activity. Other actors stepped into the vacuum of leadership at the neighborhood level.

Moving the *Barrios*: Transforming Work at the Local Level

The process of transformation of work at the local level began before the Special Period and is still ongoing. Three major stages in this process can be identified. The first covers the early emergence of neighborhood planning undertaken as pilot initiatives by the Grupo para el Desarrollo Integral de la Capital (GDIC). The second represents the height of the "neighborhood movement." It is marked by the introduction of the People's Councils and with them the legitimization of the *barrio* as an appropriate space for interventions; it involves significant methodological experimentation and systematization. The third involves the continuing growth of the number of experiences, along with some adoption of the methodologies by state agencies and urban development projects. This is also the stage during which the state re-emerges from the crisis and reclaims its primary role at the local level. In some cases, this leads to increased complementarity between the state and neighborhood actors; in others it leads to conflict and the dissolution of some successful initiatives.

The Emergence of Neighborhood-level Planning

In the late 1980s, before the economic crisis would clearly underscore differences within the city of Havana, there was a growing recognition of the need to attend to problems accumulating in the *barrios*. The most frequent issue was the quantity and the quality of housing, but its manifestations differed depending on whether the neighborhood was an inner-city neighborhood with a preponderance of tenements and overcrowding, a large housing project in the inner suburbs or the periphery without services or transportation, or a spontaneous settlement on the edge of the city without running water.

In 1988, the GDIC initiated the first long-term effort to address the specific problems of the most vulnerable neighborhoods in Havana. The GDIC organized the Talleres de Transformación Integral del Barrio (TTI, Neighborhood Transformation Workshops) in three *barrios* of Havana: Cayo Hueso, Atarés, and La Guinera. Both Cayo Hueso and Atarés are located in the central city, one in Centro Habana, in the downtown area near Old Havana, and the other in Cerro. Both are neighborhoods of great historical and cultural traditions, but both are old, poor neighborhoods with serious problems in the quality of the housing and an equally difficult set of social problems. La Guinera, in contrast, is located in Arroyo Naranjo in the outskirts of Havana and, at that time, had a large sector of its population living in marginal, precarious neighborhoods that had no water, electricity, or services. "When we started in 1988," says Regla Barbón, the director of the Taller de Transformación Integral of Atarés, "we were aware that changes were coming, but what we foresaw were positive changes, for example new technologies, new ways of working. The government had prioritized the city and . . . so we came with all our energy to try to solve those problems."[3] The multidisciplinary workshops identified the community's needs, sponsored local projects at the neighborhood level, and experimented with methods of involving neighborhood actors and the population in the work of the workshops.

The workshops gathered together six or seven *técnicos*—architects, planners, social workers—to address the problems of the neighborhood. Their appearance coincided with the rebirth of the microbrigade movement, which mobilized workers and residents to construct housing, schools, day care centers, and other buildings with social benefit. In each of the neighborhoods, the workshop worked closely with the *técnicos* in the construction of housing. In the case of Cayo Hueso and Atarés, the team worked on the removal of tenements, convincing the residents to move if the tenement was in precarious condition and working with them in the design and renovation of the housing. More than twelve tenements were repaired in the first three years.[4] By 1991, five additional workshops were working in the Havana neighborhoods of Pogolotti, Santa Felicia, Los Angeles, and Zamora-Coco Solo in Marianao, and in suburban Alamar in Habana del Este.

The early approach of the workshops consisted of identifying the main problem areas in the neighborhood and mobilizing neighborhood and outside resources to address them. This approach was quite successful. Workshops were able to reach quickly into the neighborhood in ways that were difficult for provincial or municipal entities to do: they were known in the neighborhood, they addressed issues that the residents thought were priorities, and, unencumbered by emergencies in other areas, they had the time to build the relationships and the networks necessary to address problems at the neighborhood level. The workshops provided mechanisms by which other entities (such as the mass organizations, the school principals, the family doctors, and others acting *in* the neighborhood) could focus on neighborhood-identified problems. Their role was not to do the work of the CDR or the FMC, but rather, to bring the CDR and the FMC to focus on the specific problems of the neighborhood. Adding potential to this set of new relationships was the fact that workshops were effective in bringing resources into the neighborhood. In the early years, the GDIC and the workshops enjoyed considerable government support, which overcame many barriers and permitted them to be very entrepreneurial in the search for solutions. For example, they were often able to bypass clogged municipal bureaucracies and mobilize provincial and even national resources. Leveraging resources to address problems identified at the neighborhood level by neighborhood residents would become the landmark contribution of the workshops.

But, as the economic crisis changed the city, so too changed the methods by which the workshops accomplished this. Due to the crisis, government resources and supplies disappeared, but personnel allocations were not touched—the government continued to pay workers—and the workshops kept all their professionals working in the community. "When the crisis arrived, it paralyzed everything. It stopped construction and affected healthcare, food, transportation. This affected how people feel in the neighborhood," explained the director of Alamar's Taller de Transformación. So, as the economic crisis made itself felt, the brick-and-mortar approach transitioned into interventions that focused on the broader needs of the community. "Our objectives did not change. . . . What happened is that we had to revitalize our objectives and think about them differently. We also had to incorporate new ones, because the Special Period highlighted new problems and forced us to look at other things."[5]

With the methodological support of the GDIC, the workshops began to apply participatory community planning methods that helped the activists conduct needs assessments, strategize priorities, and plan in collaboration with neighborhood residents. Projects included repairing schools and the offices of family doctors, recycling programs and reforestation campaigns, and cultural and social service programs focused on the needs of the most vulnerable: youth, the elderly, women. These projects began to attract support from the international NGOs that began to work in Cuba at this time (Sinclair 2000; Uriarte 2003, 54–55). Although implementing projects and maintaining participation has been a challenge, the experience of the workshops is generally recognized as positive.[6] With a growing track record, continued domestic and international support, and at the request of municipalities throughout the city, the GDIC expanded the number of workshops to seven in 1993, to twelve in

1997, and currently to more than twenty in the *barrios* of Havana.[7] The latter workshops have been organized in inner-city neighborhoods, in suburban marginal areas, and in neighborhoods in transition such as Vedado and Náutico.

Lo Local: Legitimacy and Systematization

Up to 1990, "local level" in Havana meant the fifteen municipalities, the lowest level in the governance structure. This changed with the appearance of the People's Councils in 1992.[8] The People's Councils are composed of fifteen to twenty delegates elected directly by the population,[9] as well as representatives of the main economic, social, and service institutions in the area, including the CDRs and the FMC. The creation of the People's Councils and their mandate to focus on the needs of much smaller geographic areas meant a redefinition of *lo local* from the former reference point of the municipality to a space that was much closer to the problems of everyday *habaneros* and much more amenable to neighborhood-level interventions. The legitimization of this "space" led to a broader acceptance of a comprehensive vision of neighborhood needs and resources and the development of horizontal relationships among the different neighborhood stakeholders. This contrasts with the more prevalent centralized and vertical perspectives that seek coordination of service areas (education, health, and so forth) along the vertical axis made up of municipality, province, and central government.

The councils' role evolves very slowly in this direction. Their mission, by law, is to monitor all entities located in their geographic area, regardless of whether they are municipal, provincial, or central government entities, for the sole purpose of improving services at the local level with the participation of the population (Roman 1999). But the economic crisis has proved a challenging context for the definition of their role. "The amount of objective problems that exist in the community and the limited capacity on the part of the government," expressed Rosales de Toro, "places the delegates and the presidents of the councils in a very difficult position" (Grupo de Investigaciones Sociológicas 1996). As the central, provincial, and municipal governments became less able to provide resources and less effective in addressing the growing local problems, the councils became, in practice, the managers of the impact of the crisis at the local level. Almost all local problems came to the People's Councils, which were then forced to improvise solutions. This, says the sociologist Jesús García Brigos, presents a conflict "between the need to obtain immediate results and the realization of their new and exceptional potential" (2001, 2).

It is in the search for local solutions that some entrepreneurial councils moved forward with aggressive community-based initiatives. Councils have sponsored environmental cleanups, brought together neighborhood actors to focus on the problems of youth and the elderly, and harnessed for the neighborhoods the resources of industries and government agencies located in their areas. More recently, as will be described later, councils have joined with the workshops and with Cuban NGOs in community initiatives.

But not all councils have taken this activist approach, and some that did have not been as effective. Research on the work of the councils reveals deficiencies in their ability to monitor services at the local level, in their ability to promote the participation of the residents, and in their capacity to strengthen the ties among those responsible for different services at the local level (Del Río Hernández 1998; García Brigos 2001; Roman 1999). Renewed work on the development of the councils emphasizes their coordinating role vis-à-vis other actors in the neighborhood and their capacity to monitor the quality of services at the local level. Attention also focuses on the transformation of the relationship of the council to the residents and the participation of the population in the work of the council.

Cubans have experimented liberally with participatory community planning methods. In the process, Cuban activists have engaged in heated debates regarding the nature of the participation that is possible in the Cuban context and the level that is required for successful community development. Cuba has a strong history of social and political participation, which, although it provides a strong framework for current efforts, has mostly entailed participation in the execution of initiatives designed centrally. Although there have been some advances in the decentralization of decision making, there is still some resistance to the promotion of a "real" participation by residents or consumers—one in which residents have decision-making power—as opposed to more formal and indirect participation mechanisms, such as participation through the mass organizations. Many Cuban community development projects have achieved a good level of participation, although, by Cuban standards, they are not optimal (Díaz Carbó, Uriarte Martín, and Dávalos Domínguez 1998; Dilla Alfonso, Fernández Soriano, and Castro Flores 1998). Community development projects make strong efforts to promote "real" participation; this is facilitated by the high level of education of the population, which permits participants to engage with a great degree of effectiveness.

The experimentation with new participatory methodologies was supported by the entry of a broad set of actors to the work at the local level. Key among these were the Cuban NGOs that emerged during this period and included, among many others, the Consejo de Iglesias (Council of Churches), the Centro Memorial Martin Luther King, the Fundación de la Naturaleza y el Hombre (Foundation for Nature and Mankind), Habitat-Cuba, and the Centro de Intercambio y Referencia sobre Iniciativas Comunitarias (CIERIC).[10] Cuban

NGOs have conducted their own projects with varied success, but their most salient contribution has been their experimentation with participatory planning methodologies and continued efforts to systematize of these methods in the Cuban context (*Mensaje de Cuba* 1998). These NGOs, together with the GDIC, supported community activists in moving from "learning by doing" to a more systematic process of skill acquisition, application, and analysis. This reflective practice allowed for the swifter and more effective adaptation of these methods to the Cuban context. Community development activists continually discuss the application of participatory planning methods and the management of community-based projects and are "accompanied" in their process of innovation by the staff of these organizations. Their work in this area has been supported by international NGOs and the United Nations.

The early process of consolidation of these experiences proceeded with some tension. One set of tensions emanated from the resistance of state agencies to a horizontal (rather than vertical) perspective and their lack of experience in collaboration at the base. The new approaches challenged established structures and practices, which often became very resistant to collaboration with community-level initiatives in the solution of local problems. The urban planner Carlos García Pleyán expressed this resistance as a missed opportunity "of having a powerful state, organized and with an ideology that supports popular initiatives," effectively linking with community-based initiatives because of unworkable structures.[11] For most of the decade, the community-based initiatives would remain marginal to policy-making processes because of this bureaucratic resistance.

Adding to this considerable tension was the fact that the domestic and the international NGOs, new actors in the Cuban environment, were deeply involved in the process. Cuba approached the emergence of Cuban NGOs and the entry of international NGOs with great caution. Its limited experience dealing with, and its distrust of, international cooperation in the capitalist world were factors that predisposed it negatively to the activity of international NGOs, which were generally regarded as paternalistic and prone to impose both their culture and their politics (Sinclair 2000).

Limited experience and distrust also marked the early relationship with Cuban NGOs. Some saw little purpose in the organization of an independent civil society since the government provided everything that individual citizens were deemed to need (Gunn 1995). Others cautioned about the potential use of independent organizations to subvert the Cuban government, a thought reinforced by the "Track II" provisions of the Torricelli-Graham law passed by the U.S. Congress in 1992.[12] Nevertheless, in the early 1990s, the number of NGOs grew significantly and some government officials even began to see some benefit to their presence, albeit one focused primarily on their ability

Rediscovering Lo Local / 107

to attract hard currency from international sources, since many NGOs were engaged in development projects (Gunn 1995; Sinclair 2000).

It is a tribute to the diligence and effectiveness of those working in local initiatives that this mistrust abated enough to give way to collaborative relationships. By the end of the 1990s, some NGOs had disappeared, victims of these tensions,[13] but effective partnerships had also emerged between projects sponsored by NGOs and local councils and municipalities that heralded some of the most fruitful relationships that would take shape in the next stage.

Growing collaboration and complementarity expanded the application of community development practice. Although the GDIC had taken an early lead, the adoption of these methods by a broader set of government agencies was set into motion by the recommendations of the Grupo Ministerial de Trabajo con las Comunidades, which in 1996 supported these methodologies in its document *Trabajo Comunitario Integrado: Proyecto de Programa* (Integrated Community Work: Draft Program) (Grupo de Investigaciones Sociológicas 1996). Large urban projects in Havana such as the Plan Maestro de la Oficina del Historiador (Master Plan of the Office of the Historian) and the Parque Metropolitano de La Habana began to use these methods, as was the case of the Centro de Cultura Comunitaria (Community Cultural Center) of the Ministry of Culture, the environmental educators in the Ministry of Science, Technology, and Environment, and others (Farncombe and Betancourt 2000; Grupo para el Desarrollo Integral de la Capital 1999a, 1999b, 2000; Oliveras Gómez 1999; Uriarte Martín and Fernández Pérez 1998).[14] Popular participation in decision making began to be perceived as intrinsic to the work of the People's Councils, a fact underscored by the specific mention of the role of popular participation in the identification of problems and solutions as well as in the planning and monitoring activities of the councils in Law 91 of the People's Councils, passed by the National Assembly in July 2000 (República de Cuba 2000). At this time, also, skills in participatory methods, facilitation, and other aspects of work at the community level were integrated into the training of presidents of People's Councils and local delegates offered by the Provincial Secretariat of People's Power in the City of Havana.[15] Although popular participation remains a goal for the councils, they continue to provide the context for ongoing experimentation in transforming relationships at the local level.

Complementarities and Barriers in Current Practice

The integration of the methods introduced by the "neighborhood movement"—small-scale, integrated, participatory, focused on the development of local resources and local leadership—into the work of the People's Councils

calls to mind the way in which Cuba, in the midst of great economic transformation, has changed its practice in key areas while retaining its values and
structures. One example is social policy, where although there is little questioning of the values and structures that drive social policy, there is growing
recognition that service improvements are required, particularly in coordination, targeting, and reach (Espina Prieto 2003; Togores González 2003; Uriarte
2003). Similarly, the introduction of mandates for more inclusive processes
by the People's Councils does not mean that there will be structural changes
to People's Power—for example the greater control of resources at the local
level—but rather it means "el Poder Popular actuando de una forma diferente"
(People's Power acting differently).[16] Although this opens the door to a broadly
more democratic process at the base, the fact is that there are clear barriers to a
council's capacity to address the conditions at the local level without resources
and without clear entry points into the policy-making process. This is particularly important now, as differences emerge among Havana's neighborhoods
that threaten the values of equity and the possibilities of development for all
(Dilla Alfonso 1998, 49).

This current stage has shown new models in the improvement of the capacity for decision making at the local level, emerging out of the collaboration
between the Peoples' Councils and the Neighborhood Transformation Workshops in strategic community planning (Oliveras Gómez 1999). Strategic community planning involves members of the People's Council, municipal staff,
and persons from the community in a process of diagnosis, broad discussion
of the findings, and assessments of strengths, weaknesses, opportunities, and
threats (SWOT exercise) faced in addressing the problems. This technique
assists the group in prioritizing those areas in which there is the potential for
success. Objectives and action plans are devised, with the hope that neighborhood entities, whether government agencies or mass organizations, will take
direction from the strategic community plan. This level of planning affords ad-
vantages to the council's delegates as they set policy and negotiate for resources
at the municipal level. According to Rosa Oliveras, who guides the work of the
workshops at the GDIC, this planning is also strengthening municipalities by
providing them with "the diversity of problems, priorities and possibilities in
its territory as well as a large number of well-trained participants, aware and
ready to offer perspectives, seek solutions, and execute them" (Oliveras Gómez 2002, 8). Strategic planning, including the assessments conducted at the
community level, informs the process of resource allocation at the provincial
(city-wide) level as the government of the city of Havana engages in its own
strategic planning, which it has done since 1994 (Oliveras Gómez 2002, 6).
Although the province does not have control over the central government's
investments in the city, which are the largest and the ones creating the great-

est transformations, a process of strategic thinking that begins with broad participation at the base is perceived as a deterrent to uneven development (Oliveras Gómez and Núñez 2004). Strategic community planning is taking place in the twenty People's Councils in Havana in which there is a workshop and is involving nine of the fifteen municipalities in the city.

Other complementary relationships between domestic and foreign NGOs reinforce and invigorate work at the community level. The story in Pogolotti, which opened this paper, is an example of collaboration between residents of a neighborhood (Pogolotti), a state enterprise (Parque Metropolitano de La Habana), a People's Council (Pogolotti-Belen-Finlay), a transformation workshop (Pogolotti), a Cuban NGO (the Martin Luther King Center), and a foreign NGO (the Canadian Urban Institute, with funds from the Canadian International Development Agency). There are many other stories throughout the city that involve these and others actors such as universities, government ministries, associations, religious groups.

But as these community processes evolve and mature, they quickly come up against barriers, also illustrated in the case of Pogolotti. Most of the barriers are institutional, one example being the policies that obstruct the development of local economic initiatives. Although many of the local projects have included economic development activities such as the production of materials for housing repair, organization and support for the work of artisans, organization of cooperatives of handymen for housing repair, and so on, these have not prospered because of regulations barring their implementation. These can be as minimal as the inability to hire using hard currency (even when exchanged with pesos) or to open a bank account.

Institutional barriers also threaten the sustainability of the initiatives themselves. At this point, community development initiatives cannot generate income, although several continue to push this envelope with proposals ranging from charging minimal fees for cultural activities such as dances or video showings to selling arts and crafts made by residents. The initiatives are sustained by local or municipal resources (the salaries of the professionals working in the workshops, for example, are paid by the municipalities); by ministries with a community mission, such as the Ministry of Culture; and by international NGOs that channel funding through Cuban NGOs or agencies such as the GDIC.

Moving Forward

Across the world, the development of community resources and community capacity is one of the weapons that poor neighborhoods and poor people wield in their defense against the vagaries of capital. This development takes place to defend the poor from economic inequality, political disenfranchisement, and social problems emanating from their position in the economic structure. The hope is by building communities' capacities to analyze their problems, develop strategies for action, and leverage resources to address their problems, communities will be transformed and social problems will be decreased.

For forty years Cuba sought to affect social problems with macro approaches: universal policies, grand initiatives, and large mobilizations propelled Cubans to a set of social outcomes that surpass those of most developing countries. Because of that, today, in spite of the economic crisis, Cuba is still far from the worst examples and results of social inequality: Cuba's safety net alone provides an important protection for all, especially the growing number of vulnerable families. Be that as it may, it is also a fact that in the urban area of the capital city, social relations are transforming, inequalities are re-emerging, and the mechanisms that once sustained an equitable distribution across areas of the city are no longer as effective in the face of this onslaught. For many Cubans, community development initiatives fall very short in comparison to the problem and in comparison to the initiatives they have been able to put in place in the past.

In 1988, Havana began an experiment in local empowerment in its poorest *barrios*. And in spite of resistance, it blossomed in the midst of crisis. Its expansion was fueled by the great needs emerging in neighborhoods and the creation of a new "space" for initiatives that were much closer to the lives of people. The diligence and energy of sustained, reflective practice transformed relationships at the local level by building on the strong social capital already in place from forty years of work at the base by mass organizations and institutions. In time, new and old actors at working at the local level established that complementary relations between the state, NGOs and local community development efforts are possible in Cuba as well, in spite of the central role of the state and even its initial resistance. As a result, Havana's *barrios*, including some of its poorest and most marginal ones, count on well-trained activists who have been informed of the community's most pressing problems, who possess the level of education and training necessary to seek viable solutions, and who have the energy and the skill to execute actions to reach these goals (Oliveras Gómez 2002, 8). Because they exist, poor *barrios* have more possibilities of being represented by informed and able voices at the municipal and provincial levels. By all measures this is successful as far as community development efforts go.

But as one observes the ease with which Cubans move through these processes, the enormous potential to which García Pleyán referred is evidenced along with the missed opportunities.[17] The tremendous organizational capacity, the ability to analyze complex problems and easily grasp the processes of

Rediscovering Lo Local / 111

planning, the history of voluntary activity and social responsibility, and the skills and "know-how" at the community level sit alongside the bureaucratic barriers, the hyper-centralist tendencies, and the fears that lessening central control of resources will result in even greater inequality. Community development processes, banned from developing local economies, are stretching the limits in the area of governance, building capacity, conducting strategic planning at the community level, and encouraging participation.

Notes

1. By 1996, there were 12,000 gardens and 18,300 producers in Havana alone according to Cruz Hernández and Sánchez Medina 2003, 31.

2. The Committees for the Defense of the Revolution (CDRs) and the Federation of Cuban Women (FMC) are two of Cuba's "mass organizations," others of which organize farmers, students, and even children.

3. Regla Barbón, interview, March 2001.

4. Interviews with Joel Díaz, the director of the Taller de Transformación de Cayo Hueso, and Regla Barbón of the Taller de Transformación de Atarés, fall 1994.

5. Sylvia López, interview, fall 1994.

6. The work of the workshops has been presented in national and international forums and has won several national awards. In 1995, the Friends of the United Nations named the Workshop of La Guinera as one of the "fifty world vanguard communities."

7. In addition to those already mentioned, there are workshops in the following neighborhoods: Los Angeles and Libertad in the municipality of Marianao; Príncipe and Vedado-Malecón in Plaza; El Canal in Cerro; Ceiba-Kohly, Buena Vista, and Cubanacán-Náutico in Playa; Alamar Este in Habana del Este; Párraga in Arroyo Naranjo; Balcón de la Lisa-Arimao in La Lisa; and Jesús María-Tallapiedra in La Habana Vieja (Coyula, Oliveras, and Coyula 2002).

8. There are 105 People's Councils in Havana, each including an average of twenty thousand residents.

9. Delegates are elected in *circumscripciones* (electoral districts) of approximately fifteen hundred electors. All are also members of the Municipal Assembly.

10. The emergence and the activities of NGOs have been controversial, leading to consistent tension with government agencies and limited possibilities for independent operations. Several have found a space to maintain their activities at the local level, collaborating with municipalities, People's Councils, and large provincial and national urban projects. Others, unable to resolve these contradictions, have been closed down by their sponsoring agencies, as was the case of Habitat-Cuba in 2001.

11. Carlos García Pleyán, interview, March 2001.

12. The Cuban Democracy Act, the official name of this bill, called for a two-track approach to the policy on Cuba. Track I was the further tightening of the U.S. embargo. The bill also provided funds for subversion that were to be channeled through U.S. NGOs and government agencies to Cuban independent NGOs; this was Track II.

112 / Miren Uriarte

13. A salient example of this is the demise of Habitat-Cuba in 2001, after a series of confrontations with its sponsor, the Institute of Housing.

14. Interviews with Fernando Rojas, the Ministry of Culture, and staff from Plan Maestro of the Oficina del Historiador de la Ciudad de La Habana, March 2001.

15. Interviews with Jesús Ramos, the secretary of the People's Power in the City of Havana, and David Díaz Carbó, March 2001.

16. David Díaz Carbó, interview, March 2001.

17. Carlos García Pleyán, interview, March 2001.

References

Campfens, H. 1996. "Partnerships in International Social Development: Evolution in Practice and Concept." *International Social Work* 39: 201–23.

Centro de Investigaciones de la Economía Mundial (CIEM). 2000. *Investigación sobre el desarrollo humano y equidad en Cuba, 1999*. Havana: Caguayo, S.A.

Coyula, M., M. Cabrera, and R. Oliveras. 1995. *Los talleres de transformación integral del barrio: Una experiencia en el planeamiento sustentable y participativo en La Habana.* Havana: Grupo para el Desarrollo Integral de la Capital.

Coyula, M., and J. Hamberg. 2003. "The Case of Havana, Cuba." In *Understanding Slums: Case Studies for the Global Report on Human Settlements.* London: Development Planning Unit, University College London; Nairobi: UN-Habitat (United Nations Human Settlement Program).

Coyula, M., R. Oliveras, and M. Coyula. 2002. *Towards a new kind of community in Havana: The Workshops for Integrated Neighborhood Transformation.* La Habana: Grupo para el Desarrollo Integral de la Capital. 16–17.

Cruz Hernández, M. C. 1997. "Agricultura urbana y medio ambiente: Ciudad de La Habana." In *¿Quiénes hacen ciudad?: Ambiente urbano y participación popular: Cuba, Puerto Rico, República Dominicana*, edited by Mario Coyula et al., 202–16. Cuenca, Ecuador: Sociedad Interamericana de Planificación.

Cruz Hernández, M. C., and R. Sánchez Medina. 2003. *Agriculture in the City: A Key to Sustainability in Havana, Cuba.* Ottawa: International Development Research Centre.

Del Río Hernández, M. 1998. "Consejos populares: Entorno comunitario de la participación política en Cuba." In *Desarrollo local y descentralización en el contexto urbano*, edited by Roberto Dávalos Domínguez, 153–61. Havana: Universidad de La Habana.

Díaz Carbó, D., M. Uriarte Martín, and R. Dávalos Domínguez. 1998. "Participación comunitaria en cuatro experiencias de los órganos locales de gobierno en Cuba." In *Desarrollo local y descentralización en el contexto urbano*, edited by Roberto Dávalos Domínguez, 93–104. Havana: Universidad de La Habana.

Dilla Alfonso, H. 1995. "Los municipios cubanos y los retos del futuro." *Comunidad* 4, no. 95. Havana: Instituto de Planificación Física.

———. 1998. "¿Por qué necesitamos municipios más fuertes?" In *Desarrollo local y descentralización en el contexto urbano*, edited by Roberto Dávalos Domínguez, 46–52. Havana: Universidad de La Habana.

Dilla Alfonso, H., A. Fernández Soriano, and M. Castro Flores. 1998. "Movimientos bar-
riales en Cuba: Un análisis comparativo." In *Participación social: Desarrollo urbano
y comunitario,* edited by A. Vázquez Penelas et al., 65–92. Havana: Universidad de
La Habana.

Dilla Alfonso, H., and G. González Núñez. 1995. "Successes and Failures of a Decen-
tralizing Experience: Cuba's Local Governments." *Canadian Journal of Development
Studies* 16 no. 1: 131–47.

Espina Prieto, M. 1998. "Panorama de los efectos de la reforma sobre la estructura social
Cubana: Grupos tradicionales y emergentes." Paper presented at the 21st Congress,
Latin American Studies Association, Chicago.

———. 2003. "Efectos sociales del reajuste económico: Igualdad, desigualdad, y procesos
de complejización en la sociedad cubana." Paper presented at the annual meeting of
the Latin American Studies Association, Dallas.

Farncombe, A. and R. Betancourt. 2000. "Canada Contributes to Sustainable Urban Development in Cuba: Revitalization of el Parque Metropolitano de La Habana." http://
www.globalexchange.org/countries/cuba/sustainable/metroPark.html.pf (accessed
28 March 2004 .

Ferriol Murruaga, A. 2001. "Apertura externa, mercado laboral, y política social." *Cuba
Siglo XXI,* no. 3 (March). http://www.nodo50.org/cubasigloXXI/economia/ferriol1_
280201.htm accessed 28 June 2007.

Ferriol Murruaga, A., G. Carriazo Moreno, O. Echavarría, and D. Quintana Mendoza.
1998. "Efectos de políticas macroeconómicas y sociales sobre los niveles de pobreza:
El caso de Cuba en los años noventa." In *Política macroeconómica y pobreza: América
Latina y el Caribe,* edited by E. Ganuza, T. Taylor, and S. Morley. Madrid: PNUD,
CEPAL, BID, Grupo Mundi-Prensa. http://www.undp.org/rblac/documents/pov-
erty/politica_macro/index.htm, accessed 3 November 2006.

García Brigos, J. 2001. "Cinco tesis sobre los consejos populares." *Cuba Siglo XXI,* no.
3 (March). http://www.cubaxxi.f2s.com/politica/brigos4_280201.htm, accessed 3
March 2002.

García Ramos, A., and X. González de la Hoz. 1999. "La promoción de la participación
social en la circunscripción 40 del príncipe, Municipio Plaza." In *Desde el barrio,* by
Grupo para el Desarrollo Integral de la Capital. Havana: Grupo para el Desarrollo
Integral de la Capital.

González de la Hoz, X. 2000. "La colaboración en el Barrio Príncipe." In *Los barrios
hacen ciudad,* by Grupo para el Desarrollo Integral de la Capital. Havana: Grupo para
el Desarrollo Integral de la Capital.

Grupo de Investigaciones Sociológicas. 1996. *Trabajo comunitario integrado: Proyecto de
programa.* Havana: Grupo de Investigaciones Sociológicas. Unpublished.

Grupo para el Desarrollo Integral de la Capital. 1999a. *Comunidades que se descubren y
se transforman.* Havana: Grupo para el Desarrollo Integral de la Capital.

———. 1999b. *Desde el barrio.* Havana: Grupo para el Desarrollo Integral de la Capital.

———. 2000. *Los barrios hacen ciudad.* Havana: Grupo para el Desarrollo Integral de
la Capital.

Gunn, G. 1995. *Cuba's New NGOs: Government Puppets or Seeds of Civil Society?* Georgetown University Cuba Briefing Paper Series 7. Washington, D.C.: Georgetown University.

De la Hoz Padilla, I., and N. Reyes Herrera. 1999. "Vamos a participar en el reciclaje." In *Comunidades que se descubren y se transforman*, by Grupo para el Desarrollo Integral de la Capital. Havana: Grupo para el Desarrollo Integral de la Capital.

Lutjens, S. L. 2000. "Restructuring Childhood in Cuba: The State as Family." In *Children on the Streets of the Americas*, edited by Roslyn Arlin Mickelson, 55–66. New York: Routledge.

Martínez Canals, E., and J. García Brigos. 2001. "Comunidad y desarrollo: Una experiencia cubana en área urbana." *Cuba Siglo XXI* no. 9 (September).

Mensaje de Cuba. 1998. "Speaking with the Goblin on Popular Education." *Mensaje de Cuba* 49/50 (February and March). Havana: Centro de Estudios Europeos.

Oakley, P., and O. Flores. 1994. "Editorial Introduction: Community Development in Latin America: The Current State of Play." *Community Development Journal* 29, no. 4: 295–97.

Oficina Nacional de Estadísticas. 1997. *Anuario Estadístico de Cuba*. Havana: Oficina Nacional de Estadísticas.

O'Gorman, F. 1994. "Where Is Community Development Going in Latin America?" *Community Development Journal* 29, no. 4: 298–306.

Oliveras Gómez, R. 1999. *Planeamiento estratégico comunitario: Método, técnicas, y experiencias.* Havana: Grupo para el Desarrollo Integral de la Capital.

———. 2002. *Propuesta para la elaboración del planeamiento estratégico en los municipios de la ciudad de La Habana.* Havana: Grupo para el Desarrollo Integral de la Capital.

Oliveras Gómez, R., and R. Núñez,. 2004. "There Will Be Reason to Keep Balance: Urban Segregation in Havana: Policies, Instruments, and Results." Paper presented at the seminar entitled "Poverty and Social Policy in Cuba: Addressing the Challenges of Social and Economic Change," sponsored by the Centro de Investigaciones Psicológicas y Sociológicas, Havana, and the David Rockefeller Center for Latin American Studies, Harvard University. Havana, January.

Pérez Villanueva, O. E. 2002. "Ciudad de La Habana, desempeño económico y situación social." *Cuba Siglo XXI* (April). http://www.nodo50.org/cubasigloXXI/economia/villanueval_310302.htm (accessed 28 June 2007).

República de Cuba. 2000. *Gaceta Oficial de la República*, 25 July.

Rodríguez, B. L. 1997. "Descentralización y participación en el ámbito local: Estudio comparativo de los consejos populares de Prado y Belén." Graduate thesis, Department of Philosophy and History, University of Havana.

Roman, P. 1999. *People's Power: Cuba's Experience with Representative Government.* Latin American Perspectives Series 20. Boulder, Colo.: Westview Press.

Scarpacci, J. L., R. Segre, and M. Coyula. 2002. *Havana: Two Faces of the Antillean Metropolis.* Chapel Hill: University of North Carolina Press.

Segre, R., M. Coyula, and J. L. Scarpacci. 1997. *Havana: Two Faces of the Antillean Metropolis.* West Sussex, England: John Wiley and Sons.

Sinclair, M. 2000. "NGOs in Cuba: Principles for Cooperation." Paper presented at the annual meeting of the Latin America Studies Association, Miami, March.

Sinclair, M., and M. Thompson. 2001. *Cuba, Going Against the Grain: Agricultural Crisis and Transformation*. Boston: Oxfam America.

Snow, A. 1998. "U.S. Dollar Takes on Role in Cuba." Associated Press, 20 July. AP-NY-07-20-980657EDT.

Togores González, V. 2002. "Cuba: Efectos sociales de la crisis y el ajuste económico de los '90's." *Cuba Siglo XXI* (January). http://www.nodo50.org/cubasigloXXI/economia/togores1_311201.htm. (accessed 28 June 2007)

———. 2003. "Una mirada al gasto social en Cuba a partir de la crisis de los noventa." Paper presented at the annual meeting of the Latin American Studies Association, Dallas, arch.

Uriarte, M. 2003. *Cuba: Social Policy at a Crossroads: Maintaining Priorities, Transforming Practice*. Boston: Oxfam America.

Uriarte Martín, M. y M. Fernández Pérez. 1998. "Acción Ambiental Urbana y la Participación: El Caso del Parque Metropolitano de La Habana." In *Participación Social. Desarrollo Urbano y Comunitario*, edited by Aurora Vásquez Penelas and Roberto Dávalos. University of Havana.

5

Solidarity Organizations and Friendship Groups

Internationalist Volunteer Work Brigades
and People-to-People Ties

NINO PAGLICCIA

The concept of general human solidarity is the highest cultural and moral concept; to turn it into reality, is the task of socialism.

Wilhelm Liebknecht (quoted in Wildt 1999, 214)

We must then begin to erase our old concepts and begin to draw closer and closer to the people and to be increasingly aware. We must approach them not as before. [All] we have done [is] practice charity, and what we have to practice is solidarity.

Che Guevara (1960)

Many would agree that there is a strong solidarity movement in Canada. The astonishingly large number of organizations that advocate some kind of support for an equally large number of causes or interests is just one indicator of the movement. But even among those who are part of that movement there is little agreement on what solidarity is, on solidarity for what or for whom, and on how solidarity should be carried out and by whom. It is fair to say that there is no solidarity within the solidarity movement in Canada. Many, among those who are familiar with Cuba, would also agree that solidarity is quite strong in that country. But this is the extent of the similarity between the two countries. Solidarity in Cuba is quite simply solid—it is a way of life, essential to and consistent with the Cuban social system.

Canadian solidarity with Cuba has gained strength particularly since the early 1990s. The range of people-to-people connections goes from providing material aid to sharing political views. The outreach has been toward the Cuban people, but there is a mutual feeling that the exchange benefits both peoples.

This chapter presents an empirical account of solidarity in Canada and Cuba, based on participant observation; it explores the issues of how solidarity is put into action and what motivates it. The first section begins with the "uses of solidarity" as a starting point to provide a framework for the concept of solidarity itself. It is suggested that the uses of solidarity do not lie on a linear scale; there are other dimensions to consider, from solidarity as resistance, which strives to change the social structure, to state-sponsored solidarity, to charity as distinct from solidarity. It is argued here that it is precisely the outlook on society that marks the difference in the expressions of solidarity in Canada and in Cuba. This will be illustrated in the second section through the examination of a Canadian solidarity project in Cuba that involves a people-to-people connection through voluntary work. Ultimately, this chapter strives to offer a critical analysis of solidarity that stems from the interface of theory and praxis when praxis is considered as the testing ground where the theory is forged.

Solidarity

Philosophers and sociologists have tried to develop different ways of explaining how solidarity arises in a society and how individuals and organizations are bound by the ideals of solidarity. Nevertheless, solidarity continues to defy the coining of a single formal theoretical definition and is often used interchangeably with charity. The difficulty in arriving at a normalizing definition stems from the existence of a great variety of expressions of that feeling of wanting to help and the underlying political nature that motivates these expressions. Practitioners of solidarity can contribute constructively to the understanding of solidarity through their exploration of their motivation and reflection on their experience. This is the underlying premise in this chapter. However, it is important to trace briefly the origin of the term solidarity and the social context in which the term arose. The "birth" of solidarity was a response to fundamental social changes, and these changes give meaning and relevance to the forms of solidarity that are practiced today.

While the usage of the word solidarity can be traced back to the eighteenth century, only more recently have there been attempts to formalize a theory of solidarity. Several thinkers can be associated with early concepts and formulations of solidarity. In 1859, Pierre Leroux attributed to himself the first use of "solidarity": "J'ai le premier utilisé le terme solidarité pour l'introduire dans la philosophie, c'est-à-dire suivant moi, dans la religion de l'avenir. J'ai voulu remplacer la charité du christianisme par la solidarité humaine" [I am the first to use the term solidarity in order to introduce it in philosophy, that is to say, in the religion of the future. I wanted to replace the charity of Christianity for the human solidarity] (Le Bras-Choppard 1992, 55). This is a clear indication that, at conception, solidarity was distinct from charity. Others consider that "solidarity" became a standard linguistic term thanks to Auguste Comte's attempted conceptual analysis of society (Metz 1999, 194).

Leroux also claims the first use of the word socialism as opposed to individualism. While charity emphasizes a one-to-one relationship between a giver and a receiver, solidarity is the relationship between a unified collective and a larger social entity. This latter relational process is the basis of socialism. Therefore one could conclude that solidarity is to socialism what charity is to individualism.

It is perhaps Emile Durkheim who is most often quoted by sociologists in relation to solidarity, especially in the context of an industrial society. Durkheim's view was a reflection of the biological approach to the science of his day. He placed the beginning of solidarity in the interdependence of individuals that was created by the division of labor (Durkheim 1965). This in turn stemmed from an acknowledgment that in a society that functions with an extreme division of labor, individuals will recognize their mutual dependency and in doing so will give rise to an active conscious solidarity in lieu of a mechanical one (Metz 1999). This is obviously reminiscent of the Marxist notion of workers' raised awareness of their own class condition and the ensuing solidarity of workers' unions that are engaged in class struggle. The correspondence between solidarity and socialism is made even more evident with the understanding that the interdependency among members of Durkheim's society implied a political extension of solidarity because,

> ... in order to become integrated and effective, solidarity has to be exemplified in contractual specifications within a framework of social laws laid down by the State. This thought leads on from theory to politics, and it was also the basis for the emergence of the solidarism doctrine, as put forward in 1896, three years after Durkheim, by the leading "radical," i.e., left-wing liberal politician, Léon Bourgeois. . . . The battle for a State social legislation was thus also regarded as a battle against Catholic charity." (Metz 1999, 196)

It was based on precisely these ideas that France contributed to the world the initial concept of *securité sociale*, a system that is still much debated today in many countries within the context of providing public (social) assistance as opposed to private charity. In fact, the major divide between conservative and more progressive political parties is around the public policy of social welfare usually associated with a more liberal viewpoint.

More recently, other thinkers have examined the notion of solidarity, expanding its meaning to include distinct concepts such as charity and state-sponsored solidarity. For example, Bayertz (1999) identifies four uses of solidarity: as a moral concept, as a social need, as a liberation movement, and as a state responsibility. Bayertz's idea of solidarity as a moral concept is largely based on the belief that humans have a natural trait for compassion and charity and react as a result of a moral obligation toward those who are seen as suffering. Typically, this moral response constitutes a bond among religious groups. Adam Smith himself wrote about the virtues of charity consistent with the Christian outlook toward helping the underprivileged.

Today, under continued, more stringent, forms of social pressure, modern societies have come to depend more and more on benevolent organizations in order to mitigate social problems such as poverty and indigence. These types of "civil society" are increasingly becoming part of the fabric of many societies. In this context, and without any intention of diminishing its value, one might say that charity *toward* the oppressed, for instance, is in contrast to solidarity *with* the oppressed; the former does not necessarily imply probing into the causes of oppression and bringing those to social consciousness.

As more complex societies evolve, in which people congregate in large communities and social structures gain alienating strength vis-à-vis individuals, mutual support, as a response to a social need, acquires a meaning of human and social cohesion as protection against perceived threats. This phenomenon first became evident with the advent of the Industrial Revolution and its tremendous impact on labor, as suggested by Durkheim. The ensuing division of labor and economic theories of capitalism helped create a kind of social solidarity, which was needed to offset individualism and the "tyranny of the market." In this context, for instance, one may speak of the "solidarity of the oppressed" as a collective position in contrast to an individualistic or passive stand on oppression.

The third use of solidarity suggested by Bayertz is a step beyond that of social cohesion for endurance and is conceptually closer to the meaning assigned to it by the forebears of solidarity. It is solidarity that implies a consciousness of a social condition, then a rejection of that condition, and finally actions leading to the overturning of that condition toward liberation. The origin of this view has been associated with Jean Jacques Rousseau in the context of the *fraternité* (brotherhood) of the French Revolution, but the more traditional, consistent, and operational use of solidarity—so explicitly named—is associated with the labor movement and class struggle on a world scale. In a reference to this more political aspect of solidarity, Engels added to the debate by stating "that the simple feeling of solidarity, based on an insight into sameness of the class position, is sufficient in order to create amongst all of the laborers of all countries and languages one large and cohesive proletariat party" (Bayertz 1999, 17). This type of solidarity identifies an opponent with which to contend, which may be perceived as oppressive, and organizes itself around a movement that demands changes through resistance.

Finally, there is the question of whose responsibility it is to ensure the well-being of a society, that is, who is to exert solidarity with those in need. According to Bayertz, the concept of the welfare state as being in solidarity with the disadvantaged stems from the French Revolution. Many continue to believe that people in need should be entitled to be supported by the state, but this notion did not make it into the Universal Declaration of Human Rights; therefore, states are often reluctant to adopt social welfare policies. This "solidarity of the state" has remained elusive in modern societies as some states refuse to take on the responsibility. While the current trend is for governments to regress toward the individualism of neoliberal policies, there is a striking exception to this trend as represented by Cuba. The solidarity of the Cuban state will be addressed in the next section.

The sequential order of the uses of solidarity that Bayertz identifies suggests a progression and a continuum in the development and practice of solidarity. The individual's innate, moral, and compassionate response to those in need acquires more social cohesiveness as societies grow in complexity. With growing societies, the inherent development of a social consciousness demands that actions be taken to counter the ills of societies that cause indigence. Consequently, the magnitude and nature of social problems elude the possibilities of individuals' actions and therefore there arises an expectation of state-sponsored solidarity.

This conceptual continuum may be more suitable for a historical analysis of solidarity (Metz 1999; Wildt 1999). It will suffice here to say that the difficulty in providing a full (and commonly accepted) concept of solidarity lies in the difficulty of reconciling charity with solidarity, with political solidarity, and with solidarity as a state responsibility outside a historical analysis of the evolution of societies. Others have already indicated that solidarity may encompass a multiplicity of empirical notions and that "it may make sense to distinguish *multiple* concepts of 'solidarity' . . . and to investigate how the designated phenomena are related to each other empirically" (emphasis in the original) (Wildt 1999, 219).

The fact that solidarity as social cohesion is a human behavior that responds to needs is not a sufficient common denominator for normalizing the concept. If that were the case then the solidarity of members of organized crime groups would lead those groups to be considered as solidarity organizations. The legitimacy of the outcome and the collective view of solidarity actions are definitely strong qualifiers of what is intuitively understood as solidarity, and the extent of acceptance of that outcome determines which solidarity actions are worthy of being supported by individuals and governments.

The four uses of solidarity identified by Bayertz (1999) try to fit qualitatively different concepts on the same scale. When the term solidarity is used as a moral concept it is more akin to charity and therefore should not be found on the same scale or dimension as the type of solidarity expressed in a liberation movement. The charity and humanitarian work of the Salvation Army, for example, as valuable as that work is, should not be placed in the same realm of work as that of Greenpeace; the latter goes to great lengths to expose the perpetrators of the perceived harm to the environment that compels them to act. The practice of compassion, charity, or altruism may not necessarily probe into the causes of social problems or even the perceived connection between a given sociopolitical system and its social problems. Typically, compassion acts upon the individual or group of individuals in hardship for the immediate relief of their suffering. This kind of altruistic practice may well be effective in the case of needs resulting from natural disasters, physical disabilities, personal inability, or temporary distress. However, it may not be a solution for regularly recurring or permanent problems that individuals do not bring upon themselves intentionally, such as poverty, marginality, and other social ills that have a more systemic and structural origin.

Furthermore, this charitable approach to helping others has sometimes been seen as a way of covering up the failure of an individualistic or profit-driven social system. Many charitable organizations in fact are perceived to overlook the root cause of social problems in order to have access to scarce funding and resources from the system itself for their altruistic work. In a market-oriented society it is precisely the availability of such resources that separates charitable organizations from more politically motivated solidarity organizations. Charitable organizations are far more likely to receive government funding in capitalist societies.

It has been argued that charity and the proliferation of charitable organizations are ideologically associated with an individualistic and capitalist society. It is not coincidental that in the crudest form of capitalism advocated by the early Protestant church the prevalent view proposed was that humankind was not capable of showing compassion and care for others (Weber 2002). Consequently, this position did not encourage altruism, which was possibly seen as interfering with the "invisible hand" of capitalism. More currently, many believe that non-interference with stringent neoliberal policies put forward today will inevitably contribute to creating more poverty and a larger gap between the rich and the poor. In a society that relies on charity, practitioners of charity silently try to cope with a job that is becoming increasingly unmanageable, albeit valuable.

Solidarity as originally conceived is—quite contrary to charity work—designed to act upon the social organization in order to change it for the benefit of the larger collective. Solidarity is directed at awareness of the condition and at social change or redefinition of power relations. As such, charity and solidarity are mutually exclusive activities and not simply the "division of tasks," as for instance Giugni (2001, 236) attempts to reduce it to.

The kind of solidarity that people and organizations practice is shaped by their belief system, their worldview, and their view of the sociopolitical system in which they live, and this in turn may compel them to embrace the politics of minorities. Therefore, "'solidarity activism' seems primarily left wing" (Fillieule 2001, 52), where left wing ideology is usually associated with an ideology of resistance. Consequently, this solidarity activism *among* a collective of individuals *for* the purpose of obtaining social change clearly rests on a dimension of resistance.

Given that solidarity as resistance frequently may have the state as an opponent, the concept of solidarity as a state responsibility lies on a third dimension. A society that has state-endorsed solidarity is one that assumes the protection and well-being of its members to be guaranteed by social welfare policies and not to be left to the uncertainty and possibly the humiliation of charity. Usually a state that practices solidarity as a collective goal is associated with a socialist ideology. Solidarity in this case becomes the antonym of individualism.

In order to visualize this three-dimensional examination of solidarity and charity, it may be helpful to imagine the space created by three perpendicular lines connected at one vertex (figure 5.1). If we assume that line 1 represents an increasing degree of charity as we move away from the vertex, then line 2 represents an increasing degree of solidarity as resistance, and line 3 represents increasing stages of state-endorsed solidarity.

It is instructive to observe the extreme cases that are possible in this "solidarity-charity space." A hypothetical society involved only in practicing charity (that is, along line 1) may be operating exclusively with a laissez-faire attitude; there are neither solidarity activism nor welfare state policies. If only solidarity activism is practiced, in the dimension of line 2, without state solidarity or charity, it may be the case of a politically struggling situation with protracted resistance movements. State solidarity with a socialist outlook (along line 3) may be viewed as a society where the state assumes the responsibility for the well-being of every individual and therefore solidarity activism is absent and charity becomes redundant.

It is possible to envision hypothetical societies with a mix of elements from different dimensions. The combination of charity with certain state welfare policies and possibly with some degree of solidarity activism could be construed as a social democratic society in terms of solidarity practice (see the arrow in figure 1). Similarly, a society largely based on charity and solidarity activism may represent a polarized society with both a liberal attitude and a class struggle movement. Finally, a society with mostly a mix of solidarity

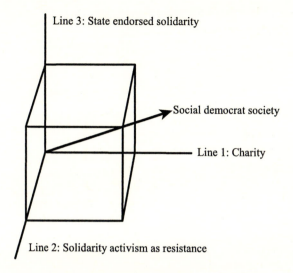

Figure 5.1. Three-dimensional solidarity-charity space.

activism and state-sponsored solidarity may reflect a more progressive society with organizations of individuals demanding social changes and a state supporting the implementation of those changes.

In conclusion, from this three-dimensional perspective it can be observed how charity and solidarity (as resistance or state-endorsed) are mutually exclusive. It could be inferred that in an ideal society, to the extent that state solidarity has a strong presence, there is no need for charity; in contrast, to the extent that there is need for charity, solidarity is likely to be seen as ideologically opposed. It can be argued that it is the mix of three basic ingredients that marks the character of solidarity versus charity in a society or organization: charity, solidarity activism, and state solidarity. This view is based on the original notion of solidarity, but it can also be substantiated from the empirical observation of the people-to-people ties of the Canadian-Cuban solidarity work brigades that will be highlighted in the next section.

Solidarity Organizations and People-to-People Solidarity

The discourse about solidarity organizations parallels that of individual solidarity, since organizations reflect and carry out the specific solidarity mandate with which they are invested in the sociopolitical context wherein they operate. While individuals can perform solidarity as a personal mission, it is a group of individuals structured in some form of collective or organic association with a common mandate that is normally recognized and recognizable.

Solidarity organizations are the catalysts of the solidarity movement and as such they have an extremely important role in society and, with it, a fundamental responsibility.

NGOs and Cuba

Nongovernmental organizations (NGOs) or "civil societies" have flourished in the twentieth century. In his analysis of social solidarity in the context of the division of labor and the role of the state, Durkheim foresaw the development of NGOs when he stated that a "nation cannot be maintained unless, between the state and the individuals, a whole range of secondary groups are interposed. These must be close enough to the individual to attract him to their activities and, in so doing, to absorb him into the mainstream of social life" (Durkheim 1984, preface).

However, in the last twenty years the growth of NGOs has been dramatic and they have had to adjust or perish in an ever increasingly competitive world chasing limited resources. In order to survive and grow, organizations have had to reinterpret their role in society, trying to fit into what is expected of them. As Berthoud (2001) so aptly stated:

> At a time when the neo-liberal catechism known as the "Washington consensus" was waxing victorious with cookie-cutter recipes for "development," the NGOs frequently filled in for the social functions of the states, which were being dismantled by those very recipes. The NGOs that maintained a critical discourse about the system and continued analyzing the causes of poverty found it ever harder to respond to a number of pressing questions in the real world of practice. (Berthoud 2001, n.p.)

Despite the fact that NGOs are not-for-profit organizations, some of them handle very large budgets. In fact, the total NGO input to the global economy amounts to billions of dollars annually. As a result, the collective impact of NGOs in the economy as another market player has prompted some to introduce "solidarity work" into the field of economics (Gottheil 1996; Arnsperger and Varoufakis 1999).

The growth and development of NGOs has not happened without criticism or skepticism. The criticism has even included a questioning of the legitimacy of the work that some civil societies undertake. For example, the use of civil societies in political covert actions through financial support and infiltration with the purpose of changing the balance of power in certain countries has been well documented for the period 1945 to 1991 by Kevin O'Brien (1995). Unfortunately, there is no indication that this practice has stopped and it certainly continues in the case of Cuba. For example, Agee (2003) reports that

U.S.-based organizations have links to terrorist activities carried over in Cuba. Saney adds: "Washington's record of aggression [against Cuba] includes sabotage, terrorist attacks, coastal raids, an invasion, assassinations, attempted assassinations against the leadership, biological warfare, an economic embargo tantamount to an economic blockade and a constant propaganda and disinformation crusade" (Saney 2004, 70).

Many U.S. NGOs that overtly oppose the Cuban government receive substantial funding from the United States Agency for International Development (USAID). Particularly noticeable is the funding to the U.S colleges, universities, and NGOs for "Civil Societies Developed," a program reportedly to facilitate access to information and "training" for Cuban NGOs. Considerable financial assistance is also provided to individuals in Cuba who are willing to organize any form of resistance or opposition to the Cuban government. This assistance is granted under Section 109 of the popularly known Helms-Burton law of 1996, which is controversially titled the Cuban Liberty and Democratic Solidarity Act.

While there may be U.S. government-sponsored destabilizing activities carried out against Cuba, this section will refer only to people-to-people solidarity activities carried out by NGOs based in Canada and the United States. A special Canadian case of the people-to-people link will be used as empirical evidence to support the concept of solidarity-charity space developed in the first section. Many international organizations have programs and activities targeting poor countries, but a focus on Cuba acquires a different meaning in light of the distinct paradigms of, on one hand, a market-oriented, hegemonic and militarily interventionist United States and, on the other hand, a revolutionary Cuba, set on defending sovereignty and socialism. Why is solidarity with Cuba so relevant today? The largest growth of solidarity with Cuba has occurred since the demise of the Communist Bloc in 1989, when Cuba, having lost about 80 percent of its trade exchange, faced the most serious economic crisis in the early 1990s that any country has ever experienced in time of peace, the Período Especial. While the U.S. government seized the opportunity to tighten the economic embargo of Cuba with the Torricelli-Graham law in 1992, in the hope that Cuba would give up its socialist path, a large number of people in many countries chose to side with the island. But to say that the renewed interest in Cuba has been a simple humanitarian response to the hardship caused by the economic crisis is an oversimplification. A seemingly far more important element has been the perception of a relentlessly increasing and aggressive U.S. foreign policy against Cuba over the last fifteen years, following an already long history of provocations since 1959 (Franklin 1997).

A U.S.-sponsored armed invasion of the island has always been considered a possibility by Cubans and by many Cuba analysts. However, never has this

126 / Nino Pagliccia

possibility been as real as it was when the U.S. government announced new measures following the recommendations of the Commission for Assistance to a Free Cuba (Powell 2004). These measures, de facto proposing the destabilization of Cuba, are seen by many as a provocation aimed at stimulating a Cuban reaction that could be used by the U.S. government to justify military action against the island (Pagliccia 2004).

Cuba has also seen a growth of so-called NGOs, as well as a reinterpretation of their role, as a response to the expanded interaction with countries outside the former Soviet bloc. A detailed and comprehensive study of the nature and development of civil societies in Cuba can be found in Gray (2003).

On the one hand, it may seem a contradiction to conceive of active NGOs in a society where the socialist state has the sole and responsible role as guarantor of well-being. However, this apparent contradiction stems from the point of view of societies that have an antagonistic model of governance in which the separation between the state and organizations (and hence individuals) is viewed as a positive and necessary requirement. Non-governmental organizations in a free market society are literally meant to be organizations that have no association with the state although they might be doing the work that the state is relinquishing.

On the other hand, the Cuban author J. L. Acanda González argues that Cuban civil society is "the breeding ground for ideological production interconnected and interwoven with political society and with the state ... [and] ... contributes to the growth of socialism" (Acanda González 2006, 34–35). Ironically, NGOs in Cuba perhaps reflect more closely the vision that Durkheim had of absorbing individuals into the mainstream of social life (Durkheim 1984).

Yet another striking characteristic of Cuban civil society or the "mass organizations," as they are called in Cuba, is their formal legal status. Saney explains that "mass organizations, unlike the Communist Party, are granted through Article 88 (c) of the [Cuban] Constitution the right to propose legislation in the areas that fall under their jurisdiction" (Saney 2004, 67). Even further, mass organizations may have elected representatives in government; this is the case, for instance, of the Federación de Mujeres Cubanas (FMC, Federation of Cuban Women), the Central de Trabajadores de Cuba (CTC, Cuban Workers' Confederation), the Federación de Estudiantes Universitarios (FEU, Federation of University Students), the Asociación Nacional de Agricultores Pequeños (ANAP, National Association of Small Farmers), and many other organizations, including professional organizations. Almost 54 percent of the members of the National Assembly from 1998 to 2003 were elected delegates of mass and professional organizations. A detailed description of the role of mass organizations in the Cuban electoral process is given by August (1999).

Within Cuba's participatory model of governance, the notion that the only true democratic representation is by giving voice to "dissident groups," advocating a return to a pre-1959 Cuba, is perceived by most Cubans as an old and failed model. As with similar legislation in most countries, any foreign financial support aiming at manufacturing an "opposition" on the island is considered a direct threat to and interference with Cuban sovereignty. This is punishable and has indeed been punished by Cuban law (Saney 2004, 74). After the signing into law of the Helms-Burton law in 1996, Cuba suspended the authorization of new organizations, virtually stopping the growth of formal civil society. It is, nevertheless, within this divergence of views and, at times, threatening backdrop that Cuba remains open to people-to-people exchanges and links.

Cuba's Solidarity

The polarized view of the "United States versus Cuba" is also present in Canada, but it is mitigated by virtue of the historical diplomatic relationship between the two countries, never interrupted after 1959, and the Canadian government's declared policy of constructive engagement with the island. However, the perceived increasing alliance of Canada with U.S. foreign policy is creating a greater divide between those advocating solidarity and those advocating charity toward Cuba.

Many, in Cuba and in Canada, believe that the Cuban Revolution is building a society that is more humane and egalitarian in spite of limited resources. They see the Cuban state as truly representing the majority of the people as, for instance, indicated by the 97.16 percent voter turnout in the elections of 2003 in Cuba, in which only 3 percent of the ballots were invalid (Saney 2004). They also see the Cuban state as securing that support with its commitment to providing social services to all as embedded in Chapter 7 of the Cuban constitution. There is a widespread perception of solidarity between the state and the people on the island. The Cuban author José Bell Lara wrote: "La seguridad social, a pesar de la aguda crisis de los noventa, ha mantenido sus características de ser un sistema universal, equitativo y solidario" [Social security, in spite of the severe crisis of the 1990s, has kept its characteristics of being universal, equitable and in solidarity] (Bell Lara 1999, 81). At the height of the Special Period in Cuba not a single basic social service was cut back. However, the cases of malnutrition that developed at this time in Cuba are not to be ignored—they were severe and devastating, but they were promptly and effectively tackled by the Cuban government with the full participation of the population (Kirkpatrick 1996, 1997).

In the international arena, Cuba has also shown an unprecedented commitment to solidarity through internationalist missions in many countries, including the United States. Thousands of Cuban doctors and teachers have

128 / Nino Pagliccia

been providing assistance in remote communities of Africa, Asia, and Latin America, where local governments are unable or unwilling to reach. Another example of solidarity beyond the borders of the island is the creation of the Latin American School of Medicine to train doctors from developing countries with Cuban scholarships. The only requirements in order to qualify for the scholarship are that the students come from poor backgrounds and that, upon getting their medical degrees, the new doctors return to their countries to practice among the poor. African-American students are also currently being trained as doctors in Cuba and they will practice in poor neighborhoods in New York City. Finally, the Cuban program Operación Milagro (Operation Miracle) is yet another example of Cuban solidarity; started in 2004, this program has provided free eye surgery to more than 295,000 visually impaired people in Latin America and the Caribbean.

Possibly the least known and most compelling act of Cuban international solidarity has been the selfless military assistance to the government of Angola to fight back the invading South African forces from 1975 to 1990. The now famous victory of the Cuban forces at Cuito Canavale led to the independence of Namibia and the dismantling of apartheid in South Africa. Nelson Mandela has publicly recognized the crucial role Cuba has played (Saney 2004, 196; Saney 2006).

Perhaps one Cuban organization typifies the importance of solidarity in Cuba: the Instituto Cubano de Amistad con los Pueblos (ICAP, Cuban Institute of Friendship with the Peoples). The ICAP is an organization that channels most of the international solidarity activities with Cuba and is a major (but not the only) gateway to Cuba for all international solidarity and friendship activities. In a country where solidarity is a national policy that runs parallel with diplomatic work, the ICAP represents and carries out that policy.[1] In this sense, it is an informal executor of government policy, but, in its administrative and operational functions, the ICAP is self-financing and autonomous, that is, independent from the government. The head office, based in Havana, has administrative divisions that cover all areas of the world, including Canada; the ICAP's Canada desk supervises and maintains links with many solidarity organizations and people in Canada. The ICAP has offices in all provincial capitals of the island that operate as hosts for visiting delegations.

Cuba is also perceived by many as exemplifying the true meaning of solidarity in its significance with regard to state responsibility and liberation movements. Virtually the whole country seems to embrace the concept of human solidarity, as stated in Article 1 of the Cuban Constitution, which is based on the value of human dignity, that is to say, the "unlimited capacity to give solidarity to our fellow human beings" (Blanco 1997, 103), therefore rejecting the notion of charity. Additionally, Cuba may be considered today as the ultimate bastion of self-determination, defiance, and resistance to the unrestrained power of the United States that seems to typify in turn the worst of liberal capitalism and imperialism. But, more importantly, Cuba is seen by many to symbolize a desired paradigm: a country truly governed by the people for the people.

Solidarity with Cuba

Cuba maintains its defiance in spite of perceived threats of military aggression. The voice of opposition of a small island to a "superpower" is also becoming the increasingly loud voice of many both inside and outside the island. The solidarity movement with Cuba has the implicit role of providing an international stage for the Cuban political struggle outside the island and helping counter the misinformation about Cuba.

There are many organizations, formally structured as registered NGOs or loosely organized, that do "Cuba solidarity work" in almost every country of the world. Their collective practice of solidarity covers the full range of the solidarity-charity space. The United States, whose government regards Cuba as an enemy state, is also home to many "Cuba solidarity" organizations.

One of the oldest organizations, known as the Venceremos (We Shall Overcome) Brigade, was formed in the United States in 1969 as a means of showing solidarity with the Cuban Revolution by working side by side with Cuban workers and challenging U.S. policies toward Cuba. The Venceremos Brigade is still active today and brings groups of Americans to Cuba to do volunteer work and also challenge the U.S. government's travel restrictions to Cuba for Americans. Similar brigades of volunteers go to Cuba in large numbers from many countries.

One organization in the United States, Pastors for Peace, typifies the kind of solidarity that is a direct confrontation with and rejection of government policy: "Pastors for Peace is a special ministry of the Interreligious Foundation for Community Organization and was created in 1988 to pioneer the delivery of humanitarian aid to Latin America and the Caribbean. Many thousands of people have participated in more than 40 caravans to Mexico and Central America, 16 to Cuba and many delegations and work brigades" (www.ifconews.org/about/about_us.htm, accessed 8 October 2006). The work of Pastors for Peace with Cuba has been remarkable and has grown beyond the simple "delivery of humanitarian aid." As the organization states on its website,

Our work on Cuba centers on our U.S.-Cuba Friendshipment [sic] Caravans, as well as our ongoing program of solidarity with the people of Cuba, which began in 1992 at the request of the Martin Luther King,

Jr. Memorial Center, in Havana, Cuba. Together with our international partners, we organize study tours, construction brigades and delegations for our members, bring Cuban religious leaders to the U.S., and educate U.S. citizens in their work with their Congressional representatives.

The work of Pastors for Peace has been relentless and directly challenging to the U.S. government because the group does not apply for licenses to travel to Cuba as required by law. The group also carries out a "reverse challenge" by bringing Cuban-made products back to the United States.

Perhaps the event that underscores the group's solidarity work and its effectiveness occurred in 1996, when "the U.S. government, in its most brutal confrontation to date, attacked the caravan and seized all the computers. In response, and in the name of reconciliation and peace, five caravan participants consecrated a 'Fast for Life' on 21 February 1996. On Day 94 of the Fast, the U.S. Treasury Department released the computers to the General Board of Church and Society of the United Methodist Church. They were delivered to Cuba in September 1996" (www.ifconews.org/about/about_us.htm, accessed 8 October 2006).

Lucius Walker, the organizer of Pastors for Peace and a participant in the fast, is a well-known figure among Cubans. The work of Pastors for Peace is becoming more international, including Canadian participation.

Another project has a special place in the solidarity movement of the United States and Canada that brings the Cuban people closer to the North American people. It is a campaign that demands the freedom of five Cuban men sentenced to very long prison terms in the United States for "conspiracy to commit espionage," while the Cubans claim that they were acting in response to the wave of violence directed at Cuba by "mercenary groups" from the Cuban exile community in southern Florida. Since they were sentenced in December 2001, many "Free the Cuban Five" committees have sprung up, bringing together North Americans who are sympathetic with the cause of the "Cuban Five" and Cubans who are concerned about the unfairness of the trial and the sentences (www.antiterroristas.cu, accessed 8 October 2006).

Also, in the United States, the National Network on Cuba (NNOC) "is the umbrella organization for several dozen separate organizations that advocate for the end of Washington's hostility towards Cuba, including activist solidarity groups in various major cities." The group's first principle is to "uphold and defend the right of the Cuban people to determine their own destiny and to freely pursue their own social, economic and cultural development. The Cuban people have a right to self-determination and national sovereignty. This is an inalienable right." And the group's first goal is "to build public pressure and influence U.S. public opinion in order to bring about an end to the criminal

U.S. blockade of Cuba, including working against the U.S. prohibition of the sale of food and medicines to the people of Cuba, ending the travel restrictions, and promoting cultural and educational exchanges" (www.cubasolidarity.com 2006).

In Canada, solidarity with Cuba had its beginnings right after the Cuban Revolution. In 1961 the Canadian Cuban Friendship Association (CCFA) was founded in Vancouver, and it still works today to initiate and promote activities and the continued growth of friendship and cooperation between the Canadian and Cuban peoples. Over the years, the CCFA has helped Cuban professionals, scientists, and cultural groups to come to Canada on tours in order to break the wall of misinformation about Cuba. Several other CCFAs have been founded across Canada over the years with a similar mandate.

Since the early 1990s, the solidarity movement in Canada has strengthened its links with the Cuban people, both in terms of the number of organizations involved and in terms of the intensity of solidarity work. At present, there are more than twenty solidarity organizations in major Canadian cities that are involved in promoting exchanges and informing the Canadian public about Cuba's affairs.

In September 2002, a pan-Canadian umbrella organization, the Canadian Network on Cuba (CNC), consolidated not only the work of traditional solidarity organizations but also solidarity work carried out with Cuba by other organizations such as labor groups. Currently the CNC has a membership of about twenty-four organizations with a collective constituency of close to sixty thousand people. A similar network has also been founded in Quebec—La Table de Concertation de Solidarité Québec-Cuba (Quebec-Cuba Solidarity Coordinating Committee). The stated principles of the CNC emphasize "friendship and solidarity between the people of Canada and Cuba" as well as equality in solidarity: "We uphold the right of the Canadian and Cuban peoples to self-determination and national sovereignty, the right to choose their own social, political, economic and cultural development" (www.canadiannetworkoncuba.ca/CNC/constitution.shtml 2006). One of the objectives of the CNC is to dialogue on a continual basis with the Canadian government in order to ensure that its policies with regard to Cuba remain more independent from U.S. policies.

People-to-People Links

The lack of overt political hostility between Canada and Cuba has allowed closer exchanges and links between the two societies where solidarity plays a relevant role. A unique model of a people-to-people link is represented by the volunteer work brigades to Cuba.

132 / Nino Pagliccia

Brigades are formed by a group of people committed to travel to Cuba for a period of time to perform manual labor alongside Cuban workers. In exchange, they benefit from close contact with Cuban workers and professionals of all walks of life and from meetings with representatives of Cuban mass organizations. Volunteer work brigades worldwide started in the 1960s as a response to the U.S.-imposed isolation of Cuba after the triumph of the Revolution. Numerous countries now organize brigades of volunteer workers that go to different parts of Cuba and in hundreds at a time.

The first Canadian volunteer work brigade went to Cuba in 1993 and it has been going every year for the last fourteen years without interruptions. The brigade project was initiated as a response to Cuba's call for solidarity in the wake of the collapse of the Communist Bloc and as a public rejection of the U.S. economic blockade of the island. It is a non-profit people-to-people solidarity project of the CNC, in cooperation with the ICAP, which brings together Canadians and Cubans during three weeks in Cuba to share work, space, time, experiences, values, and ideology. Its mandate is one of solidarity that includes upholding the UN declaration against the U.S. blockade of Cuba and encouraging Canadians to support the Cuban people in upholding their national sovereignty, self-determination, and social system without any foreign interference (http://www.canadiannetworkoncuba.ca/brigade 2006).

The Canadian brigade is known by its full name, the Ernesto Che Guevara Volunteer Work Brigade. It was named after the legendary revolutionary who inspired generations of Cubans and others to perform selfless work for the greater benefit of society.

Fundamental to the understanding of this exchange is the understanding of the concepts of work and worker in the socialist society. Work "acquires a new condition, that of connecting the worker to the object of work and, at the same time, creating the awareness of the importance of creativity" (Ariet 1993, 122). Che Guevara believed that it was possible to create a "new man" in a truly socialist society. This new "man of the twenty-first century" would grow up from the Cuban youth: "Our . . . students do physical work during their vacations or along with their studying. Work is a reward in some cases, a means of education in others, but it is never a punishment. A new generation is being born" (Guevara 2001, 157). Che Guevara himself performed voluntary work as an example to others even when he was a member of the revolutionary government. Article 45 of the Cuban Constitution states: "Work in a socialist society is a right and duty and a source of pride for every citizen."

The Canadian volunteer work brigade constitutes both a symbolic gesture of solidarity and real productive labor. This gesture is highly appreciated by Cubans who marvel at the dedication of foreigners who are spending their time to work in Cuba. The original intent of the brigade was to help provide resources to a population in need, but it also hoped to raise consciousness among Canadians about Cuba as something other than just a tourist destination. While Cuba's opening to tourism has allowed many Canadians to travel and vacation in Cuba, the volunteer work brigade provides the means for a more intimate view of Cuba and its social system.

Visits and meetings are also an important part of the brigade program, as they give an opportunity for a closer one-to-one contact through dialogue, questioning, and a more focused exchange of ideas. Organizations that are usually visited are mass organizations, of which Cubans are very proud, schools and hospitals, political organizations, such as the Union of Young Communists, and government institutions such as the People's Power Assembly—the Cuban Parliament.

This is by far the best direct means of learning about and understanding Cuban society, the Cuban Revolution, and socialism. At the same time, it gives an opportunity to exchange experiences and viewpoints. It is a coming together of those who have only experienced the capitalist system and may wonder about socialism and solidarity, and those who live socialism and solidarity daily.

In this context certain questions may be expected: How can Canadian solidarity be compared to Cuban solidarity? How is Canadian solidarity reciprocated from Cuba, if at all? What is the outcome of two social systems interacting from two quite different sociopolitical perspectives? Ultimately, how does Canadian-Cuban solidarity reflect the multidimensional view of solidarity-charity described in the first section?

More accurate answers to these questions can be provided not by the analysis of government policies or by measuring the magnitude of the trade exchange between the two countries, but rather by observing how people connect, what people value in each other, and how people-to-people bonds are formed.

Individually, Canadian *brigadistas*, as the brigade participants are called in Cuba, are generally a very heterogeneous group. Among them there are students, professionals, workers, immigrants to Canada, young, old, men, and women. They are a fairly representative cross-section of Canadian society. Similarly, the Cuban *brigadistas* include workers, students, and other people representative of Cuban society. Cubans generally have a high educational level, have a good knowledge of Canada, and welcome the opportunity to meet Canadians personally; they are genuinely curious, interested, and engaging. Often they are passionate about their culture and willing to share some of their major cultural assets: music and dance. It is through this basic sharing that friendship and trust start to grow, but it is through shared work and ideas that a true bonding happens.

Ideologically, there is more diversity of sociopolitical views among Canadian *brigadistas*. There may be some who are openly socialist and are in Cuba to live and learn from the socialist experience. Others are political activists in Canada who are in Cuba to bring their personal message of solidarity to their Cuban comrades. However, many others are not politically active but are very sympathetic to the Cubans on the grounds of a human concern for their scarcity of material goods and lack of economic affluence.

Among the Cuban *brigadistas* there seems to be a greater ideological homogeneity. They reflect the societal conception of international solidarity through their acceptance of Canadian *brigadistas* as well as their pride in their stories about the many endeavors Cubans have undertaken for the benefit of other countries. Their narrative reveals a concept of solidarity that is embedded in the makeup of Cuban society in the most fundamental meaning as a state responsibility toward its citizens as well as a political tool.

Understandably, the range of views about world outlook, political awareness, and approach to solidarity is quite different between Canadian and Cuban *brigadistas*. This may be largely due to the different life experiences and historical development. Among Canadians, the humanitarian support for the deprived fellow human beings, as expressed by different individuals, coexists and is quite distinct from solidarity. The delivery of donations brought from Canada is one indication of human compassion. This sentiment is by no means the only one, but it is a prominent dimension in the solidarity-charity space. Among Cubans, the solidarity-charity space is mainly active in two dimensions: state-endorsed solidarity and solidarity activism. The remarkable level of well-being, in spite of material scarcity, and general satisfaction and knowledge can only be associated with state solidarity by means of social services and other provisions Cubans freely receive. Solidarity activism is experienced in their interaction with the rest of the world and more directly with those who are perceived to be oppressed by social injustice. Examples of this are given by the many Cuban *brigadistas* who speak of their participation in international missions.

The reciprocal nature of solidarity between Canadian and Cuban *brigadistas* takes advantage of the synergies at play. Cubans do not keep a secret of their critical need for political solidarity, friendship, acceptance in the world community, and humanitarian support. These are things that Canadians are willing to give and capable of giving. Participation in the brigades in fact constitutes an opportunity for Canadians to fulfill in a modest way those needs. Canadians in turn may have a need for a cause, a different model of a working social organization or a partnership in what is perceived as a joint struggle for global survival; this is reflected in the promises that Canadian *brigadistas* make to promote the Cuban cause in Canada. Cubans in turn offer diversity, dignity in deprivation, and a promise that they will continue their Revolution as Cuba's contribution to the world struggle.

The empirical observation provided by the volunteer work brigade indicates that there is no final single outcome from the coming together of two peoples representing two different social systems and political views. A people-to-people link is a process rather than an immediate short-term goal. In fact, over the fourteen years of being in operation, the Che Guevara Volunteer Work Brigade clearly has shown itself to be an open-ended process. The only expectation is the establishment of a sustained process of building human solidarity based on dignity and self-determination. This process recognizes the differences, bases itself on the common ground of mutual respect, and allows the full range of camaraderie. In conclusion, a full understanding of people-to-people ties has to begin from an analysis of the underlying motivation that causes people to want to establish ties.

Charity has been used as the inherent human trait that motivates people to provide help and support to others in need. This humanitarian action has indistinguishably been used as synonymous with solidarity. However, a review of the origin of the term solidarity suggests that it contains a more political element and, even more precisely, a left-wing political nuance. This continues to be true today by virtue of its use in the Cuban context and in the Canadian solidarity movement. Consequently, charity and solidarity are not on the same continuum; they are qualitatively different concepts and they interact to form a three-dimensional space of human concern as depicted in figure 5.1.

The increasing number of NGOs with a wide range of people-to-people interactions tries to fill the equally wide solidarity-charity space as NGOs translate their mandates into action. The Canadian volunteer work brigade illustrates the multidimensional view of solidarity; in addition, it illustrates that this view is not divisive. On the contrary, it provides a unique experience of human connectedness.

The brigade often produces a transformative process in participants. Two accounts from former Canadian *brigadistas* made to the author may capture the full scope and extent of solidarity:

1. I have decided to bring Cuba to my daily life so every day I spend some time thinking about people who are living there (singing, dancing, smiling, struggling, surviving, resisting). The trip to Cuba was a wonderful experience for me because it helped me understand better the revolutionary process. My comprehension of the Cuban reality is much clearer now.

2. I remember how the brigade arrived in Cuba as Canadians, but left with Cuba inside of them. Indeed everybody left a bit of their soul in Cuba, and I will soon be back to recapture the essence of the Cuban soul. I remember a people who are driven by a moral incentive, rather than one of material gain. I remember seeing happy kids, knowing that they had a bright future, I remember seeing seniors living in dignity, I remember seeing women treated with respect, and I remember seeing all Cubans living their lives with purpose. Finally, I remember committing myself to the people of Cuba to tell everyone I met about my experience in Cuba. I will work to eliminate the bias and misconceptions, and explain what Cuba really is; a land of diverse beauty, where social justice holds top priority, and its people are the warmest in the world.

These emotive accounts are representative of the volunteer work brigade's transformative experience, and these words are symbolic of the building blocks that go into building Canadian solidarity with Cuba. Finally, it is the rediscovery of the human and political nature of solidarity together with the cumulative and collective efforts of individuals that create and sustain solidarity organizations and friendship groups. The people-to-people ties established as a result of participating in a brigade give a human face and a political expression to international solidarity and contribute to promoting a more fair and just world.

Author's Personal Statement

There is a high school in a small city in Venezuela that has the bust of two students who were shot dead by the Venezuelan police during a protest in 1961. They were my schoolmates—young but already seasoned activists. I was nineteen years old when they were killed and for the first time I had participated in a protest "against the government."

I had emigrated from Italy less than a year before and I was immediately thrown from a politically sheltered life into a very politically dynamic Venezuelan activism. I had quickly learned some basic facts about Venezuela: extreme poverty existed in spite of huge oil revenues; the pro-U.S. government had no diplomatic relationship with Cuba at the time; the communist party was illegal, and the Venezuelan guerrilla movement was quite active. Almost all other Latin American countries had similar sociopolitical situations. Any news of events happening in the region, such as the invasion of Playa Girón (Bay of Pigs) in Cuba by a group of U.S.-supported Cuban émigrés, spread very quickly among students, and the news felt very close and "personal." The young Cuban Revolution of course was seen as the hope for all of Latin

America and a sense of solidarity with the Cuban people was pervasive among progressive and left-leaning students. I participated in many protests after that first one and more students were killed. I owe my political formation to my years in Venezuela and to those courageous Venezuelan activists.

I have now lived in Canada almost as long as I did in Venezuela and I have participated in Canadian rallies and protests. I have become very familiar with Cuba through many visits and, not least, through my Latin American formation and affinity. My professional life as a researcher in joint Canadian-Cuban collaborative projects on global health is yet another learning experience about what I call "academic solidarity." Over the years I have observed and practiced solidarity in different contexts and have been very active in solidarity organizations concerning Cuba.

Note

1. Enrique Román, the first vice president of ICAP, personal communication, 15 August 2004.

References

Acanda González, J. L. 2006. "Cuban Civil Society: Reinterpreting the Debate." *NACLA Report on the Americas* (January–February): 32–36.

Agee, P. 2003. "Terrorism and Civil Society: The Instruments of U.S. Policy in Cuba." 9 August. http://www.counterpunch.org/agee08092003.html, accessed 8 October 2006.

http://www.antiterroristas.cu, accessed 8 October 2006.

Ariet, M. 1993. *Che: Pensamiento político*. Havana: Editora Política.

Arnsperger, C., and Y. Varoufakis. 1999. "Beyond Altruism, Duty, or Collusion: Introducing Solidarity into Economics." Université Catholique de Louvain, Institut de Recherches Economiques et Sociales (IRES), discussion paper with number 1999030.

August, A. 1999. *Democracy in Cuba and the 1997–98 Elections*. Havana: Editorial José Martí.

Bayertz, K., ed. 1999. "Four Uses of 'Solidarity.'" In *Solidarity*, edited by K. Bayertz, 3–28. Philosophical Studies in Contemporary Culture. Dordrecht: Kluwer Academic Publishers.

Bell Lara, J. 1999. *Cambios mundiales y perspectivas: Revolución cubana*. Havana: Editorial de Ciencias Sociales.

Berthoud, O. 2001. "NGOs: Somewhere between Compassion, Profitability, and Solidarity." *Envío* 233 (no page numbers). Universidad Centroamericana, UCA, Managua, Nicaragua. http://www.edinter.net/docs/index.htm, accessed 7 November 2006.

Blanco, J. A. 1997. *Talking about Revolution*. Melbourne: Ocean Press.

http://www.canadiannetworkoncuba.ca/brigade, accessed 8 October 2006.

138 / Nino Pagliccia

http://www.canadiannetworkoncuba.ca/CNC/constitution.shtml, accessed 8 October 2006.

http://www.cubasolidarity.com/aboutnnoc/index.htm, accessed 8 October 2006.

Durkheim, E. 1965. *Montesquieu and Rousseau: Forerunners of Sociology*. Ann Arbor: University of Michigan Press.

———. 1984. *The Division of Labor in Society*. Basingstoke: Macmillan.

Fillieule, O. 2001. "Dynamics of Commitment in the Sector known as 'Solidarity.'" In *Political Altruism?: Solidarity Movements in International Perspective*, edited by M. Giugni and F. Passy, 51–66. Lanham, Md.: Rowman and Littlefield.

Franklin, J. 1997. *Cuba and the United States: A Chronological History*. Melbourne: Ocean Press.

Giugni, M. 2001. "Conceptual Distinctions for the Study of Political Altruism." In *Political Altruism?: Solidarity Movements in International Perspective*, edited by M. Giugni and F. Passy, 235–44. Lanham, Md.: Rowman and Littlefield.

Gottheil, A. 1996. "Redefining Marketing: Self-interest, Altruism, and Solidarity." Master's thesis, Faculty of Commerce and Administration, Concordia University, Montreal.

Gray, A. 2003. "Deconstructing Civil Society in a Revolutionary Socialist State: The Genesis of NGO Participation in Contemporary Cuba." Ph.D. diss., University of Limerick.

Guevara, E. 1960. "On Revolutionary Medicine." In *Obra revolucionaria* 24. Havana: Imprenta Nacional. http://www.marxists.org/archive/guevara/1960/08/10.htm, accessed 8 October 2006.

———. 2001. "Socialism and Man in Cuba." In *Che Guevara Speaks*, 142–60. New York: Pathfinder Press. http://www.ifconews.org/about/about_us.htm, accessed 8 October 2006.

Kirkpatrick, A. F. 1996. "Role of the USA in Shortage of Food and Medicine in Cuba." *Lancet* 348: 1489–91.

———. 1997. "The U.S. Attack on Cuba's Health." *Canadian Medical Association Journal* 157: 281–84.

Le Bras-Choppard, A. 1992. "Metamorphose d'une Notion: La solidarité chez Pierre Leroux." In *La solidarité: Un sentiment Républicain?*, edited by J. Chevalier et al., 55–69. Paris: Presse Universitaire de France.

Metz, K. H. 1999. "Solidarity and History: Institutions and Social Concepts of Solidarity in Nineteenth-Century Western Europe." In *Solidarity*, edited by K. Bayertz, 191–207. Dordrecht: Kluwer Academic Publishers.

O'Brien, K. A. 1995. "Interfering with Civil Society: CIA and KGB Covert Political Action during the Cold War." *International Journal of Intelligence and Counterintelligence* 8, no. 4: 431–56.

Pagliccia, N. 2004. "Cuban Hardship—Courtesy of America." *National Post* (9 July): A12.

Powell, C. L. 2004. *Commission for Assistance to a Free Cuba: Report to the President*. Washington: Department of State.

Saney, I. 2004. *Cuba: A Revolution in Motion*. Blackpoint, N.S.: Fernwood Publishing.

———. 2006. "African Stalingrad: The Cuban Revolution, Internationalism, and the End of Apartheid." *Latin American Perspectives,* vol. 150, issue 33, no. 5 (September): 81–117.

Weber, M. 2002. *The Protestant Ethic and the Spirit of Capitalism and Other Writings.* Edited, translated, and with an introduction by Peter Baehr and Gordon C. Wells. New York: Penguin Books.

Wildt, A. 1999. "Solidarity: Its History and Contemporary Definition." In *Solidarity,* edited by K. Bayertz, 209–20. Dordrecht: Kluwer Academic Publishers.

6

"A Space within the Revolution"

Religious Cubans and the Secular State

CHRISTINE AYORINDE

Wouldn't it be ironic if history remembers the Cuban revolution because it successfully exported Santería instead of revolution?
Anonymous Cuban writer (cited in Landau 1999)

Ay Mamá Inés, ya los cubanos tenemos la fe.
Cuban nursery rhyme

The international isolation and internal economic difficulties that followed the collapse of Communism in Eastern Europe forced a rethinking of the Cuban revolutionary project. One of the changes was the removal of religious intolerance. It is now acknowledged that the adoption of scientific atheism as the national religion was a mistake of an earlier period.[1] The Communist Party (PCC), formerly the promoter of materialist ideology, opened its membership to religious Cubans.[2] Amid the growing deprivation and ideological disorientation of the Special Period there has been a visible increase in religious practice. In spite of several decades of atheist indoctrination, it emerged that an estimated 85 percent of Cubans were religious to some degree.[3]

For outside commentators the recent proliferation of relatively autonomous spaces in Cuban society reflects a "shrinking of the state" and a "ripening of civil society" (Espinosa 1999; Crahan 2003). In this context, religious associations are seen to perform an important role as they are among the few remaining institutions of the prerevolutionary civil society (Espinosa 1999, 348, 355). For decades they represented an almost unique social forum outside of state-controlled political and social organizations. Today religious associations range from officially recognized NGOs such as the Consejo Cubano de Iglesias (Cuban Council of Churches), the Martin Luther King Jr. Memorial Center, and the Asociación Cultural Yoruba (Yoruba Cultural Association) to informal networks of believers including Pentecostalist *casas de culto* (houses of worship) and Afro-Cuban temple houses.

"A Space within the Revolution" / *141*

However, the debate as to what constitutes civil society, covered in detail elsewhere in this volume, sometimes questions whether religious institutions may be considered part of it. While there may not be consensus on this, it should be noted that Cuban Catholics were instrumental in initiating the debate around civil society on the island. Since then, religion has rarely been absent from the discussions in and outside of Cuba.[4] The U.S. government has also identified religious institutions and individuals as important for promoting its own preferred version of a civil society in Cuba.[5]

The state, for its part, has enlisted the support of religious groups. It has sought to use the moral force of Christianity to counter any reversal of revolutionary values that followed its measures to resolve the economic crisis. It has also attempted to formalize the role already played by many religious organizations in providing social services. Thus, rather than simply enjoying greater freedom of religious expression, religious associations of all types currently enjoy a capacity for civic action not held in Cuba since 1959 (Hearn 2004, 81). As in other areas of Cuban life, external actors and transnational links are exerting influence on the activities of religious groups.

Religion and Revolution

While most analyses of religion in Cuba have tended to focus on the Christian denominations, the religious scene is extremely diverse. During colonial times, alongside the official Roman Catholicism, enslaved Africans perpetuated their religious and cultural traditions. Over time, the encounter with popular Catholicism created the Cuban religions that became known as the *regla de ocha* or *santería*, the *reglas congas* or *palo monte*, and the Abakuá secret society.[6] Associated predominantly with the urban elite and the Spanish ruling class, the Catholic Church lost acceptance among the population when it sided with Spain during the wars of independence. At that time, both Kardecan spiritism and Freemasonry gained ground and a number of Protestant denominations entered from the United States.[7] At various points other religions reached the island with the migration of Chinese, Jews, and Arabs. There is thus both a diversity of religious practices and a popular religious spectrum that is difficult to quantify. People dip in and out of different traditions, managing to combine apparently incompatible beliefs. An individual may go to a Catholic church, then on to a Masonic lodge, visit a *palero* (a practitioner of *palo monte*), attend a *plante Abakuá*, and end up at a Communist Party *nucleo* (branch) meeting. Although the adoption of Marxism-Leninism naturally implied a move away from religion, of all the socialist states Cuba had the least aggressive policy toward religious believers and institutions. At various times, Fidel Castro insisted that the government should not appear to be the enemy of religious

142 / Christine Ayorinde

practitioners, nor give them grounds for claiming persecution. However, although no churches were closed, their social space was reduced when some religious organizations were abolished as part of the dismantling of the previous civil society. The nationalization of education in 1961 took schools away from religious congregations and church access to the media was forbidden (Gómez Treto n.d., 44–45).

Despite its predominantly urban, middle-class membership, which gave Cuban Catholicism limited possibilities for popular mobilization, the church was attacked by revolutionaries as a pressure group (Cárdenas Medina 1995, 8; Crahan 1979, 161). Some churches and individuals did become involved in counterrevolutionary activities. During the religious procession in honor of the Virgen de la Caridad del Cobre in 1961, four thousand people shouted antirevolutionary slogans. Public religious events were no longer permitted from that point onward.

There was less confrontation between the state and the Protestant denominations in the early years of the Revolution. However, their ties to the United States meant that conflict was inevitable, although most denominations rarely adopted a counterrevolutionary stance. After 1963, only those denominations inscribed in the register of the Office of Religious Affairs were authorized to hold regular worship and some *casas de culto* were closed.[8] As with the Catholics, the Protestants' social space was curtailed by the closing of schools.

Although the Cuban Jewish community declined sharply after 1959 through emigration, the government was careful to ensure that it did not experience any particular discrimination. Religious and communal buildings were given maintenance by the state. Kosher butchers were the only enterprises not nationalized eventually, and state rations for Jewish Cubans replaced pork with beef and extra poultry. At times, however, the government's evolving anti-Zionist stance created tension and may have discouraged practice of the Jewish faith, leading many to become more integrated into the wider community (Kaplan 2000; López Levy 2003).

The government's curtailment of its spheres of influence, combined with the exodus of many of the faithful, including religious activists, soon reduced the capacity of organized religion to threaten the Revolution (Crahan 1979, 166).[9] Even before any atheist propaganda had begun, the counterrevolutionary stance of some churches and religious individuals led many Cubans to oppose all organized religion (Arce Martínez 1985, 26; Cárdenas Medina 1995, 8).[10]

If doubts about the political trustworthiness of practicing Christians were raised by the fact that some churches sided with foreign counterrevolutionaries, the Afro-Cuban cults profited from their history as cultures of resistance to slavery, the colonial regime, and the Catholic Church. Also, their practices

"A Space within the Revolution" / *143*

were not connected with institutions, like the churches, which could be threatened by the new structures.[11] The revolutionary leadership thought that the sector most strongly associated with these religions had benefited the most from the social transformations of the Revolution and was thus more likely to support it. For practitioners of Afro-Cuban religions, their beliefs posed no moral dilemma about participation in the revolutionary project. They were perceived as being more readily disposed to accept the new political ideas (Cárdenas Medina 1995).

However, after the political threat represented by the Christian churches was neutralized, religion as an ideology came under greater attack. With the increasing reliance on Soviet models in the 1970s, the theories of scientific atheism gained greater currency in Cuba. The state continued to uphold freedom of conscience and the First Congress of the Cuban Communist Party asserted that religious and atheist Cubans were united in the battle to build a new society. Yet, as the instrument of mass education, the party's aim was to overcome religious beliefs in the population.

Religion was deemed to be a private matter, but it had implications for life's opportunities. With the dismantling of existing intermediary organizations in an attempt to redirect loyalty from churches and Afro-Cuban religions to the party, believers were encouraged to join the mass organizations.[12] People known to have religious beliefs were barred from joining the Communist Party and the Union of Communist Youth (UJC). Membership in either was important for obtaining a university place and certain administrative and managerial posts. Those individuals who were applying to university had to undergo a political-moral interview to determine not only if they, but also any members of their families, were religious.

The Constitution of 1976 permitted freedom of assembly and association for the mass organizations only. Public order dispositions dictated when and where a religious ceremony could be held. Only registered churches were authorized to hold regular worship. Like the Jehovah's Witnesses, and some other Protestant denominations,[13] most Afro-Cuban religious groups were denied official registration and thus were technically illegal.

As all religions became regarded as unrevolutionary, practices that did not require regular attendance at church were easier to hide from official scrutiny. As Fernández Robaina has noted, the *doble moral* has its origin in the historical concealment of the practice of *santería* (1998, 8). People hid their beliefs in order to obtain material benefits such as certain consumer goods and better housing. At the same time, it was recognized that members of Afro-Cuban religions were more likely than Christians to participate in social tasks and belong to the mass organizations (Cárdenas Medina 1995, 10).

While some practitioners of Afro-Cuban religions managed to accommodate the double identity of believer and revolutionary, this position gradually also became more comfortable for both the state and the Christian churches. In 1969, Cuban bishops' pastoral letters condemned the U.S. blockade of Cuba and stated the need to respect the state's atheistic position (Crahan 1979, 175; Departamento de Estudios Socioreligiosos 1990, 50). The Papal Nuncio to Cuba, Monsignor Zacchi, recommended that Christians should integrate into the Revolution through the mass organizations as this would allow them to introduce Catholic ideals into the Revolution (López Oliva cited in Crahan 1979, 177). The Protestant denominations that belonged to the Consejo Ecuménico Cubano (formed in 1977 and later called the Consejo Cubano de Iglesias), once they had been cut off from their U.S. mother churches, were essentially in sympathy with the Revolution. They encouraged their members to participate in revolutionary activities and endeavored to make Christian and Marxist ethics converge in the New Cuban Theology.

The example of the Nicaraguan Catholics and of liberation theology then demonstrated to the Cuban leadership that revolutionary thinking and Catholicism were not incompatible. Fidel Castro's interviews with the Brazilian priest Frei Betto, published as *Fidel y la Religion* (1985), became a bestseller in Cuba. In 1986, the Third Communist Party Congress stated that believers should be encouraged to participate voluntarily and consciously as citizens and patriots in the construction of socialism.

However, the thaw in church-state relations was not immediately accompanied by a rise in religious observance among Christians. By 1988 attendance at Sunday mass was only 2 percent as compared to 24 percent in 1954.[14] In striking contrast, the Revolution appeared to have given a new impulse to the Afro-Cuban religious practices.[15] Ironically, this was a result of social and economic transformations, in particular the ending of discrimination toward the practitioners of these religions. After 1959, attending church was regarding as less acceptable than attending a *toque de santo*. The revaluing of African-derived culture was also a factor. Another was that increased employment opportunities meant that more practitioners could afford religious initiations. As the researchers of the Departamento de Estudios Socioreligiosos of the Academia de Ciencias noted, this vitality of the so-called syncretic cults indicated that they were not leftovers from the past (*rezagos*) but in fact had "considerable weight in the field of the struggle of ideas." They were also no longer solely associated with the marginal sectors of society. Further, the growth in membership indicated that some people felt the need to express religious beliefs without this necessarily implying a distancing from the revolutionary process (Argüelles Mederos and Hodge Limonta 1991, 144, 217–18).

In 1992 the Constitution was modified, making discrimination against believers illegal. The state was defined as secular rather than atheist. In the

"A Space within the Revolution" / 145

early 1990s the Christian denominations saw a rise in baptisms and Sunday attendance.[16] The visit of Pope John Paul II in 1998, which had been under negotiation since the late 1980s, represented an important milestone for both religious and atheistic Cubans.

The turn to religion represented a search for spiritual consolation amid the difficulties of the Special Period and also a search for new values in the face of the collapse of "real socialism." For young people it offered a way of not conforming. In contrast to the predominantly elderly congregations of the 1970s and 1980s, Christianity now enjoys popularity among youth. The role of churches in distributing material goods is also a factor in attracting membership. The festive nature of *santería's* ceremonies, at which there is music, dance, food, and alcohol, makes them an important social element in the absence of other affordable entertainment and limited public transport. Because of rationing, many will only eat meat such as goat or lamb at the banquets following the ritual sacrifice of these animals. Perhaps significantly, Christian denominations also offer music and a celebratory atmosphere and sometimes opportunities for travel abroad.

An Increasingly Civil Role?

Although some of the adjustments to the revolutionary project brought new freedoms and greater tolerance, the "dollarization" of the economy and the reliance on tourism have had negative effects. Support for the Revolution in its current form is diminishing, especially among young people who associate socialism with privation. For the leadership, the *doble moral* represents not a political response to the situation but indicates a decline in moral values (Domínguez García and Ferrer Buch 1996, 49). The government's rapprochement with the Christian churches was motivated by a need to enlist their support in combating social ills. It became less important who was promoting positive values as long as they contributed to the formation of an "hombre integral" (Perera Pintado 1995, 12). The pope and Fidel Castro notably coincided in their criticism of capitalist evils such as individualism and consumerism during the visit of the former to Cuba in 1998.

While, previously, the utilitarianism and amorality of the Afro-Cuban practices were seen to be in conflict with the ideal of the New Man, now there were attempts to find in them positive values that could be used to promote social change (Perera Pintado 1996, 4, 8ff.). Carlos Samper of the Oficina para Atención a los Asuntos Religiosos (Office for Religious Affairs) emphasized that members of the Afro-Cuban religions are fully integrated into the Revolution and that nowadays there are hardly any Abakuá members in jail. He did note, however, that the government is working with religious groups to

146 / Christine Ayorinde

dissuade them from using religion to shelter those who commit crimes. The Office for Religious Affairs is also involving Afro-Cuban religious leaders in the government's campaign against drugs.[17] In neighborhoods where Catholic priests are a rarity, *babalawos*,[18] as figures of some standing within their communities, can play an important role in inculcating moral values. Nevertheless, it is important to state that much of the appeal of *santería* lies in its tolerance of the full range of human behavior. Its absence of moral indignation contrasts not only with Christianity but also with revolutionary criticism and self-criticism.

Those who practice the Afro-Cuban religions are also hopeful of material as well as spiritual compensation for their devotion.[19] As the *babalawo* Ricardo Guerra stated, using a phrase also favored by the Communist Party, these religions offer "*nivel de solución*" (means of finding a solution).[20] The fact that *los orichas resuelven* (the *orichas* provide results) explains why *santería* is gaining members in Cuba of the post-1990s.

The growing decentralization has enabled religious groups to extend their role in meeting social needs. This is perhaps ironic, given that religion was previously regarded as one of the ideological influences likely to hinder the revolutionary social development program.[21] Now religious groups are helping to shore up the Revolution. The organization Cáritas, which distributes humanitarian aid, is run by lay Catholics and headquartered in Rome. It was officially established in Cuba in 1991. The Italian Catholic Church contributes to social and humane projects in rural areas. Although they no longer run schools, religious orders such as St. John of God provide healthcare for the elderly and psychiatric patients, while the La Salle Brothers now oversee the education of priests and carry out pastoral work with youth.

The Protestant churches play a similar social role via the Cuban Council of Churches. The Martin Luther King Jr. Memorial Center, an NGO with close ties to the government, runs projects that include the rehabilitation of housing and the development of alternative energy sources. The renowned Pastors for Peace, a ministry of the Inter-Religious Foundation for Community Organization based in New York, collaborates with the Martin Luther King Center on projects including help with nutrition and work in hospitals, old people's homes, and nursery schools. Through their charitable work, the Christian denominations are significant providers of humanitarian aid and not only to churchgoers. This has also enabled them to increase their social space as lay people, priests, and nuns gain access to areas where they can wield influence within the community.

Like their Christian counterparts, synagogues also work with outside organizations to provide social welfare for Jewish Cubans. These include the American Joint Distribution Committee (JDC), which began operations in

Cuba in 1992, the Canadian Jewish Congress, and B'nai Brith. In addition to providing religious items and humanitarian supplies, foreign organizations and individuals donate funds for restoring synagogues, as does the Cuban government. The outside support has also helped to resuscitate community organizations, including those for youth, women, and senior citizens (Kaplan 2000).

Adrian Hearn (2004) describes the collaboration between local government authorities and community groups rooted in Afro-Cuban religions in Atarés and Old Havana. The projects attempt to address social problems such as drug use, prostitution, and housing decay, recognizing that Afro-Cuban religious groups and leaders are influential within their communities and already play a role in providing welfare.

Hearn describes how the projects were intended to facilitate social objectives by working through informal networks of community support and religious allegiance. However, he notes that folkloric performances came to dominate the activities, leaving the social objectives neglected in favor of quick returns from the tourist market (Hearn 2004).

The involvement of Afro-Cuban religious communities in official projects indicates their growing capacity for civic action. Such projects also enable the Afro-Cuban groups to acquire legitimacy. In some cases they attracted the interest of foreign NGOs, which began to donate money. Hearn concludes that both state and civil society actors contributed to the successes of the projects, but that both also shared responsibility for initially allowing commercial activities to fall out of balance with community interests (Hearn 2004, 85).

The role played by external actors in Afro-Cuban religious communities is a growing phenomenon. While Christian churches in Cuba historically received material and moral support from mother churches elsewhere, the Afro-Cuban practices were believed to have fewer international affiliations. However, with the exodus of a large number of Cubans after 1959, *santería* spread to the United States and other parts of Latin America. The lifting of restrictions in the 1990s on Cubans living in the United States who wished to travel to the island allows members of religious families that originated in Cuba to visit the island for initiations and ceremonies. In the same period, the expansion of tourism and the focus on Afro-Cuban cultural expressions as part of the "tourist package" have increased the numbers of foreigners who have become exposed to the religions.

The practice of *santería* in particular is a lucrative source of income and foreign exchange. Cuba is promoted as the Mecca of *orisha* worship. Foreign practitioners go there in search of religious orthodoxy, believing the practice to be purer and better preserved than elsewhere in the diaspora. Antonio Castañeda, the president of the Asociación Cultural Yoruba (ACY), an NGO

148 / Christine Ayorinde

that promotes Yoruba religion and culture, spent several minutes of our interview complaining that fees for religious initiations have risen steeply because those who sell animals and ritual items are pricing them for clients from outside the country.[22] This has led to commercialization and attempts by sectors, including the government, to gain a share of the profits.[23] Practitioners speak disparagingly of *ocha turs* and *diplobabalawos* (by analogy with the hard currency shops for foreign diplomats called *diplotiendas*).

As with other sectors of Cuban society, Afro-Cuban religious and cultural centers have come increasingly to rely on foreign money. The ACY raised some funds for the repair of its building from foreign supporters. The international conferences on Yoruba culture and religion, hosted by the ACY, also provide a source of income. The Eighth World *Orisha* Conference was held in July 2003 at the luxurious International Convention Center in Havana and was sponsored by the Cuban government.[24] Seminars on religious themes were presided over by Cuban practitioners and scholars but also by the same functionaries of the Communist Party who had once predicted the disappearance of the religion.

The state sees the fact that even a limited number of Afro-Cuban religious institutions now have official recognition as an indication of the degree to which the religions have gained in prestige. The ACY, originally founded by a group of *babalawos*, became a registered association in 1991. Its building on the Paseo de Martí (known as the Prado) in Old Havana was renovated at the cost of $2 million and was partly funded by the Ministerio de Cultura and soft loans facilitated by the government. It houses a cultural center, conference rooms, a library, a shop selling religious items, and a museum exhibiting life-size statues of the Yoruban deities. Furthermore, the official body representing members of the Abakuá society, the Asociación Abakuá de Cuba (Abakuá Association of Cuba), was officially registered in 2003.

Becoming a registered association brings with it certain benefits, including the opportunity to buy goods at a lower price than in normal state shops, the right to purchase a vehicle, and the right to publish a magazine. Yet many Cuban religious associations are not permitted to register with the Ministry of Justice. Carlos Samper explained that the ACY and the Abakuá Association of Cuba are intended to be representative umbrella organizations for their respective practices. Branches of the ACY will be created in other provinces where there is a nucleus of practitioners with the necessary level of organization.[25] According to Samper, *palo monte* is not likely to follow this route as it is the least institutionalized of all the practices. Yet it seems unrealistic to claim that the ACY can represent all *santeros* and *babalawos*. Some are put off from joining because they believe the ACY is too "political" and thus not sufficiently

"A Space within the Revolution" / 149

"religious," given that it is one of the few Afro-Cuban religious associations listed in the Registro de Asociaciones (Register of Associations).

Nevertheless, while in earlier historical periods, the absence of a unified hierarchical structure enabled practitioners of Afro-Cuban religions to evade unwelcome official scrutiny, today some believe their lack of institutions places them at a relative disadvantage. Until recently the Christian denominations and the Jewish community had a more public dialogue with the state as there were no obvious representatives to speak on behalf of Afro-Cuban religious groups. This is changing. On 25 December 2000, a *mesa redonda informativa* (informative round table) on the participation of religious Cubans in the social life of the country was broadcast on television.[26] Participants included representatives of the Protestant Council of Churches and the Coordinating Committee of the Jewish Faith, as well as also Antonio Castañeda of the ACY and Ángel Freire Fernández of the Supreme National Council of Abakuá.[27]

Uncivil Responses

Even though it has granted greater space to religious groups of all denominations, there is no doubt that the government is conscious that these groups could spread beyond the confines of their allocated space. Like other NGOs, religious associations play an important role in helping ordinary Cubans survive the pressures of the Special Period, which is why the state has enlisted their cooperation. Yet the extent of their intervention in social relief has already raised doubts as to whether they are cooperating with the state or usurping its role. The government has responded by imposing a number of restrictions on the activities of registered religious institutions.[28]

The growing disaffection due to the influence of capitalism and increasing inequality in Cuban society has meant that membership in mass organizations has fallen. Meanwhile, the number of religious Cubans has grown. Formal and informal religious networks help to assuage personal and societal problems by offering material as well as spiritual sustenance. Such work can help to reduce overt opposition to the regime. Yet in a context where religious activity is the most rapidly expanding and least regulated social activity, and the social welfare activities of religious associations are strengthening transnational ties, there is state concern that religious groups could, like other NGOs (especially those with outside links), become launching pads for political activism (Crahan 2003).

Carlos Samper argues that Cuba is a country at war and that the United States seeks to use religious institutions against the Revolution.[29] The role of the Office for Religious Affairs is to ensure that religious institutions remain just that, rather than becoming counterrevolutionary political parties.[30] Mindful of earlier periods of the Revolution when the suspicion of counterrevolutionary activity was used to clamp down on religious activities, many religious leaders hasten to express pro-revolutionary sentiments or dissociate themselves from politics. Cardinal Ortega stated in a homily in 1995 that the church has a religious mission, not a social or political one. Yet the role of the Catholic Church in particular clearly goes beyond spiritual matters. Catholic publications comment on controversial issues, including *balseros* (boat refugees), and maintain dialogue with the exile community, often expressing views at odds with those of the state.[31] Lay Catholics, such as Dagoberto Valdés, have been prominent in the debate around the need to reconstruct a civil society that is more independent of the state.[32] The Proyecto Varela, led by the Catholic Oswaldo Payá of the dissident Movimiento Cristiano de Liberación, attempted to force a referendum on reforms by presenting a petition of over ten thousand signatures at the National Assembly in 2002. Its aim was to get people to participate in the process of change needed in society, but it also called for religious rights such as the freedom to build churches and offer religious education. The movement has little evident support, however.

None of the practitioners of Afro-Cuban religions with whom I spoke would admit to having an overtly political agenda. Lucas Aberasturis, the secretary of the ACY, thought that the self-contained nature of each *casa templo* (temple house) would impede attempts (by outsiders) to manipulate practitioners politically. In fact, attempts at creating a central body to represent the interests of the practitioners of *santería* have largely failed because the various groups cannot reach agreement on religious issues.

Previously it was claimed that the so-called syncretic religions "do not necessarily influence political conduct as this would require a theoretical systematization which it had been established does not exist" (Argüelles Mederos and Hodge Limonta 1991, 94). However, the DESR, which has monitored the annual pilgrimage to the shrine of San Lázaro since 1983, noted that the event acquired increasingly sociopolitical connotations in the 1990s.[33] The saint was petitioned not just for health issues but for his intervention to improve the situation in the country (Perera Pintado 1995, 10).

Also often mentioned in this context is the Letra del Año (Year's Letter), the predictions produced by Ifá divination at the beginning of each year. These have been issued since 1988 and copies are distributed locally and abroad. They are taken seriously by the foreign media, including the *Miami Herald*, which view the Letra as a barometer for the Cuban social and political situation. Two competing Letras are issued. One is issued by the ACY, and some claim that the government ensures that this Letra is either favorable to the government or at least neutral. The other Letra is divined by Ifá priests belonging to the

"A Space within the Revolution" / 151

other main religious families who gather in a *casa templo* on the Avenida Diez de Octubre.

It has been suggested that religious groups with looser organizational structures are more likely to cooperate with the state because they run a greater risk of being closed down (D. J. Fernández 2003).[34] This would apply to Afro-Cuban religious groups and also Protestant, mainly Pentecostal, *casas de culto.* But even those that do not directly challenge the authorities can, as before, subvert official policies by functioning as an arena for illicit practices. One reason for the state's collaboration with Afro-Cuban community organizations was to preempt unregistered economic activity (Hearn 2004, 79).

Nevertheless, for religions with a history of resistance, and which played an important role in bolstering black self-esteem, there is clearly the potential for a gathering movement of opposition. Although the exodus of many white Cubans after 1959 means that the island has become more obviously black and mulatto, racism has intensified in the 1990s. The Special Period has undermined social equality and Afro-Cubans are at a particular disadvantage in the hard-currency economy, as they are less likely to receive remittances from relatives abroad and also tend to be excluded from the jobs in tourism.

One effect of increasing contact with the outside world is the exposure to a more radical African diasporic discourse. *Santería* represents one strand of a transnational Yoruban religious complex and practitioners are now able to explore these links. In Cuba this has led to calls by some for a re-Africanization of *santería*. This means replacing local practices with "African" ritual forms and eliminating syncretic (Roman Catholic) elements. This trend is decried by cultural nationalists who claim *santería* as an autonomous cultural form (Menéndez Vázquez 1995; Guanche Pérez 1996). *Santería* is increasingly hailed by white and black Cubans, of all social backgrounds, as an important representation of national identity and of raceless *cubanía*. Its inclusiveness is an important selling point both inside and outside Cuba and therefore it is important that it be seen to remain apart from racial politics.

However, in Brazil, where the Afro-Brazilian religions have a longer history of appropriation by the entire nation, the tide has turned back and traditional expressions of black culture such as *candomblé*, are being used in the affirmation of a black identity (Hanchard 1999). In Cuba too, within a context of growing disaffection, there is a potential for religious groups to once again become spaces for asserting a separate Afro-Cuban identity.

The removal of intolerance has also created a space for religious practices not previously found in Cuba. Rastafarianism and the Nation of Islam have established themselves on the island; both are race-based religious movements. While Samper dismissed the Nation of Islam as a minority movement, he noted that Rastafarianism was an example of the transposition of forms of behavior developed in a society where people experience marginalization and discrimination. In Cuba, where the official line is that blacks are not discriminated against, he thinks that such rebellion is not justified. This echoes the perception by the leadership and many white Cubans that their black compatriots should be particularly grateful for the benefits bestowed on them by the Revolution. As at earlier periods in Cuba's history, attempts by Afro-Cubans to organize along racial lines are condemned as unpatriotic and face severe restriction.

Religious organizations of all denominations play an important role in helping ordinary Cubans survive the pressures of the Special Period. In many cases they do this in cooperation with the state and are broadly in agreement with revolutionary objectives. Where this is not the case, even though religious associations probably represent the strongest element of civil society, as Crahan (2003) notes, the multiplicity of beliefs has created a competitive religious environment. Cuba differs from Poland, where 90 percent of the population is Catholic and the Catholic Church expressed the wishes of the popular majority and was linked with the struggle for independence. The Cuban Catholic Church still relies heavily on foreign clergy and Afro-Cubans are underrepresented among the laity.[35] While some Protestant denominations have expressed more wholehearted support for the Revolution since the 1960s, one Cuban pastor expressed concern that the charismatic Pentecostal movement, which stems from North America, is gaining ground.

Cubanía is the terrain on which people and government meet. It is acknowledged that Afro-Cubans played a crucial role in the consolidation of the Revolution, which drew on the cooperative traditions of prerevolutionary Cuba that were rooted in the Afro-Cuban religions (Kapcia 2000; Cárdenas Medina 1995). Practitioners of Afro-Cuban religions have both survived on the margins of the revolutionary project and been fully incorporated into it. Today, for the first time, the socialist state is willing to celebrate their religious expressions as an important facet of a collective Cuban identity.

One effect of this has been to revive antagonism between Christian denominations and *santeros*. During his visit, Pope John Paul II insisted on at least three occasions that the true Cuban tradition is Christian. At the end of his visit, he cautioned against putting the Roman Catholic Church on par with *santería* and other Afro-Cuban religions.[36]

The Christian churches largely refuse to engage with the issue of religious syncretism. Most churches do not welcome *santería* worshippers and are doing little to encourage the participation of Afro-Cubans generally. With a few exceptions, statements made by clergy over the years seemed to be aimed at rousing animosity rather than promoting ecumenism. Cardinal Ortega has stated that *santería* is not a religion. Defending his refusal to grant Afro-Cu-

"A Space within the Revolution" / 153

ban religious representatives an audience with the pope in 1998, Ortega complained about the government's attempts to promote Afro-Cuban rites, both as a political alternative to Catholicism and as a tourist attraction (Tamayo 1998).[37]

Conclusion

Since the late 1980s, there has been greater tolerance of all religions, even those, like the Jehovah's Witnesses, that experienced the greatest repression during an earlier period of the Revolution.[38] The easing of restrictions on religious practice was part of an attempt to widen assent for an increasingly beleaguered regime. I questioned Carlos Samper about the Communist Party's apparent elasticity with respect to ideology and he explained that the Communist Party is a political party, not a philosophical one.[39] Internal and external conditions compelled the party to acknowledge different perspectives and find a way to make them work together. It has moved on from enforcing unanimity and homogeneity to seek to create a more pluralistic and participatory civil society, without abandoning the project of building socialism.

The churches and other religious groups have more operational space than before. The role of the Christian churches, curtailed in the 1960s, has been extended. Although some of the spaces occupied by Afro-Cuban practices remained untouched and even expanded after 1959, today these religious expressions enjoy greater visibility and status, both nationally and internationally.

Even though they enjoy greater freedoms, for some the pendulum has not swung sufficiently far. Some years after the euphoria of the pope's visit, Cardinal Ortega stated in 2003 that he thought there had been no substantial change in relations with the Cuban government. He complained that the Catholic Church is not recognized as a public entity and that its sociopolitical space is limited and often ignored.[40] According to him, Cubans are allowed freedom of religious belief but no corresponding freedom of religious expression. There is also frustration at the unmet expectations of further concessions, such as regular access to the media and allowing the church to operate schools. Ortega subsequently announced that the prospects for real religious freedom were foundering and that despair was setting in. Protestant denominations have been less critical of the government and relatively content to seek space for carrying out social projects. While the presence of three Protestant ministers in the National Assembly is a significant development, they have limited possibilities for influence.

For all NGOs in Cuba, even those that are registered, the margins of action are unclear. All remain subject to state control at the practical level. The

154 / Christine Ayorinde

state continues to block the construction of new churches, impose limits on the numbers of foreign priests, and refuses to recognize most new Christian denominations as well as existing Afro-Cuban groups. As at earlier periods, restrictions are often presented as part of general limitations on the freedom of expression, association, and assembly rather than as specifically targeting religious associations.

Religious associations are the most autonomous sector of society and also have the potential to act as pressure groups. Furthermore, as at earlier times in history, they provide a spiritual refuge or a site of internal exile as well as a means of resolving material problems. The state's response to religious organizations, as to secular ones, seeks to widen participation in the socialist civil society while at the same time retaining control over an increasingly independent civil society.

Notes

1. Carlos Samper, Oficina para la Atención a los Asuntos Religiosos, interview, 24 January 2003. At the Fourth Party Congress, Fidel Castro declared that "we are a Party not a religion and at a certain moment we converted the Party and atheism into a religion" (Partido Comunista 1992, 103).

2. In fact, the admittance of religious believers to the PCC only applied to the fewer than 5 percent of the population who were *militantes* (members).

3. The Departamento de Estudios Socioreligiosos, which was set up by the Communist Party in 1982 to study religion in society, concluded that around 15 percent of Cubans are "defined believers." The rest (70 percent) are "vacillating" or "nondefined believers," that is, they fall outside what the researchers defined as a formal religious system (Díaz Cerveto, Pérez Cruz, and Rodríguez Delgado 1994); the remaining 15 percent are atheist.

4. See Gunn 1995, Tobin 2004, and Crahan 2003. Cuban commentators on the religious revival also regard religious institutions as a part of civil society; see Del Rey Roa and Castañeda Mache 2002, Ramírez Calzadilla 2003.

5. Tobin notes that, historically, the United States has considered religion to be a significant contributor to a more civil society. In pressing for changes in Cuba, U.S. policymakers promote the idea of religion as playing a similar role there (Tobin 2004, 78).

6. The *regla de ocha* is the Cuban version of the West African Yoruba religion in which *orishas* or gods are the object of worship. *Palo monte* originates from a wide area of west central Africa, and Abakuá came from the eastern region of Nigeria.

7. Initially identified with the cause of Cuban independence, Protestantism later became linked to the growing U.S. political and economic domination of the island as Protestant missionaries attempted to inculcate American values.

8. This was the year when the Ley de Asociaciones (Law of Associations) was implemented, a legacy of Spanish colonial laws by which Protestant denominations were con-

"A Space within the Revolution" / 155

sidered associations and were required to register, pay taxes, and give an annual account of membership (D. Fernández 1965).

9. There was a dramatic reduction in clergy (70 percent of Catholic priests, 90 percent of nuns). The remaining laity was composed primarily of women, the elderly, and children. There was a fall in Protestant congregations, often because members abandoned the church. Some denominations lost more pastors than others, particularly those that had been more dependent on U.S. missionaries. By 1973, around 90 percent of the fifteen thousand members of the Jewish population had left Cuba, including religious leaders.

10. One example cited is the Bay of Pigs invasion in 1961. The American invasion force included three priests and because of this churches in the area were subjected to spontaneous demonstrations by the local people (Felipe Carneado cited in Cárdenas Medina 1995, 9).

11. Nevertheless, the revolutionary leadership continued the pattern of previous eras by linking membership of the Afro-Cuban religions with criminality and social pathology. The First Party Congress referred to the specific need to curb antisocial attitudes and behavior associated with the "syncretic cults" (Partido Comunista de Cuba 1976, 304, 316).

12. The Comités de Defensa de la Revolución and the Milicias de Tropas Territoriales y Defensa Civil had a high percentage of religious members: 93 percent and 57 percent respectively. By the 1980s, 80 percent of Cubans belonged to the CDRs and over 60 percent of women to the FMC (Del Águila 1994, 175–76).

13. These sects displayed the most extreme examples of noncompliance with the revolutionary process: some refused medical treatment and military service; the Seventh Day Adventists would not work or let their children attend school on Saturdays; the Jehovah's Witnesses were believed to be backed by the CIA (see *La verdad sobre la secta Testigos de Jehová* 1977).

14. The number of Protestants was estimated at sixty thousand in 1959–60 and fifty thousand in the 1980s.

15. The Matanzas Registry of Associations showed that initiations into *santería* in Matanzas quadrupled between 1959 and 1970 (cited in Argüelles Mederos and Hodge Limonta 1991, 157).

16. An estimated 40–45 percent of the population is baptized, though the number of practicing Catholics is estimated at around 250,000. The figures also reflect the fact that most *santeros* are baptized as this is a requirement for initiation. Also, until recently, the Catholic churches tended to be packed on the annual festivals of the popular religious saints San Lázaro and Santa Bárbara rather than at Christian feasts such as Christmas and Easter. The Protestant denominations grew rapidly from the 1980s onward to reach 250,000. There are approximately 2,000 Jewish Cubans (Washington Office on Latin America 2004).

17. Carlos Samper, interview, Havana, 24 January 2003.

18. *Babalawos* are priests of the Ifá divination cult. Ifá, also known as Orúnmila, is the Yoruban deity of wisdom.

19. Guanche has defined *santería* as "el culto del más acá" (the cult of the here and now). Guanche, interview, 30 January 2003.

156 / Christine Ayorinde

20. Ricardo Guerra, personal communication, January 1997.

21. Jorge Ramírez Calzadilla, interview, Havana, 3 February 1997.

22. Antonio Castañeda, interview, Havana, 28 January 2003.

23. Fernández Robaina, interview, 19 January 2003. See also "In Cuba, Black Culture Becomes Tourism Lure," *Miami Herald*, 16 January 1998. http://www.herald.com/americas/carib/cuba/digdocs/051761.htm, accessed 17 January 1998.

24. An indication of the changing response of the state to Afro-Cuban practices is the fact that prospective foreign delegates for the International Workshop on Yoruba Culture in 1992 were refused visas.

25. Carlos Samper, interview, Havana, 24 January 2003.

26. This was reported in *Granma*. http://www.granma.cubaweb.cu/temas7/artículo205.html.

27. Freire used the media opportunity to emphasize the participation of Abakuá members in the defense of the Revolution and his association's contribution to the Cuadernos Martianos. Castañeda thanked the Revolution for exporting *santería* to the world. "La participación de los religiosos cubanos en la vida social del país," *Tabloide especial* 30: 4, 6.

28. At a meeting that was held between Caridad Diego, the director of the Oficina para la Atención a los Asuntos Religiosos, and over one hundred religious leaders in May 1997, Diego referred to the unauthorized distribution of donations from abroad and the abuse of travel permits obtained through her office. Subsequently, the Ministerio de Comercio Interior issued Resolution 144–97. This prevented registered religious institutions from purchasing fax machines, photocopiers, and other electronic items (Tamayo 1997).

29. In June 2004, the U.S. President's Commission for Assistance to a Free Cuba (CAFC) issued a report that resulted in increased funding for "democratic opposition and civil society" in Cuba. This gave religion a primary role. See Commission for Assistance to a Free Cuba 2004.

30. Carlos Samper, interview, Havana, 24 January 2003.

31. Catholic publications include *Palabra Nueva* from the Diocese of Havana, *Vitral* from the Centro de Formación Cívica y Religiosa of the Diocese of Pinar del Río, edited by Dagoberto Valdés, and *Vida Cristiana*, which is distributed at mass, has a national reach, and has been in existence since the 1960s. Protestant titles include *Caminos*, produced by the Martin Luther King Jr. Center, *La Voz Bautista* from the Baptists, and the *Heraldo Cristiano* from the Presbyterians. Most of the writers are not journalism graduates as this was a career denied for a long time to those who professed religious beliefs.

32. Dagoberto Valdés, the agronomist and editor of the independent Catholic journal *Vitral*, together with Luis Enrique Estrella Márquez, wrote a report entitled "To Rebuild Civil Society," which was presented at the Second Catholic Social Week in 1994. This report stated that only the church and a few symbolic associations filled the vacuum of civil society.

33. San Lázaro is a saint of the popular Catholic calendar who became linked with the Yoruba *orisha* Sòpònnón, who, in Africa, both spreads and cures smallpox. In Cuba, where he is known as Babalú Ayé, he is supplicated for health matters. Numbers of pilgrims rose steadily from almost thirty-five thousand in 1983 to a peak of ninety-four

"A Space within the Revolution" / 157

thousand in 1995. The number of whites attending also increased. The attendance figures are cited in Zamora 2000, 245–46.

34. Some U.S. commentators have suggested that the regime has attempted to co-opt *santeros* since the 1980s and the fact that many of their activities were illegal may have induced some to comply (Oppenheimer 1993, 352).

35. In his interviews with Frei Betto, Fidel Castro noted there had been no Afro-Cuban pupils at the Catholic schools he attended (Betto 1987). Enrique López Oliva, who was formerly a professor of the history of religion at Havana University, told me that the first black priest was ordained in Cuba in 1941 (interview, January 1997). In the late 1990s, there were still only six black and seven mulatto Catholic priests out of a total of over three hundred (López Oliva and Faguaga 2001).

36. Associated Press, 26 January 1998. http://www.cubanet.org/Cnews/y98/jan98/26e91.htm 16, accessed 16 September 1999.

37. In the same article, one priest in Havana was quoted as saying that "this government has promoted *santería* as a virtual official religion, giving oxygen to friendly *babalawos* to earn tourist dollars while trying to asphyxiate the church."

38. "Se abre espacio para los Testigos de Jehová," *El Nuevo Herald*, 26 December 1998, 6A.

39. Carlos Samper, interview, Havana, 24 January 2003.

40. "Cuban Cardinal Says Church's Situation Has Not Improved," CWNews.com, 13 January 2003; "Hopes Dim for Religious Freedom in Cuba," CWNews.com, 12 January 2003. http://www.cwnews.com/news/storytools.cfm, accessed 13 January 2003.

References

Arce Martínez, S. 1985. *The Church and Socialism: Reflections from a Cuban Context.* New York: Circus.

Argüelles Mederos, A., and Ileana Hodge Limonta. 1991. *Los llamados cultos sincréticos y el espiritismo: Estudio monográfico sobre su significación social en la sociedad cubana contemporánea.* Havana: Editorial Academia.

Ayorinde, C. 2004. *Afro-Cuban Religiosity, Revolution, and National Identity.* Gainesville: University Press of Florida.

Betto, Frei. 1987. *Fidel y la Religión: Conversaciones con Frei Betto.* Havana: Oficina de Publicaciones del Consejo del Estado.

Cárdenas Medina, R. 1995. "Religión, producción de sentido y Revolución." *Temas* 4: 6–12.

Commission for Assistance to a Free Cuba. 2004. *Hastening Cuba's Transition: Report to the President* (6 May): 12, 17–20. http://www.state.gov/p/wha/rt/cuba/commission/2004.

Crahan, M. E. 1979. "Salvation through Christ or Marx: Religion in Revolutionary Cuba." *Journal of Interamerican Studies and World Affairs* 21, no. 1: 156–84.

———. 2003. *Religion, Culture, and Society: The Case of Cuba.* Conference report. Woodrow Wilson Center Reports on the Americas 9, Washington, D.C.

Del Águila, J. M. 1994. *Cuba: Dilemmas of a Revolution.* Boulder, Colo.: Westview.

Del Rey Roa, A., and Y. Castañeda Mache. 2002. "El reavivamiento religioso en Cuba." *Temas* 31: 93–100.

158 / Christine Ayorinde

Departamento de Estudios Socioreligiosos (DESR). 1990. *La religión en la cultura*. Havana: Editorial Academia.

Díaz Cerveto, A. M., O. Pérez Cruz, and M. Rodríguez Delgado. 1994. "Religious Beliefs in Today's Cuban Society." *Social Compass* 41, no. 2: 225–40.

Domínguez García, M., and M. E. Ferrer Buch. 1996. *Jóvenes cubanos: Expectativas en los '90*. Havana: Editorial de Ciencias Sociales.

Espinosa, J. C. 1999. "Civil Society in Cuba: The Logic of Emergence in Comparative Perspective." In *Cuba in Transition*, edited by Jorge Pérez-López and José F. Alonso, 346–67. Washington, D.C.: ASCE.

Fernández, D. 1965. *Persecución religiosa en Cuba comunista*. n.p.

Fernández, D. J. 2003. "The Greatest Challenge: Civic Values in Post-transition Cuba." Cuba Transition Project Paper. University of Miami: Institute for Cuban and Cuban-American Studies.

Fernández Robaina, T. 1998. "La cultura y la historia afrocubana valorada por Juan René Betancourt, Gustavo Urrutia y Fernando Ortiz, entre otros." Paper presented at Antropología 98, Havana, 7–10 April.

Gómez Treto, R. N.d. *La Iglesia Católica durante la construcción del socialismo en Cuba*. 3rd ed. Havana: CEHILA.

Guanche Pérez, J. 1996. "Santería cubana e identidad cultural." *Revolución y Cultura*: 43–46.

Gunn, G. 1995. *Cuba's NGOs: Government Puppets or Seeds of Civil Society?* 7 (February). Washington, D.C.: The Caribbean Project, Center for Latin American Studies, Georgetown University.

Hanchard, M. G. 1999. "Black Cinderella: Race and the Public Sphere in Brazil." In *Racial Politics in Contemporary Brazil*, edited by Michael George Hanchard, 59–81. Durham, N.C.: Duke University Press.

Hearn, A. 2004. "Afro-Cuban Religions and Social Welfare: Consequences of Commercial Development in Havana." *Human Organization* 63, no. 1: 78–87.

Kapcia, A. 2000. *Cuba: Island of Dreams*. Oxford: Berg.

Kaplan, D. E. 2000. "A Jewish Renaissance in Castro's Cuba." *Judaism* (spring). http://www.findarticles.com/p/articles/mi_m0411/is_2_49/ai_64332275, accessed 13 September 2006.

Landau, S. 1999. "The Revolution Turns Forty." *Progressive* (March): 24–30. http://www.findarticles.com/p/articles/mi_m1295/is_4_63/ai_54246111, accessed_3 November 2003.

La verdad sobre la secta Testigos de Jehová. 1977. Havana: Editora Cultura Popular.

López Levy, A. 2003. "The Jewish Community in Cuba in the 1990s." In *Religion, Culture, and Society: The Case of Cuba, edited by* Margaret E. Crahan, 79–92. Conference report. Washington, D.C.: Woodrow Wilson Center Reports on the Americas.

López Oliva, E., and M. E. Faguaga. 2001. *Interreligious Dialogue in Cuba*. Georgetown University Cuba Briefing Paper Series 26. Washington, D.C.: Georgetown University.

Menéndez Vázquez, L. 1995. "Un cake para Obatalá?" *Temas* 4: 38–51.

Oppenheimer, A. 1993. *Castro's Final Hour*. New York: Simon and Schuster.

"A Space within the Revolution" / *159*

Partido Comunista de Cuba, Departamento de Orientación Revolucionaria. 1992. *IV Congreso del partido comunista de Cuba: Discursos y documentos*. Havana: Editora Política.

Pedraza, S. 2001. "Democratization and Migration: Cuba's Exodus and the Development of Civil Society—Hindrance or Help?" Paper delivered at the Social Science History Association, Chicago, 15–18 November; updated July 2002. http://www.pdc-cuba. org/DEMO_MIGRA.htm, accessed 11 January 2004.

Perera Pintado, A. C. 1995. "Cuba: Valores religiosos y cambio social." Mimeograph. Havana: DESR.

———. 1996. *"La regla ocha: Sus valores religiosos en la sociedad cubana contemporánea*. Mimeograph. Havana: DESR.

Pérez, L. A. 1999. *On Becoming Cuban: Identity, Nationality, and Culture*. Chapel Hill: University of North Carolina Press.

Ramírez Calzadilla, J. 2003. "Cultura y reavivamiento religioso en Cuba." *Temas* 35: 31–43.

Ramos, M. A. 2002. *Religion and Religiosity in Cuba: Past, Present, and Future*. Cuba Occasional Paper Series 2. Washington, D.C.: Trinity College.

Tamayo, J. 1997. "Cuba impone restricciones a las iglesias." *El Nuevo Herald,* 18 October, 1A.

———. 1998. "Afro-Cubans Say Catholics Have Slighted Their Religions." *Miami Herald* 12 January, 1A.

Tobin, K. 2004. "Whose Civil Society?: The Politicization of Religion in Transitional Cuba." *Journal for the Study of Religions and Ideologies* 8 (summer): 76–89.

Valdés Hernández, D. 2002. "Cuba: Hacia una nueva república desde la sociedad civil." *Vitral* 49. http://www2.glauco.it/vitral/vitral48/cent2.htm, accessed 21 December 2003.

Valdés Hernández, D., and L. E. Estrella Márquez. 1994. "Reconstruir la sociedad civil: Un proyecto para Cuba." II Semana Social Católica, Havana, 17–20 November 1994.

Washington Office on Latin America. "Religious Freedom in Cuba." http://www.wola. org/cuba/religious_freedom.htm, accessed 25 January 2004.

Zamora, L. 2000. *El culto de San Lázaro en Cuba*. Havana: Fundación Fernando Ortiz.

7

The Genesis of NGO Participation in Contemporary Cuba

Perceptions from the Field, as Reported by Local and Foreign NGO Representatives

ALEXANDER I. GRAY

There is no clear line in Cuba between civil society and the state. However, with the economic strife resulting from the disintegration of the Soviet bloc and the simultaneous tightening of the U.S. economic embargo, international donor agencies and nongovernmental organizations (NGOs) entered Cuba, altering the makeup of civil society. These interventions have brought about a social context where the revolutionary socialist view of civil society comes into close contact with a more Western conception. Cuban civil society is intriguing because it offers an alternative approach to Western perceptions of social development. Inspired by revolutionary socialist principles, the state centrally manages the scarce resources available for social projects and through this practice becomes intimately involved in shaping civil society.

Since Gillian Gunn's (1995) informative study of NGOs on the island, little else of empirical substance has been published. The aim of this chapter is to provide information on, and thus illuminate, Cuba's emerging NGO community. While it is recognized that mass organizations are the traditional, and perhaps the most appropriate, actors in Cuban civil society, this study uses NGOs as a mechanism to assess the new context of social development initiatives. This is largely achieved by assessing the experience-based opinions of individuals currently working within Cuban civil society, principally in an effort to create knowledge about the relationship between NGOs and the socialist revolutionary state and the changing dynamic of Cuban civil society. The study is informed by primary data collected during fieldwork between March 2001 and April 2004. This fieldwork consisted of formal interviews with representatives from Cuban and foreign NGOs, solidarity organizations, independent study centers, academic researchers, international donor agencies, and religious organizations. Members of the national media, Cuban and foreign diplomats, healthcare professionals, teachers, and members of mass organizations were also interviewed at a more informal level. Consequently, this chapter is constructed around a variety of experience-based opinions and may read as "voices from Cuba" in that it captures and explains the perspective of actors intimately participating in social development on the island. The "voices" belong to both Cubans and foreigners; it is suggested that both are equally valid, if for different reasons. Cubans have intimate experience with the character of the country's social development initiatives; foreigners are not tainted by personal experience of Cuba and arrive with fresh views. Knowledge was also gained by engaging in numerous informal conversations with Cubans and observers of Cuba both inside and outside the country. The principal objective of the work is to attempt to determine the extent to which NGOs either conform to, or conflict with, the state's conception of civil society. In undertaking this task, this chapter gives attention to the challenges that arise out of the differing and sometimes conflicting approaches to social development as espoused by the state and NGOs.

The Traditional Actors

To judge from certain successful experiences, a guerrilla unit leaves something—or at least someone—behind it . . . for the purpose of organizing what is to become a base of solid support . . . to explain the new organization to the populace.

R. Debray

This quote illustrates the phenomenon that mass organizations are supposed to emerge naturally following a revolution; they are what revolutionaries leave in their wake. Such organizations arise following the success of guerrilla warfare and are made up of the people, fueled by popular support, and carry on the implementation of the revolutionary cause. In Cuba, the traditional mass organizations, otherwise known as the Big Seven,[1] play this administrative role and "have historically been utilized by the government to convey instructions, report citizens' opinion, and rally support for government policies" (Gunn 1995). Theoretically, the future success of the Revolution rides on the people's involvement in the new society through active participation in mass organizations. This reality has occurred in Cuba as evidenced by the participation of the majority in the undertakings of the Big Seven. For example, membership of the Cuban Federation of Women comprises 85 percent of all women over the age of fourteen. This gives an impression not only of the size of mass organizations, but also of their voluntary nature. Mobilizing the population, the Big Seven are the instruments through which the state has directed the growth of Cuban civil society.

Since 1989 there has been a change in the identity of Cuba's mass organizations. This change may only have been of a semantic nature, as some of these groups were simply relabeled as NGOs. In many cases, the bureaucracy-cum-staff remains unchanged. One obvious reason for this change in nomenclature was to acquire funds from foreign NGOs and governments that were encouraging Western-style social development in Cuba following the collapse of the Soviet Union. Nonetheless, given their former association with the Central Committee and their inclusion in the Cuban Constitution, it is questionable whether these relabeled mass organizations and think tanks are now autonomous. For the most part they continue to employ top-down approaches to development, passing the requests of the state down to the people. While this system has boasted many successes, the point to be made here is that it differs from the mainly bottom-up approaches employed by Western organizations.

There have been examples of mass organizations representing the demands of the people to the state, as in the case of the Central de Trabajadores de Cuba (CTC, Cuban Workers' Confederation). In 1994, the CTC had a significant impact on national policy when it prevented the government from imposing a personal income tax that was to go into effect that year. Trade unions can exert direct influence on high level decision making, in this case by allowing individuals to organize in defiance of a decision by the government. This example demonstrates that trade union members sometimes act independently of the state and can be successful when doing so. By responding to its members' needs, the CTC put itself in the position wherein it was not merely executing tasks as determined by the government, but rather was also entering into the arena of formulating state policies. This is the proclivity, if not the duty, of civil society, to ensure that the activity of the state creates a social setting that reflects the desires of the general population.

This example might quickly be undermined if one looks at the overall relationship between the state and labor. According to the internationally recognized Human Rights Watch, labor rights continue to be abused in Cuba, this stemming from the reality that there is only one official confederation of state-run unions, namely the CTC (De Cosse 1999, 9–10). Small unofficial independent unions are appearing across the island; however, none has yet achieved legal status. In limiting the role that they can exercise, the state effectively excludes these unions from participation in official civil society. Independent labor activists have been known to come into direct confrontation with state security forces, thus frustrating the emergence of labor organizations outside the confines of state sponsorship. As the above income-tax example demonstrates, the mass organization in charge of labor has acted in defiance of the state, deferring instead to the will of its members. If independent trade unions are permitted to form outside the confines of the CTC, workers might well experience increased bargaining power vis-à-vis the state.

The New Actors

As mentioned in the introduction to this volume, the mass organizations are the most relevant actors in Cuban civil society. An examination of civil society on the island would be meaningless without the inclusion of traditional actors. However, this chapter concentrates on the new actors, namely the NGOs.

Redefining Civil Society

The topic of nongovernmental participation in the country's social development was virtually absent from public debate throughout the Cold War. It was not until Fidel Castro's introduction of the topic during a speech at the Rio Summit in 1992 that Cubans thought that they had been given the signal not only to open public debate on the subject but also to engage in nongovernmental activity. Over the past decade or so there has been provocative discussion within Cuba regarding the appropriateness of participation by NGOs in a revolutionary culture, although the state's support of such debate diminished somewhat toward the end of the 1990s. In spite of this, the Cuban government is evidently no closer to solidifying consensus regarding its approach to dealing with NGOs than it was ten years ago. The genesis of participation by NGOs merits further inquiry as these new actors have arguably acted to alter the conception of civil society on the island.

Adapting to the context of the Special Period, a public declaration in 1996 of the Central Committee of Cuba's Communist Party defined civil society as a "socialist" construct, which included the official mass organizations *and* NGOs "that acted within the law, did not attempt to undermine the system . . . and together with the revolutionary state, pursued the common objective of constructing socialism" (Dilla 1999). Inherent in the party's definition is the contention that civil society represents the collective face of society and works to ensure that the rights of a society are protected. In putting the rights of a society before those of the individual this definition is in keeping with the conception of society that the Cuban government has projected, one of equality and solidarity. What is most striking about this definition is the implicit declaration that civil society is necessarily a "socialist" construct. While this idea has merit, it betrays a not so subtle warning that the state remains cautious about the active involvement of nongovernmental actors in the country's social development. Thus, while the party's definition of civil society now includes NGOs, it still promotes mass organizations as the most appropriate and relevant type of group for Cuba's socialist system. Even though mass organizations continue to be the major actors in Cuban civil society, NGOs have begun to play a significant role and can be used as a mechanism to assess the new context of Cuban civil society.

Cubans' growing interest in civil society participation may be evidenced by the significant increase in civil society organizations throughout the Special Period. The Ministry of Justice currently has a total of 2,200 legally registered civil associations or NGOs (Dilla 1999; Gunn 1995). Theoretically, a list of these organizations is a matter of public record; in reality the ministry is seemingly unwilling to part with this information, dismissing the requests of both Cubans and foreigners. Examining these organizations from a critical perspective demonstrates that the majority are sports, cultural, or social organizations that have little influence outside their membership. Looking specifically at developmental NGOs, some observers put their number at around fifty, while in reality there are probably only half this figure (Dilla 1999). At the same time, there are other more publicly active groups, such as the Masons and Cáritas Cubana (the Catholic Church's charity), that are not legally registered with the Ministry of Justice, yet contribute significantly to the country's social development (Gray 2002).

Foreign NGOs first entered Cuba in response to the economic crisis on the island; that is, they entered in a capacity of humanitarian aid rather than one of social development. At that time, they were embraced by the state. However, now that time has passed and the economic situation is much improved, the continued presence of NGOs is being questioned. To complicate this situation, it appears that there are differing opinions within the state and its bureaucracy on how the relationship between the state and NGOs ought to be approached. There are state functionaries who believe that NGOs ought to be completely controlled, as they are incompatible with socialism. These functionaries believe this because socialism assures everything; there is no place for organizations that operate outside of the structures and apparatuses that the state has for answering the people's needs.[2] There are also state functionaries who perceive NGOs as a necessary evil that can potentially answer the needs of the people. These functionaries believe that NGOs have some positive value and can aid in the development and strengthening of socialism. They perceive that the presence of NGOs can potentially answer the short- to medium-term needs of the people, but that NGOs should not remain in the long term. Then there are state functionaries who believe that socialism and NGOs are compatible and complementary. They believe that NGOs can help to preserve and to build upon the gains of the Revolution. A lack of consensus within the state regarding the usefulness of NGOs results in the state having no clear policy for their management. Those currently working within Cuban civil society identify this as a major source of aggravation (Gray 2002).

Official Status of NGOs in Cuba

Until 1993, Cuban civil society organizations, including sports and cultural clubs, bird-watchers' associations, and so on, were regulated by Law Number 54 of 1985, which pertains to "Associations and their Regulation" and is commonly known as the Law of Association. Accompanying this law are Articles 39, 396, and 397 of the Civil Code of 1985. When Cuban NGOs began to proliferate many had difficulty registering under Law 54 as the existence of nongovernmental organizations was practically unknown. This is when Law 54 was revisited and revised and reappeared in 1993 under the new Association Act.

To be eligible for official recognition an organization must fulfill the following requirements:

- Provide the names of thirty members, together with the names, addresses, telephone numbers, and ages of the top leadership.
- Prove that the organization is self-financing.
- Submit a written statement of goals, together with an explanation of the institution's internal structure.
- Obtain a "negative certificate" from the Ministry of Justice stating that there is no other registered NGO with a similar purpose. If there is a duplicate organization, the new applicant must associate with the one already registered.
- Obtain the sponsorship of a "state reference institution," which affirms that the establishment of the NGO is in its interest. The reference institution subsequently has the right to attend the NGO's board meetings and inspect its accounts to confirm that it is carrying out its stated purpose (Gunn 1995).

The essential difference between the new law and the old is the introduction of self-financing (previously, all organizations were financed by the state, as they were state organizations) and the requirement that each NGO submit a written statement of goals with an explanation of the organization's internal structure. The restrictions related to the last point—the right of state representatives to attend the organization's meetings and to audit the organization—might seem strict. However, the state has rarely enacted this point, this perhaps indicating encouragement of participation by ordinary Cubans in the direction of the country's social development.

Having a written statement of goals may be useful toward coordinating the activities of civil society and the state in order to avoid the reproduction of efforts. To this end, if it is later determined that an NGO is no longer performing its original purpose, the Ministry of Justice has the right to dissolve it. Further to this coordinated effort, and for other obvious reasons, an organization is not permitted to register if its goals violate the Cuban Constitution or involve activities that, according to the Ministry of Justice, "are properly the role of the state." This rule effectively bans the registration of political parties as the Cuban Constitution provides for a one-party system. A somewhat more controversial point is the denial of registration to human rights organizations, as these have the potential to operate as covert political parties.

It is also worth mentioning that in 1992 the socialist Constitution of the National Assembly of 1976 was revised to some degree. For the first time religious people, *creyentes* (believers), were permitted membership in the Communist Party of Cuba and the Union of Communist Youth. Prior to this constitutional revision, university admittance and certain posts in the bureaucracy were not fully open to believers. With the official removal of religious intolerance from the Constitution there was an immediate increase in religious activity, including the number of spiritually based organizations. Simultaneously, discrimination based on sexual orientation was removed from Article 7 of the Constitution. The Revolution's attitude toward homosexuality has traditionally been not uniformly but occasionally repressive, this despite the open homosexuality of some of those in mid- and high-level leadership positions.[3] The release of the film *Fresa y Chocolate* (Strawberry and Chocolate) aided enormously in reforming public opinion with respect to homosexuals. At the same time, there are seemingly no gay organizations in Cuba, official or otherwise, although there was a brief period in 1994 in which the Gay and Lesbian Association of Cuba (Asociación Cubana de Gays y Lesbianas) was formed; it soon transformed itself to become the Action Group for the Free Expression of Sexual Choice (GALEES). However, neither of these groups, despite their enthusiasm, ever had large numbers, and GALEES soon disappeared from view. It may be that such organizations are not permitted on the grounds that they are unnecessary, given that the rights of homosexuals are already laid out in the Constitution as being the same as those rights enjoyed by any other Cuban citizen.

How NGOs Operate in Cuba

Cuba's NGO community grew in the mid-1990s, as international developmental organizations, donor agencies, and foreign governments became willing to fund their activities. A simplified view of how NGOs operate in Cuba might be described in the following way: the foreign NGO comes to Cuba and contacts either the state through the Ministerio para la Inversión Extranjera y Colaboración Económica (MINVEC, Ministry of Foreign Investment and Economic Cooperation) or more often a Cuban NGO directly; the foreign NGO cannot engage in any activities of its own but has to have a Cuban partner; the Cuban NGO proposes a project to the foreign NGO; the foreign NGO brings the finance and technical assistance in the form of a field representative; the Cuban NGO offers the people and expertise to carry out the project; the Cuban NGO goes to the state to get what are known as the "terms of reference" for the project; once the state gives the terms of reference, the project can start. The Cuban NGO is supposed to go to MINVEC with a project proposal and secured funding from a foreign NGO. The MINVEC will evaluate the project and give its *criterios* (judgment), outlining the conditions under which permission for the project will be granted. Determining the terms of reference for a project is the state's way of getting involved in the direction a project will take. Once the project is approved, the Cuban NGO can interact with all the local actors, including the People's Council, people in the municipality, various government agencies, and so on.

In theory, this would seem to be a good model. There is central management of scarce resources, which in the case of foreign NGOs means state supervision of foreign cooperation with Cuban NGOs. The state keeps an inventory of, and administers, the use of all available resources, eliminating waste and overlapping. In practice, this means that neither foreign nor Cuban NGOs act independently; the state is always close by, monitoring and managing the use of all resources that come into the country. A particular area of controversy arises in the state's appropriation of donations addressed to NGOs. Foreign NGOs are more accustomed to acting autonomously and therefore find it difficult when the state dictates how their resources are to be used. The state's argument is that the revolutionary government is in closer touch with the country's needs and can therefore divert donations in a more appropriate manner than can NGOs.

The above is a simplification of the way that NGOs function in Cuba. In reality, there are exceptions to this model. For example, a major stumbling block is that state approval for a project comes easily for some Cuban NGOs and with more difficulty for others. Some NGOs report waiting only a few weeks to get their terms of reference from the state, while others report waiting up to one year without getting them. Evidently, the state is cautious in approving certain social development projects, taking all the time necessary to ensure that the project is in keeping with the overall goals of the revolutionary socialist project. Those that contribute in this manner are approved more quickly than those that raise new initiatives.

Reception of Western Organizations

International developmental NGOs started entering into partnerships with Cuban NGOs in the early to mid-1990s when the country was experiencing its worst ever economic crisis. Despite the introduction of the 1993 Association Act, legislation of foreign NGOs continues to be unclear to most people working in the NGO community, this posing a challenge to their fuller inclusion in Cuban society. When speaking with representatives of NGOs, the question of whether or not their organizations have official NGO status rarely evokes "yes" or "no" answers. Instead, a variety of responses are given, indicating ambiguity with respect to the question of official standing. In fact, it became clear through the interview process that most NGOs were unsure of their official status in Cuba and offered comments indicating that under some circumstances they enjoyed official status and under other circumstances they did not.

Taking a reverse approach to this issue, Ana María Béjar Miranda, the representative of Save the Children U.K., asked the pertinent question "In what sense aren't we official?" and then proceeded to answer: "We do not have legislation to outline the rules for an international NGO. Your margins for action are part of a personal research that you have to do everyday. It is a research with MINVEC, with other NGOs, and with the Cuban people around you about what you can and cannot do, what you can bring into the country and what you cannot."[4]

Foreign NGOs have had to learn how to conduct themselves in Cuba. For most it has been a learning process, getting used to working without a clearly defined set of rules. Many NGOs report that they try to do everything in the most formal way, to follow all the norms and requirements. Nonetheless, requirements are not always clear. While many find assistance in MINVEC, especially upon arrival in the country, there are some questions to which even MINVEC does not have the answers. As a result, NGOs in Cuba have adapted themselves to working blindly, learning the boundaries of permissible behavior and activity with little official guidance. Foreign NGOs emphasize that having an uncertain status remains an obstacle to their participation in issues regarding the country's social development.

Some Cuban organizations stress their polemical status in the country. The Cuban Masons represent a membership of over thirty thousand and their numbers are growing, yet they have not been considered relevant actors since 1959 when the state suspended their official status. There is evidence of more recent attempts by the revolutionary government to improve the traditionally poor relations with the Masons. For example, on 28 January 2001 (the anniversary of the birth of the Cuban national hero and Freemason José Martí) the

Masons were permitted to hold an event in Havana's Central Park in which over eight hundred citizens participated. Gustavo E. Pardo Valdés, the leader of a Masonic lodge in Havana, explained that no such state tolerance of the Masons had occurred at any other point during the years of the Revolution.[5] The whole process of obtaining official recognition is in fact a difficult and sometimes arbitrary one. The state is reluctant to confer such recognition and seemingly has not done so since well before the pope's visit to the island in 1998, this date representing a watershed in the state's attitude toward NGOs. During the mid-1990s, while international media attention was focused on the pope's upcoming visit to the island, the state was vocal in its encouragement of Cuba's emerging NGO sector. Nongovernmental organizations were in the limelight and on display to the international community. Many representatives of NGOs expressed the view that, soon after the pontifical visit, the state took a step back in its attitude and previous support to religious groups and NGOs diminished somewhat.

The lack of clarity surrounding the treatment of NGOs is seemingly indicative of the state's policy to limit the growth of NGOs, while at the same time making it difficult for existing NGOs to gain official status. This policy contributes to strained relations in that NGOs think that the state does not always recognize their contributions to the country's social development, although at the same time the policy supports official efforts to have NGOs harmonize their objectives with those of the state. Through close management, NGOs can be guided toward initiating projects that the state deems necessary. There are examples of the state giving permission for projects that do not fall under official objectives, although the states does this infrequently. Consequently, NGOs generally undertake only those projects that promote the state's overall objectives toward the country's social advancement.

Another factor highlighting the uncertain situation of NGOs is the fact that no foreign NGOs in Cuba can say that they have an office. Officially, it is not permitted. Unofficially, some foreign NGOs are lent office space by their Cuban counterparts. However, most foreign NGOs work out of the private residences of the representatives of the NGOs. Some representatives of NGOs described feeling somewhat ridiculous in that they were operating, sometimes with large budgets, in a foreign country that attributed no certain status to them. Evidently, the state's unwillingness to apply a certain status to foreign NGOs results in disappointment for these organizations, while at the same time hindering their ability to operate efficiently within Cuban civil society. At the same time, Save the Children U.K. indicates that over the 2001–4 period the process of formalization of its office has improved significantly and that this has improved its general working conditions.[6] Perhaps, and it may yet be

170 / Alexander I. Gray

too early to tell, the longevity of an NGO's presence and the formalizing and consolidation of its commitment to the country's developmental needs may result in greater acceptance by the state of the NGOs.

An unclear policy toward NGOs could be evidence of the state's interest in seeking foreign cooperation with respect to economic matters rather than social ones. This is not to say that the economy is a priority and that social concerns are not. On the contrary, social matters are of the utmost concern to the Cuban state. This is perhaps the reason the state is apprehensive about permitting foreign involvement in this area. Possibly there is a fear that if foreign actors are given too much social space, Cuba will experience a shift toward ideals of social development based on Western, or nonsocialist, conceptions. By maintaining a vague policy with respect to NGOs, the state is not dismissing their social importance; rather it is sending a clear message to the NGO community that it is unwilling to give them free rein to reshape Cuba's model for social development.

Measure of Autonomy

For NGOs, civil society is normally characterized by its independence from the state. Applying this prerequisite to the case of Cuba, many organizations emphasize that they have autonomy in decision making and do not believe that anyone imposes any type of program upon them. The Spanish nongovernmental organization ACSUR las Segovias initiated projects that were funded by the European Union that were not considered a priority by the Cuban government; the program to repair hostels is one example. José (Pepe) Murillo, its representative, explained that the Cuban state does not tell the NGO what type of projects to undertake. "We are the ones who identify the proposals and coordinate projects, and always with our Cuban counterparts, whether they are NGOs or [state] institutions."[7] This last comment highlights the state's co-ordination of civil society activity, in that NGOs must first liaise with the state to gain permission before implementing projects. In this way, the state has the final decision on whether or not a particular project is approved.

While many NGOs report autonomy in decision making, most qualify their responses by explaining the limitations, emphasizing the need to have enough tact to know which particular themes had to be approached in a delicate manner. Ana María Béjar Miranda of Save the Children U.K. gave the example of domestic violence or the rights of children and explained, "We have autonomy that needs to be approached with diplomacy, subtlety, and caution. Nobody prohibits us anything, but inasmuch as we want to work in development here we have to work in combination with the State and Cuban institutions."[8] Save the Children U.K. has been cooperating in this respect and is now seeing the results of its efforts. The theme of family violence is one that was approached little by little over the course of a whole year before receiving a letter endorsing the project from the Federation of Cuban Women, a mass organization. Béjar Miranda reiterated the approach that needs to be taken by foreign NGOs: "We have been able to realize this work, but it has been a cautious undertaking. It also has to do with respecting where we are, and not in the name of autonomy to break down or to impose certain things that we think are important but our counterparts do not yet see as important. To achieve that these themes are viewed as important we have to work little by little with discussion and mutual accompaniment."[9]

The only organization to answer immediately that the state dictated its level of autonomy was the European Commission Humanitarian Office (ECHO), which maintained, "Everything we do is with consent from the authorities." The organization insists that it has been clear from the beginning that it came to Cuba to employ a parallel system, to take advantage of what was already established. When it thinks that there is a better way to do something, it discusses and argues about it with the state. José Eugenio Roca Rivas, its representative, stressed, "It is not always easy; sometimes it is difficult here. We have a very global view; they have a vision that is much narrower than what we wish, and within the context these things obey other types of questions."[10] Nonetheless, there is a belief that the degree of autonomy enjoyed by donor agencies and NGOs has been increasing each year: "This is not an easy system, with everything so centralized; with time we have been gaining. . . . I cannot say that it has been highly satisfactory in this sense, but on some levels there have been instances of satisfaction."[11] The organization ceased programming in Cuba at the beginning of 2002 when it was sensed that the urgent need for humanitarian intervention had disappeared.

NGO Integration into the Revolutionary Project

The relationship between Cuban and foreign NGOs and among NGOs, the state, and the para-statal[12] mass organizations is at times cohesive and at others problematical. To begin with, the partnership between foreign and local NGOs is not always an equal one. José (Pepe) Murillo of Paz y el Tercer Mundo, perceives that "it is often a vertical relationship, a donor-recipient relationship, and much work must be done to create an equal relationship and not a relationship of dependence." He thinks that the creation of a balanced relationship is contingent on Cuban NGOs and depends on their security, confidence, and experience. Trust between Cuban and foreign NGOs has been increasingly consolidated and has permitted some successes. At the same time, NGO work in Cuba is difficult, he says, "because if Cuban NGOs do not understand that there is an attitude of respect, transparency, and solidarity then they do not open up very much and there is not a fluid relationship."[13] Representatives of foreign NGOs tend to emphasize that Cuba's NGO community operates in an environment distinct from elsewhere, stressing the challenge of being confronted with a system that utilizes top-down approaches for solving social development issues.

One can distinguish between the relationship between foreign and Cuban NGOs and that which these have with other parts of Cuban society. Specifically, the work of foreign NGOs is carried out through local partners and, typically, foreign organizations do not carry out any action apart from collaborating with local NGOs. If value were added by the foreign NGO it would be in design, monitoring, and evaluation. As a result, a foreign NGO's direct relationship with beneficiaries is a second-hand one, coming through its local partner. In terms of local NGOs, Care International sees them as having a low profile in Cuba, to the point that the average citizen would be unaware of the concept of an "NGO," since an entity lying outside the confines of the state is practically unheard of in Cuba. Another important aspect, and a powerful limitation, of Cuban NGOs is that there are very few and almost all of them are based in Havana. Moreover, according to Steve Gilbert of Care International, Cuban NGOs typically have "a leader of a certain age who has a connection to the elite in the government, which provides the original space to form the organization, and provides the aegis under which the organization operates."[14] While it may be true that Cuban NGOs with state connections, including the Asociación para la Unidad de Nuestra América, AUNA, Centro Memorial Dr. Martin Luther King Jr., and Centro de Información y Estudios sobre las Relaciones Internacionales, CIERI, found it easier to gain official recognition, it does not necessarily imply that these organizations are under the influence of the state.

The representatives of the Centro Memorial Dr. Martin Luther King Jr. believe that the relationship between the Revolution (socialism) and NGOs "is a difficult relationship in that there are fears, some founded, that the enemy will enter through NGOs."[15] This is a logical concern considering the publicly expressed initiatives of the U.S. government to infiltrate Cuban civil society with the aim of undermining the Revolution and the Cuban government. At the same time, there is a certain understanding that the grave problems in the population that the state is emphasizing are also being stressed by NGOs. While in some social programs NGOs and the state "speak the same language and are working in the same area," in other cases "the government is preoccupied with NGOs and because of this they are working with certain reservations."[16] Nonetheless, there is the feeling that the state and NGOs do share common social goals. Fabio Laurenzi of the joint Cuban-Italian NGO, Havana

Ecopolis, reports that the Italian NGOs are in Cuba because they are genuinely interested in the Cuban Revolution and in Cuban socialism: "I think one of our motives for being here is because this is a country where one can still try an alternative solution. . . . Cuba has to stop being looked at from the outside as the third way, as the last island, because it has affected Cuba very much. . . . Liberalism has demonstrated itself to not be an alternative. . . . I think that here there is still a chance for an alternative."[17]

Thus, while NGOs and the state may serve similar social causes, they do not always share a harmonious relationship. To avoid conflict, some NGOs undertake to implement programs only in areas where the state is not working. For example, Habitat-Cuba[18] claimed to employ this policy frequently in order to avoid entering into any contradiction or misunderstanding.

In the Cuban case, there is an official realization that NGOs occupy a space within society and that they complement the efforts of the state to achieve its objectives; this rejects the notion that NGOs are a counterproposal to official government policy. There is also an unofficial view that NGOs are simply filling the gaps that were being left behind by the state following the economic crisis of the early 1990s. Following this line of reasoning, Steve Gilbert of Care International claims:

I have seen a number of different and interesting examples from people who are quite revolutionary, who describe society as a pyramid with different blocks representing different government organizations and the Big Seven social organizations that are covering the needs of Cuban society. And they have represented that those blocks have all shrunken a little bit and opened up fissures in the pyramid, and that these organizations [new NGOs] are sprouting up to cement together these building blocks of the Revolution.[19]

Conjuring up a graphical depiction of the role of new NGOs within Cuban society, we might consider the illustrations below (figure 7.1). The pyramid on the left illustrates the situation in Cuba before the Special Period (prior to 1989); the pyramid on the right represents the current situation and includes the new NGOs. In the left-hand pyramid, the state and mass organizations are the principal actors in civil society and are responsible for the country's social development. This situation changes in the right-hand pyramid where, in response to the economic hardships of the Special Period, the role of the state and mass organizations diminishes somewhat. The right-hand pyramid depicts the new NGOs as filling in the spaces left as a result of the diminishing activity of the state and mass organizations. In this sense, the new NGOs are seen to be filling the gaps wherein the state and mass organizations are no longer able to operate.

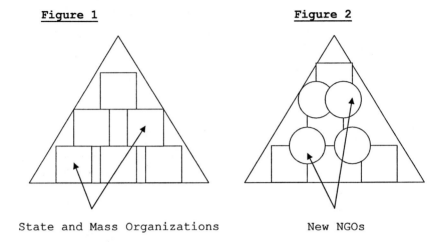

Figure 7.1. The role of new NGOs within Cuban civil society.

However, there are others who say that all of these organizations are a disruption. Steve Gilbert of Care International explained: "Let us face it, NGOs are not part of the Revolution, they represent a change . . . whether that is counterrevolutionary or evolutionary. . . . It is one of the things that I believe is why there are a lot of people in the government that are afraid of NGOs; because it is really hard to predict what the change would be."[20]

Many foreign organizations claim to support Cuban NGOs because they believe that the Cuban NGOs are doing excellent work at promoting change to make Cuba an open society, not a counterrevolutionary one but one that is more open with more access to information. There is a sense that people are slowly taking the initiative to solve their own problems, which is promoting some diversity in the way of doing things. Notwithstanding, there is little doubt that NGOs are having a disruptive effect on traditional civil society. They have no direct links to the state and function with a bottom-up approach to development. However, they represent the new reality of Cuban civil society and are therefore being accommodated by the state. While this is not a smooth process, many successes are evident, signaling that NGOs could represent an evolution, a solidification, or a change.

The distinction between civil society and the state is often blurred in Cuba. At times, the two function in cohesion and with shared priorities; at other times the relationship between them is marred by tensions. Some perceive that Cuba's revolutionary socialist state is managing civil society to such an extent that NGOs are puppets of the state. In contrast, some think that NGOs are acting autonomously of the state. The relationship between civil society

The Genesis of NGO Participation in Contemporary Cuba / 175

and the state, as conceived by Marx, is in some ways similar and in other ways distinct from the reality of Cuba in the period after the Cold War. Civil society has expanded to play an important role in revolutionary Cuba. However, the state has not disappeared with this expansion.

Official Social Policy and NGOs

Representatives of NGOs tend to say that their sentiments are very much allied with those of the state. They want to make clear that their organizations do not condone sentiments that act in opposition to the state. Ironically, some identify the close relationship that NGOs share with the state as the reason why they are not generating changes in state policy; however, a few indicate a belief that NGOs have generated changes in state policy. It is significant that even a minority of representatives express this view. This suggests that there is a willingness, if only by the few, to express the sentiment that the actions of NGOs are directly influencing decision making with respect to social policy at the state level.

Organizations that are certain that they do not generate any change in state policies tend to be Cuban (local NGOs) and suggest that the information they provide to the state might be used indirectly in decision making. Within the Cuban context, this recurring opinion is a politically correct one; perhaps these organizations are apprehensive about drawing attention to the influence they have on state policy, preferring to maintain a low profile in this respect. Foreign NGOs tend to be more forthright about the influence they have on social policy; perhaps it is in the interest of foreign NGOs to provide evidence to their donors that their actions result in influence at official levels. However, discrepancy in claiming influence may be grounded in differing conceptions of civil society. Where some Cuban NGOs may not distinguish between Cuban society as a whole and civil society as a separate domain within society, foreign NGOs absolutely identify civil society as a separate domain. As a result, some Cuban NGOs would not attribute their influence with regard to changing state policy because they would perceive themselves as working in conformity with the objectives of the state, whereas foreign NGOs would identify their influence on official social policy.

State suspicion of NGOs is understandable, given the real threat that dissident elements can enter through civil society. In this respect, the United States continues to pose a major threat to Latin American sovereignty in general and the Cuban Revolution in particular. The U.S. Agency for International Development's report of 1997, *Support for Democratic Transition in Cuba*, offers a shining example of efforts to subvert the Cuban government through the provision of financial and other assistance to the dissident elements of civil so-

176 / Alexander I. Gray

ciety. More recently, the U.S. President's Commission for Assistance to a Free Cuba issued a 500-page report containing harsh recommendations that were immediately adopted as official U.S. policy (Commission for Assistance to a Free Cuba 2004). Support for the "pro-democracy" movement (that is, forces trying to undermine the Revolution) increased from $7 million to $36 million and funding will go toward the training, development, and empowerment of a Cuban "democratic opposition and civil society." One of the island's leading dissidents, Osvaldo Payá, met this particular measure with disappointment on the basis that it went too far and would only make the work of dissidents more difficult. The end result in Cuba is diminished political tolerance toward organizations that lie outside state sponsorship. Many Cubans think that they are "dealing with an undeclared war that the U.S. is waging against [them]. So obviously you don't get the kind of tolerant environment you might find in Switzerland. You get a kind of anger, a kind of intolerance in dealing with dissent" (Blanco and Benjamin 1997, 55–56). At the same time, the state has to act prudently to ensure provision of sufficient space for social expression. In a situation where "development policy continues to deny individuals' interest and 'human nature,' social unrest is the inevitable outcome" (Cole 1998, 26). In approaching the problem of diminished political tolerance in Cuba, NGOs must avoid behavior that could be misinterpreted as a rejection of official social policy.

If one examines NGOs in neighboring Central America it is understandable that Cubans have more than sufficient reason for lacking confidence in the altruistic role of foreign NGOs. During the 1980s and 1990s there was a proliferation in the number of NGOs working in Central America. Today, there are thousands of NGOs in Central America and they work independently of the state; they do not have the state as a body of reference in terms of carrying out or completing their projects. As a result, there is no cohesion between the state's social development project and that of NGOs. There are NGOs or "private voluntary organizations" with purely political aims that have placed themselves in Central America. To give only one example, the American Institute for Free Labor Development (AIFLD) was closely tied to USAID's foreign policy strategy. The AIFLD engaged in labor union organizing to support U.S. initiatives in the region.[21] Being conscious of this potential risk, the Cuban state acts in a preventative fashion with respect to generalized access for NGOs. However, this method also works against NGOs with friendly intentions. Ultimately, not permitting generalized access for NGOs enables the Cuban state to maintain close management of the NGO community. The downside of this policy is the potential for it to deter some NGOs that could make a significant contribution from entering Cuba.

A comment that came up a few times during interviews is that the state takes over successful NGO projects. This is surely evidence of NGOs effecting changes in state policy. If the state replicates an NGO's way of carrying out a project or takes over and continues to operate an NGO's project, it demonstrates state approval of the project, if not a compliment to the NGO. Evidently, the GDIC—the Grupo de Desarrollo Integral de la Capital (Group for the Integrated Development of the Capital)—and Habitat-Cuba have affected state policy significantly. The state is now running the GDIC's housing reconstruction project in Central Havana and Habitat-Cuba's Arquitectos de la Comunidad project. In the context of Cuba, this could well mean that these projects were successful. These NGOs showed the state how a particular social problem could be addressed; the state looked at the example of the NGOs and adopted it. The fact that the state totally undermined the autonomy of the GDIC and Habitat-Cuba does not alter the fact that these NGOs affected changes in state policy. Apparently neither NGO harbors animosity toward the state for taking over its projects. Over the years the GDIC and Habitat-Cuba have undoubtedly influenced the state's decision making with respect to policy. These NGOs may well be realizing a road of development along with the state, but because they are nongovernmental organizations it is surprising that they are not more forthright about the influential role they play in Cuban civil society. Perhaps this has to do with the fact that these NGOs are working with the same social development goals as the state and as a result some employees of GDIC and Habitat-Cuba may not see themselves as working in a sphere that is outside the state. To such employees, any influence that their NGO yields may not be considered to be divorced from the state. Whether or not each of these NGOs or the state officially recognizes their contribution to social development, it is clear that the GDIC and Habitat-Cuba provide clear examples of civil society influencing official social policy.

The Future of Cuba's NGO Community

The Question of Sustainability

A major problem faced by NGOs working in Cuba is sustainability. Not knowing the state's intentions vis-à-vis NGOs results in a lack of certainty about future programming. Thus, NGOs are less likely to consider long-term programming and more likely to consider medium- or short-term programming. In this situation, NGOs find that it is especially difficult to know where to channel scarce resources. During their interviews, some representatives of NGOs indicated their organization's new willingness to engage in medium-

178 / Alexander I. Gray

term planning; however, this is not the general rule for NGOs in Cuba. It is clear that the state's lack of long-term commitment in terms of NGOs is affecting the decision making of NGOs with respect to their future work in Cuba.

The sustainability of current projects by Cuban NGOs, in the absence of funding from foreign NGOs, is a particularly relevant point. Many Cuban NGOs receive funding from a foreign NGO, and it is relatively certain that much of their programming would cease if foreign NGOs and donor agencies were to halt funding.

Working with Socialist Principles

Nongovernmental organizations do not operate in the margins of a problem; they enter into the center of a problem, tackling specific social development issues from a grass-roots position. In Cuba, they can enter harmoniously if they are prepared to work in agreement with the socialist principles of solidarity and respect the country's laws and ideology. Many NGOs do not have a political identification with the Cuban system, but they do identify specific themes with which they are prepared to help. To function within Cuban civil society, NGOs do not have to be socialist organizations; they only have to be organizations that are prepared to help in specific areas as identified by the state. This may be the crux of the matter; that is, specific areas are not chosen by NGOs, but rather are chosen by the state. Some NGOs hold this as a point of contention, as they would like to work in areas that are of interest to them but are under pressure to work only in specific areas as identified by the state.

A Call for Increased Dialogue between the State and Civil Society

When the representatives of foreign NGOs are asked how they would like to see Cuban civil society develop if they could "wave a magic wand" most respond that they want more independence and more dialogue. They would like to see change in the relationship between NGOs and the state in a way that would allow them more autonomy over their own affairs. This cannot be construed as a call to divorce the state from interaction with the NGO community. On the contrary, it is a call for independence from the state in terms of decision making surrounding daily operations and areas of programming. Most representatives of NGOs understand and appreciate the necessity for dialogue between the state and civil society. However, they think that the dialogue is mostly unilateral, with the state dictating how social development will be managed in Cuba.

Will Foreign Organizations Stay?

There are those who believe that foreign NGOs will always be external actors in Cuban civil society. This seems somewhat wishful, as it is undeniable that foreign NGOs have played a strong role in shaping Cuba's NGO community since the mid-1990s. Foreign NGOs may have started off by playing an external role in Cuban civil society with their intervention in a humanitarian aid capacity, but today their role is arguably more internal as they are engaged in development aid. The fact that many of them arrived to pursue emergency projects but are now engaged in development programming indicates an intention to remain in Cuba beyond the short term, this despite the fact that they do not engage in long-term planning. If they remain, it is likely that foreign NGOs will continue to play an increasingly influential role in Cuba's evolving civil society.

Conclusion

This chapter sought to determine the extent to which NGOs either conform to or conflict with the state's conception of civil society, and some preliminary conclusions may be drawn. Cuba's NGO community exists in a tightly managed environment, characterized by state regulation of all resources and areas open for social development programming. Those currently working within civil society think that the state is by far the more influential partner in this relationship. Opening social space for civil society may ensure survival of the revolutionary project as more ordinary Cubans vocalize their concerns and engage in efforts to defend the gains of the Revolution.

In the context of the Special Period, the degree of reliance on the state was diminished, as Cubans seemingly became more self-reliant. Through NGOs, Cuba has a community participation that permits the contribution of a bottom-up strategy for social development; however, the state employs a top-down strategy. There is evidence that this may be changing, if only marginally, as NGOs are working both from the grass-roots level and in consultation with the state. Traditionally, the state put out the message to its mass organizations about projects it wished to see undertaken; today, people are employing NGOs as a mechanism for approaching the state with proposals for projects they perceive as necessary. This new method of social development is still searching for firm ground, but it has seemingly gained acceptance in some pockets of government opinion. Initiatives by NGOs such as the soup kitchens operated by Cáritas Cubana may be empowering Cubans to search for solutions to their problems rather than having them rely on the now financially debilitated state.

In working toward an equal relationship, Cuban NGOs have created a discourse and have developed potential, all in a very short time. However, there is still a lack of consolidation among Cuban NGOs; they are not a cohesive group. This is in part due to controls pertaining to freedom of association that make "illegal" the gathering of NGOs outside state-sponsored venues. There is not only a need for consolidation, but above all there is a need to create more social space for these organizations. There have to be new actors in Cuban civil society, and these already exist; they do not have to be invented. There are unofficial groups that are prepared to get involved in Cuba's social development. The state needs to provide the space for these actors to express views and to share their approach to development. Unfortunately, and perhaps understandably, the state has only permitted a select group of Cuban NGOs to enjoy strong relationships with foreign organizations and to participate in events both inside and outside Cuba. However, many of these NGOs are working toward opening the social space that the state allows civil society.

The future of civil society in Cuba has three possible outcomes: it could represent a revolution within the Revolution; a revolution against the Revolution; or a building up of the Revolution. A preliminary outcome of this study indicates that while all three outcomes are possible, Cuba's new civil society, with its emerging NGO community, has the potential to represent a building of the Revolution.

Notes

1. Cuban mass organizations include Comités de Defensa de la Revolución (CDRs, Committees for the Defense of the Revolution), Central de Trabajadores de Cuba (CTC, Cuban Workers' Confederation), Asociación Nacional de Agricultores Pequeños (ANAP, National Association of Small Farmers), Unión de Jóvenes Comunistas (UJC, Union of Communist Youth), Federación de Estudiantes de la Enseñanza Media (FEEM, Federation of Middle Level Students), Federación de Mujeres Cubanas (FMC, Federation of Cuban Women), and Federación de Estudiantes Universitarios (FEU, Federation of University Students). Additionally, there is the more recent creation of the Asociación de Combatientes de la Revolución Cubana (ACRC, Veterans Association of the Cuban Revolution).

2. It is essential to study contemporary Cuban civil society within the context of the economic crisis. Before the 1990s there was little need for organizations outside the structures of the state. Throughout the 1990s, and especially during 1993–94, the need for NGOs and donor agencies became urgent.

3. For a comprehensive analysis of Cuba and homosexuality, see Lumsden 1996.

4. Ana María Béjar Miranda, interview, March 2001.

5. Gustavo E. Pardo Valdés, interview, March 2001.

6. Ana María Béjar Miranda, interview, March 2001.

7. José (Pepe) Murillo, interview, March 2001.

8. Ana María Béjar Miranda, interview, March 2001.

9. Ibid.

10. José Eugenio Roca Rivas, interview, March 2001.

11. Ibid.

12. Para-statal organizations are those that simultaneously might be considered as either state or nonstate organizations. They are a blend of the two and at times it may be difficult to identify them as strictly one or the other.

13. José (Pepe) Murillo, interview, March 2001.

14. Steve Gilbert, interview, March 2001.

15. Joel Suárez and Daisy Rojas, interview, March 2001.

16. Ibid.

17. Fabio Laurenzi, interview, March 2001.

18. Habitat-Cuba disappeared in 2001 when the support of its sponsoring agency was withdrawn.

19. Steve Gilbert, interview, March 2001.

20. Ibid.

21. For more information on the political purposes of USAID to NGOs in Central America, see Barry, Wood, and Preusch 1993.

References

Barry, T., B. Wood, and D. Preusch, eds. 1983. *Dollars and Dictators: A Guide to Central America.* New York: Grove Press.

Blanco, J. A., and M. Benjamin, eds. 1997. *Cuba: Talking about Revolution.* Melbourne: Ocean Press.

Cole, K. 1998. *Cuba: From Revolution to Development.* London: Pinter.

Commission for Assistance to a Free Cuba. 2004. *Hastening Cuba's Transition: Report to the President* (6 May). http://www.state.gov/p/wha/rt/cuba/commission/2004/, accessed 30 June 2004.

Debray, R. 1967. *Revolution in the Revolution? Armed Struggle and Political Struggle in Latin America.* New York: Grove Press.

De Cosse, S. A., ed. 1999. *Cuba's Repressive Machinery: Human Rights Forty Years after the Revolution.* New York: Human Rights Watch.

Dilla, H. 1999. "The Virtues and Misfortunes of Civil Society." *NACLA Report on the Americas* 32, no. 5 (March/April): 30–35.

Gray, Alexander I. 2002. "Deconstructing Civil Society in a Revolutionary Socialist State: The Genesis of NGO Participation in Contemporary Cuba." Ph.D. diss., Centre for Peace and Development Studies, Limerick, Ireland.

———. 2004. "The Changing Dynamic of Cuban Civil Society: Traditional Priorities, New Approaches." Discussion Paper IPS-DPUL-0401. *UL Perspectives: Journal of Political Studies* 3. http://www.skynet.ie/~peacesoc/read/dp/cubaNGO.pdf.

Gunn, G. 1995. *Cuba's NGOs: Government Puppets or Seeds of Civil Society?* Washington, D.C.: The Caribbean Project, Center for Latin American Studies, Georgetown University. http://www.trinitydc.edu/Academics/depts/Interdisc/International/caribbean%20briefings/Cubas_NGOs.pdf, 1–21, accessed 20 May 2002.

Lumsden, I. 1996. *Machos, Gays, and Maricones: Cuba and Homosexuality.* Philadelphia: Temple University Press.

Rieff, D. 1999. "The False Dawn of Civil Society." *The Nation* 22 February. http://www. thenation.com/doc/19990222/rieff, accessed 15 May 2002.

Sampson, S. 1996. "The Social Life of Projects: Importing Civil Society to Albania." In *Civil Society: Challenging Western Models*, edited by Chris Hann and Elizabeth Dunn, 121–42. London: Routledge.

Seligman, A. B. 1992. *The Idea of Civil Society*. New York: Free Press.

U.S. Agency for International Development (USAID). 1997. *Support for Democratic Transition in Cuba*. 28 January. http://www.info.U.S.aid.gov/countries/cu/english. htm., accessed 29 November 1999.

Interviews

ACSUR las Segovias: José (Pepe) Murillo (March 2001).

AUNA, Asociación para la Unidad de Nuestra América (Association for the Unity of Our America): Mario Molina Monteagudo and Mayra Rivero Loo (March 2001).

Care International: Steve Gilbert (March 2001).

Cáritas Cubana: Maritza Sánchez Abillud (March 2001).

Centro Memorial Dr. Martin Luther King Jr.: Joel Suárez and Daisy Rojas (March 2001).

CIERI, Centro de Información y Estudios sobre las Relaciones Interamericanas (Center for Information and Studies about Interamerican Relations): Rigoberto Fabelo Pérez (March 2001).

ECHO, Oficina de Ayuda Humanitaria de la Comisión Europea (European Commission Humanitarian Office): José Eugenio Roca Rivas (March 2001).

GDIC, Grupo para el Desarrollo Integral de la Capital (Group for the Integrated Development of the Capital): Miguel Coyula (March 2001).

Habitat-Cuba: Abel González and Teresa Vigil (March 2001).

Havana Ecopolis: Fabio Laurenzi (March 2001).

Masons (Gran Logia de Cuba de A.M. y A.M.): Gustavo E. Pardo Valdés (March 2001).

Oxfam Canada: Karen Bernard and Angela Laird (March 2001).

Paz y el Tercer Mundo: José (Pepe) Murillo (March 2001).

Save the Children: Ana María Béjar Miranda (March 2001).

Temas magazine: Rafael Hernández (March 2001).

Conclusion

ALEXANDER I. GRAY AND ANTONI KAPCIA

The aim of this book has been to fill a perceived gap in our knowledge about Cuba's NGO community and its role in, and relationship with, civil society in Cuba. It therefore has focused on the effects on that civil society of the Cuban state's necessary adaptation to dramatic change, largely approaching the subject by assessing aspects of the relationship between NGOs and religious groups on the one hand and the state on the other. As suggested in the introduction, we hope that the book has offered a possible reconceptualization of the whole question of civil society within a political system that is traditionally defined by centralized decision making and extraordinarily high levels of grass-roots participation.

It is customary in the literature on Cuba to see the post-1991 context in terms of a tension between pressures on Cuba to change and Cuban resistance to change. However, we have argued that the context is more complex than this, both in terms of the nature of the state and political system (past and present) and also in terms of the relationship between that state and the newly emerging manifestations of a different and marginally more autonomous civil society. The complexity is demonstrated, we hope we have shown, not least when we consider the question of civil society in Cuba in the light of the NGOs' underlying principle of working in cooperation with the state; this principle obviously represents something of a challenge to the Cuban system, which has long seen such external contacts in terms of solidarity rather than cooperation. Indeed, while internationalist solidarity brigades have been visiting the island since the beginnings of the Revolution, the relationships between Cuban and foreign NGOs are still relatively new, most of them starting around 1995, and the formation of these relationships has therefore been a complex affair, with the concept of working in cooperation rather than in solidarity still to find firm acceptance among Cuban organizations.

This point is fundamental to the tensions underlying those relationships, for there is an essential difference between solidarity and cooperation: solidarity involves shared ideology, and cooperation involves shared objectives. Cubans are well used to engaging in solidarity with foreign actors, as demonstrated by the impressive history of receiving and sending internationalist missions, as

184 / Alexander I. Gray and Antoni Kapcia

discussed in Nino Pagliccia's essay. For anyone who has an understanding of Cuba's widespread efforts at solidarity, it might seem ironic that they would be suspicious of foreigners who wished to cooperate with Cuba. However, given a history of sustained external attempts to subvert the Revolution by working through civil society, it is perhaps understandable that Cubans come by their suspicion honestly.

This confusion between solidarity and cooperation can be related to the normative language of the Revolution, in particular the idea that words have different and sometimes stronger meanings in Cuba than elsewhere. As highlighted in Alexander Gray's essay, cooperation is new territory for Cubans as they seek to work with those who may not necessarily share the same ideology but are interested in the same objectives. As a result of Cuba's experience, while many Cuban NGOs view their relationship with foreign NGOs as one of solidarity, those foreign NGOs view their relationship with Cuban NGOs as one of cooperation. The result is often a certain awkwardness or difficulty, as NGOs, which are used to operating in one way, have to find a new modus operandi in Cuba. Ultimately, despite differing agendas, these two types of entity are starting to work alongside each other and successfully complete projects, whatever their agenda, developing methods for carrying out social development projects if often on an ad hoc basis.

The book also, we hope, has both general and specific implications for the discussion of civil society. As has been argued in these pages, by the 1990s, apart from those who persisted in applying Cold War models and analogies to Cuba in the assumption and expectation that Cuba was simply and inevitably to become the last domino to fall, it had become clear that conventional models could no longer explain the Cuban phenomenon. This became even more obvious the longer the 1990s went on, as it became clear that the whole system's survival and adaptation was challenging many expectations and readings. Hence, more subtle analyses began to focus on the system's lack of system and on its essential complexity and contradictions, or on its underlying patterns of "passion." Indeed, as we have seen, Cuban political scientists themselves began to address the question of civil society in new ways, as part of the whole reassessment that the crisis necessarily engendered. Hence, we hope that the fieldwork-based research that has underpinned the contributions by most of the book's essayists will offer new perspectives in the light of this need to rethink our understanding of the Cuban system, perspectives that may, indeed, have implications beyond the Cuban case.

In fact, the book generally seems to suggest that the meaning of civil society as put forth by those working within and with Cuba is often in keeping with the conception put forth by non-Cuban political and social scientists: as a binarism between two social domains, the state and civil society. However,

Cuban commentators often prefer to refine this model, arguing that civil society is a domain within society that can be characterized by individual citizens *voluntarily* coming together for a common cause or purpose. Hence, while conventional Western models of civil society see decision making as a bottom-up process and not a top-down one, this definition results in some difficulties with official Cuban perspectives, although it is also clear that within the ranks of officialdom there are varying degrees of support for the emerging NGO community.

Specific models to understand how NGOs and religious groups operate within the context of Cuban society have therefore emerged in the book; they are often the result of field research and are occasionally intended as theoretical guides to describe how civil society operates in Cuba. The more convincing of these models suggest that the domains of the state and civil society in Cuba necessarily overlap. In this model the mass organizations, officially relabeled as NGOs, fall under the auspices of the state, while other NGOs and religious groups function in a somewhat more independent capacity with respect to relations with foreign NGOs and international donor agencies.

This therefore returns us to a point strongly suggested at the start of the book, namely the need to bring a fresh perspective to bear on the still evolving Cuban system and to seek to explain or understand an essentially complex phenomenon with complex tools of analysis and not with preordained models. Indeed, the argument that Cuba should be understood as a sui generis system and phenomenon is very much the driving force behind the two essays by Alexander Gray (with his notion of the pyramid) and Antoni Kapcia (with his picture of a fundamental process of constant negotiation and debate), and it underlies all of the essays in this volume, whether explicitly or implicitly.

However, all of the essays also make clear that the Cuban system is an evolving one, not least adapting painfully and occasionally clumsily to the demands of a changed world and to the emerging demands of ordinary Cubans. For example, those working within NGOs have witnessed at first hand the degree to which the state and the mass organizations have shrunk over the last decade or so, and there is a general awareness among Cubans that, because the state is no longer able to cover all of their needs, there are things that they themselves must seek to attain through their own initiatives. Thus, the Cuban state's current inability to satisfy all of the people's needs may be giving NGOs more of an opportunity to be a justifiable option, and, in this process, NGOs are usefully careful to emphasize that they are not an alternative to the state, but, rather, work alongside the state.

Hence, if, as Kapcia argues at the start, one of the most evident features of the Cuban system at any time since 1959 is how little it corresponds to preconceptions of "monolithism" or personalism, the studies in this book have all indicated that truth is even starker now, after more than a decade and a half of crisis, reform, and adaptation. For, however restricting, controlling, and centralizing the state has been at moments in the past, the fact is that at the grass roots it is now more frequently characterized by a surprising number and array of what several writers have termed "spaces," allowing ordinary Cubans an opportunity to operate independently.

As the book has made clear, this is so because social changes occurring in Cuba over recent years have resulted in a certain restlessness in the Cuban population. Not only have all Cubans experienced dramatic and occasionally disconcerting social changes, aware also that more such changes are inevitable, many have seen the positive results brought about by the country's decreased isolation and increased contact with foreign actors (from tourists to NGOs) and are eager to see more. It is precisely within the context of this restlessness that there is perhaps a clear role for NGOs to play, since there is clearly little prospect now of Cuba going back to the halcyon years of the 1980s, when there was much greater, and perhaps more evenly spread, material prosperity, but also when Cuba was generally a more closed society. Therefore, it must be difficult and perhaps politically destabilizing to withdraw permission for the continued active role of NGOs. In particular, Cuban NGOs will be reluctant to forego the social development projects they are currently able to undertake as a result of their cooperation with foreign NGOs and international donor agencies.

This has reinforced the argument put forward at the start of the book: that the 1990s so challenged traditions and beliefs as to force the whole Revolution to reassess its ideological bases and its essence, and to develop a clear consensus on what that "essence" actually was in order to agree about what should be "saved" during the Special Period. Given the rise of a survivalist and atomizing individualism that threatened patterns and principles of communal action and solidarity, given the increase in petty crime, informality, and *jineterismo*, given the decline of the system's underlying "moralism" and principles of social cohesion, the emergence of a new *solidarismo* (rather than solidarity), of a new emphasis on youth and family, all point to a new context in which a coalition of ordinary Cubans, the state, and the NGOs are actually able to work together usefully.

It is of course notoriously difficult to arrive at confident conclusions about what ordinary Cubans are actually thinking in any systematic way. However, on the basis of the primary research underlying most of the studies, we are confident enough to make some generalizations. One is that enough Cubans seem to retain a genuine interest in building on (rather than sacrificing) what are still seen as the achievements of the Revolution, this evidence arising from the scope of voluntary organization among ordinary Cubans to protect these

Conclusion / 187

achievements, including the increased participation in NGOs. Another generalization is that Cubans who grew up in the egalitarian environment brought about by the Revolution seem genuinely fearful of the social divisions that are resulting from current economic conditions and changes.

Hence, a third generalization is that the NGOs currently working in Cuba have the capacity, and possibly the intention, to help those Cubans in their desire to preserve and protect. While non-Cuban NGOs generally do not support Cuba's political system, the majority of them do seem to acknowledge the "social gains" and seem to be pressing for social space wherein they can continue to build upon them. At the same time, most NGOs seem to want to continue a process of building (society, civil society, and thus "the Revolution") outside the confines of state-directed programs; the research in this book seems to indicate that NGOs seek more autonomy in terms of daily operations and in decision making related to areas of programming. Therefore, ultimately, reconciling differences in the approach to development is the challenge facing both the state and NGOs.

Nongovernmental organizations clearly seem to want to distinguish themselves as belonging to the domain of civil society, subscribing to the notion that civil society ought to be autonomous and act independently of the state. Cuban and foreign NGOs, religious groups, foreign donor agencies, and others have indeed been active in creating social space for civil society to participate in the country's social development. While NGOs have claimed that they act autonomously in terms of decision making, they are vocal in seeking less state intervention in their affairs. Nongovernmental organizations want to remedy the unequal relationship between themselves and the state through active engagement in dialogue and debate with the state and with each other with respect to issues concerning civil society.

When they began arriving in the early 1990s, NGOs were a novelty in Cuba, a country unprepared for this type of independent actor; hence the following years have seen a nervous but often productive process of familiarization. Starting with caution, then moving through to a necessary stage of mutual recognition, with fears, reservations, and doubts in the face of new proposals and new approaches to solving problems, this process has continued to be a learning experience for both the Cuban state and the NGOs.

Cooperation between foreign NGOs and international donor agencies on the one hand and Cuban NGOs, mass organizations, and the state on the other hand has inevitably created a changed civil society domain in Cuba. Marx's ideal of the state withering away and civil society becoming the cohesive entity holding society together may be less apparent today than before the Special Period. Moreover, it is clear that those currently working within Cuban civil society think that the state is by far the more influential partner in this relationship. However, the continuing pace of change in Cuba means that Cuba's leaders seem to have recognized that the social space for civil society must continue to be opened and defined in different terms in Cuba if the government, and more importantly the Revolution, are to maintain popular support. The evidence of developments since 1998 seems to indicate a growing official awareness of the possibility that an enhanced and self-confident Cuban civil society can ensure the survival of the revolutionary project as more Cubans vocalize their concerns and engage in efforts to defend the gains of the Revolution.

As suggested in Alexander Gray's essay, the future of civil society in Cuba has three possible outcomes: it could represent a revolution within the Revolution, a revolution against the Revolution, or a building of the Revolution. An outcome of this research indicates that while all three outcomes are possible, Cuba's new civil society, with its emerging NGO community, has the potential to represent a building of the Revolution. The policy implications of this research, for the Cuban state and for the NGOs working within Cuba, are therefore considerable, ranging from the potential need for new laws to the need for greater communication among NGOs and between the NGOs and the state, perhaps via round tables sponsored by MINVEC, or independently of the state.

Glossary

Abakuá – All-male secret society with its origins in West Africa.

Apagones – Blackouts, brownouts, power outages.

Babalawo – Priest of the Ifá cult, see also *Ifá*.

Balsero – Person attempting to leave Cuba on a raft (*balsa*) or other improvised small vessel.

Barrio – Neighborhood.

Bloqueo – Blockade (the Cuban term for the U.S. economic sanctions on Cuba).

Brigadista – Volunteer participant in a work brigade.

Casa de culto – Small houses of worship for Protestant denominations.

Casa particular – Private guesthouse.

Casa templo – Literally "temple house," usually the home of a *santero*, where the shrines to the *orichas* are located; also called *ilé ocha* and *microtemplo*.

Consejo Popular – People's Council.

Crisis de valores – Moral crisis.

Cuba Libre – A free Cuba.

Cubanía – Cubanness, and the ideological belief in Cubanness. Hence, *Cubanía Rebelde* (pre-1959) and *Cubanía Revolucionaria* (post-1959).

Cuentapropista – Self-employed person.

Diplotienda – A once exclusively diplomatic shop where goods are priced in hard currency.

Doble moral – Moral ambiguity.

Ifá – Deity also known as Orúnmila, the Yoruban god of wisdom, and the related divination system.

Ilé ocha – See *casa templo*.

Internacionalista – Someone who has participated in one of Cuba's civilian or military missions in other countries.

Jineterismo – Hustling, therefore *jinetero* (masc.) and *jinetera* (fem.).

Martiano – Following the ideas of José Martí.

Militante – A member of the Cuban Communist Party.

Oricha/orisha – Deity of the *regla de ocha*.

Palera/o – Person initiated into *palo monte*.

Paladar – Family-run private restaurant.

Palo monte – Cuban religion of central African origin.

Patria – Homeland.

190 / Glossary

Plante Abakuá – Major ceremony of Abakuá.

Regla de ocha – Cuban religion with its origins in West Africa, also called *santería*.

Reglas congas – See *palo monte*.

Santera/o – Person who has undergone initiation into the *regla de ocha*.

Santo – "Saint," also used to refer to *oricha*.

Sociolismo – Pun on *socialismo* and *socio* (friend); refers to a tendency to favor one's friends.

Solidarismo – Communal solidarity.

Toque de santo – Religious ceremony in honor of an *oricha*, with drumming and dancing.

About the Contributors

Christine Ayorinde has written extensively on *santería*. Her works include *Afro-Cuban Religiosity, Revolution, and National Identity* (2004); "*Santería* in Cuba: Tradition and Transformation," in *The Yoruba Diaspora in the Atlantic World*, edited by Toyin Falola and Matt Childs (2005); and "Afro-Cuban Culture: Within or Outside of the Nation?" in *Contesting Freedom: Control and Resistance in the Century after Emancipation in the Caribbean*, edited by Gad Heuman and David Trotman (2005). She has also translated works by Cuban authors.

Francisco Domínguez teaches politics, Latin American studies, and Spanish at Middlesex University, where he is the Program Leader for Latin American and Spanish and the head of the Centre for Brazilian and Latin American Studies. He has recently published *Mercosur: Between Integration and Democracy* (2003); "The U.S. and Latin America," *Soundings: A Journal of Politics and Culture* (fall 2004); and "Violence, the Left, and the Creation of Un Nuevo Chile," in *Political Violence and Identity in Latin America*, edited by Will Fowler and Peter Lambert (2006).

Alexander Gray works in the field of democratic development, participating in international election observation missions with the European Union, the Organization for Security and Co-Operation in Europe, and the Organization of American States. He is president of Professors without Borders, an international NGO.

Antoni Kapcia is a professor of Latin American history and the director of the Cuba Research Forum at the University of Nottingham. He has been working on Cuba since 1971 and publishing on the subject since 1975. His recent books include *Cuba: Island of Dreams* (2000) and *Havana: The Making of Cuban Culture* (2005).

Michelle Marín-Dogan, Ph.D., is an executive search consultant in a leading consultancy firm in London and has taught at the Universities of York and East Anglia.

192 / Contributors

Nino Pagliccia manages Canadian-Cuban collaborative research projects as a statistician in the Institute of Health Promotion Research at the University of British Columbia in Vancouver. He is active in the Canadian Network on Cuba, the Canadian-Cuban Friendship Association-Vancouver and the Che Guevara Volunteer Work Brigade.

Miren Uriarte is a sociologist in the College of Public and Community Service and is the director of the Gaston Institute for Latino Community Development and Public Policy at the University of Massachusetts, Boston. Uriarte's recent publications on Cuba include *Cuba: Social Policy at a Crossroads: Maintaining Priorities, Transforming Practice* (2002); "Cuban Social Policy Responses to the Economic Crisis of the 1990s," in *Cuban Studies* (2004); "Holding to Basics and Investing for Growth: Cuban Education and the Economic Crisis of the 1990s," in *The Journal of Pedagogy, Pluralism, and Practice* (2003), and (with Lorena Barberia and Xavier de Souza Briggs) "The End of Egalitarianism," in *The Cuban Economy at the Start of the Twenty-First Century*, edited by Jorge Dominguez et al. (2004).

Index

Abakuá secret society, 141, 145, 148, 154n6
Aberasturias, Lucas, 150
academic circles: campaign against ideological subversion, 54–57; debates over civil society, 40–44, 47; "problem" of alternatives, 59–60; Special Period, 184; think tanks on civil society, 18, 54–57
academic solidarity, 137
Acanda, Jorge Luis, 41–42, 57–58, 62n6, 126
accountability assemblies, 95
ACSUR las Segovias, 170
Action Group for the Free Expression of Sexual Choice (GALEES), 11, 166
administrative controls over civil society, 55
Africa, 70
Afro-Cuban religions, 142–43; accommodation, 143–44; cooperation with state, 151; discrimination ended, 144, 155n15; early views of, 13, 155n11; foreign NGOs, 147; foreign support, 148, 156n24; institutionalization, 14; legality, 143, 155n13; material benefits, 146; political agendas, 150; positive values, 145–46; social problems, 147; temple houses, 140; visibility and status, 153. *See also* santería
Agricultural Production Cooperative (CPA), 73, 75, 76t, 77t
agricultural sector, 73–78; Asociación Nacional de Agricultores Pequeños (ANAP), 84; state ownership, 74
Alonso Tejada, Aurelio, 58
altruism, 121
American Institute for Free Labor Development (AIFLD), 176
American Joint Distribution Committee (JDC), 146–47
Angola, 3, 128
apagones (brownouts), 92
Asia, 70, 71, 72
Asociación Abakuá de Cuba, 148

Asociación de Combatientes de la Revolución Cubana (veterans), 32
asociaciones económicas (AEs, joint ventures), 68–70, 71, 71t
Asociación Nacional de Agricultores Pequeños (ANAP), 84
Asociación para la Unidad de Nuestra América (AUNA), 172
Assemblies of People's Power, 82
Assembly to Promote Civil Society, 21
Association Act (1993), 12, 154–55n8, 165, 168, 179–80
Association of Veterans of the Cuban Revolution, 9
atheism, scientific, 13, 140, 143, 144
ayudantes (assistants), 79, 81t
Azcuy Henríquez, Hugo, 51–52, 52–53, 55
Aznar, José María, 68

babalawos, 146, 148, 155n18
Batista, Fulgencio, 21, 23
"Battle of Ideas," 19n1
Bay of Pigs, 24, 155n10
Béjar Miranda, Ana María, 168, 170
beneficence, 32
Betto, Frei, 144
Big Seven mass organizations, 161, 173
black market, 4, 5, 74, 75, 86n6, 96, 99
bloqueo, use of term, 17
B'nai Brith, 147
Brazil, 144, 151
brigadistas, 133–36
Brothers to the Rescue incident, 31, 57
Bush, George Herbert Walker, 66

Canada: constructive engagement, 7; diplomatic relations, 127; investment, 70. *See also* solidarity movement in Canada
Canadian Cuban Friendship Association (CCFA), 131

Canadian International Development Agency, 90

Canadian Jewish Congress, 147

Canadian Network on Cuba (CNC), 131

Cardoso, Fernando Henrique, 86n3

Care International, 172

Cáritas Cubana, 146, 164, 179

Casa de las Américas, 26

casas particulares (guesthouses), 5

Cason, James, 34, 87n10

Castañeda, Antonio, 147–49, 156n27

Castro, Fidel: dictum (1961), 25–26, 35; on religion, 141–42, 144, 154n1; Rio Summit speech, 49, 163

Castro, Raúl, 22, 53–54, 55, 56

Castroism, 16, 25

Catédra de Estudios Antonio Gramsci, 58

Catholic Church, 12–13; Afro-Cubans, 152, 157n35; complaints, 153; defending *Revolución*, 31; foreign clergy, 152; historical role, 141; influence, 13; lay Catholics, 150, 156nn31, 32; membership, 13, 142, 155n15; official positions, 144; pope's visit, 14, 33, 145, 169; role of, 141, 150, 156n31; social projects, 146; use of civil society concept, 48–49, 61; Vatican links, 13

caudillismo, 16

CCS. *See* Credit and Service Cooperative

Central America, 176

Central de Trabajadores de Cuba (CTC), 32

centralization, of political system, 94–95, 105, 183, 186

Centro de Cultura Comunitaria, 107

Centro de Estudios Europeos (CEE), 54

Centro de Estudios sobre América (CEA), debates, 18, 54–57, 60, 62n8

Centro de Información y Estudios sobre las Relaciones Internacionales (CIERI), 172

Centro de Intercambio y Referencia sobre Iniciativas Comunitarias (CIERIC), 91, 105

Centro Memorial Dr. Martin Luther King Jr., 58, 90, 91, 105, 109, 129, 140, 146, 156n31, 172

charity: among Cubans, 134; root causes of social problems, 121; solidarity compared, 117–18, 120, 135; three-dimensional view, 122–23, 123f

children's rights, 170–71

China, 70, 70t, 86n4

Christian churches, 13–14

Christian values, 141

church-state relations, 12–14, 144

civil defense, 32, 37

civil society: charity and the oppressed, 119; increase in number of organizations, 164; meaning contested, 20; new actors, 163–70; official definition, 53–54, 55; possible outcomes, 177–78, 188; state role, 160; traditional actors, 161–63

civil society concept: described, 43–44; differing views, 160; as metaphor for social change, 60–61; provenance of, 41; as socialist construct, 163; Track II policy (U.S.), 48, 111n12

class struggle, 119

coercion: inclusivity and, 35; participation and, 9

Committees for the Defense of the Revolution (CDRs): creation, 10, 22; decline, 9; functions evolving, 29; neighborhood functions, 100, 103; night guard-duty, 32; religious members, 155n12

Communism: assumptions about, 16; exiles on, 16; Venezuela, 136

Communist Party: on alternative discourses, 52, 53; believer restrictions, 13, 140, 154n2, 166; dogmatists and Gramscians debate, 55; first congress, 2; institutionalization after 1970, 2–3; membership turnover, 3; need for argued, 85–86; participation, 24; on philosophy, 153; reduced mobilization, 32; on religion, 153, 154n1; religious believers in, 11, 143

community: defining, 35–36; new roles and modalities, 46

community development, 92

community movements, debate over civil society, 47

comrade investors, 65

Comte, Auguste, 118

consensus: importance of maintaining, 85; rearticulation of, 42

constructive dialogue, 7

convertible peso, 19n2, 81

cooperation, *versus* solidarity, 183–84

cooperatives, 73–78

Coordinating Committee of the Jewish Faith, 149

corruption, 11, 23
Council of Churches, 105, 140, 144, 146, 149
Council of Ministers, 94
Council for Mutual Economic Exchange (CMEA), 1
CPA. *See* Agricultural Production Cooperative
Credit and Service Cooperative (CCS), 73
crises, nature of, 60
Cuba Libre, 15, 24, 38n10
Cuban Democracy Act (1992), 6, 31; Tracks 1 and 2, 111n12. *See also* Torrecelli-Graham law
Cuban Federation of Women. *See* Federation of Cuban Women (FMC)
Cuban Five campaign, 130
cubanía: Afro-Cubans, 151, 152; and *santería*, 151, 157n37
cubanía rebelde (rebel Cubanness), 15
cubanía revolucionaria, 15
Cuban Liberty and Democracy Act. *See* Helms-Burton Law (1996)
Cuban NGOs: caution with, 106; cooperation with foreign NGOs, 109, 184, 187; limits, 172; participatory approaches, 105–6; religious (list), 140; social development policy, 175, 186; with state connections, 172; sustainability, 178; as "Trojan horse," 53. *See also* foreign NGOs; NGOs (nongovernmental organizations)
Cuban Revolution, seen in Venezuela, 136–37
Cuban Workers' Confederation (CTC), 162
Cuba Socialista journal, 57, 60
cuentapropismo, 78–81
cultural magazines, 51
cultural vanguard, 26–27, 51

debates: insider, 25; intervening, neglected, 25; "losers" in, 27; motivation, 27–28; patterns of, 25–28; rectification, 27; sugar harvest of 1970, 26
debates over civil society: contours, 40–44; general tendencies, 42–44; interplay of political strategies and events, 46–48; landmarks, 48–50; offensive against concept, 52–53; philosophical aspects, 43; principal spaces for, 50–52; publications engaged in, 41; responses of the party-state, 52–54; restructuring hegemony of revolutionary

socialist power, 42; scholarly controversy, 41–42; sectors participating, 41
Debray, Regis, 161
decentralization, 7–8
Decree-Law 141 of September 1993, 79
defections, 27
defense, 32
democracia, use of term, 17
democracy, use of term, 8, 17
democracy promotion, 48
democratic centralism, 28
Departamento de Estudios Socioreligiosos, 154n3
Dilla, Haroldo, 18
diplotiendas (hard currency shops), 4–5
dissent, managing, 34–37
dissidents: association with Bush administration, 36–37; four activities, 34; nationalist reaction to, 31–32; problems in 2003, 34; state view of, 126–27; transgression of rules, 36–37
doble moral, 143, 145
dollar economy: access to, 86n6; access to hard currency, 97, 98, 99–100; self-employed, 79
dollarization, 4–5, 19n2, 81, 145
domestic violence, 170–71
drug use, campaigns against, 146
dual economy, 96
dumping sites, 90
Durkheim, Emile, 118, 119, 124, 126

Eastern Europe: civil society as resistance, 47; civil society strategy, 42; as neoliberal, 42; paradigm of, 9–10, 20–21, 25
economic crisis of 1990s, 3–6; background to, 1–2; crisis of change, 4; Havana's *barrios,* 92–93; at local level, 5; political response, 7–9; recovery, 32, 85; regulation, 32. *See also* Special Period
economic development strategies, 26, 109
economy: background, 1–2; foreign direct investment, 68–73; most vulnerable households, 98; patterns of evolution, 25
education, 23, 32, 142
egalitarianism, 5
Eighth World *Orisha* Conference, 148
electoral reforms, 32–33, 82–83

196 / Index

electoral turnout, 127
embargo: NNOC, 130–31; tightening after Soviet collapse, 6, 30, 66–67, 160; use of term, 17; volunteer work brigades, 132
emergency response, 32
emigration, 35–36; emergency agreements, 30
employment, 65–66
empowerment: early 1960s, 9; Havana experiment, 110; momentum of, 24; use of term, 8
Engels, Friedrich, 119
entrepreneurial councils, 104–5
environmental education workshops, 90
Ernesto Che Guevara Volunteer Work Brigade, 132
Escalante, Aníbal, 26, 27, 38nn11, 13
estado, use of term, 17
Estrella Márquez, L. E., 49
Europe, 70, 71
European Commission Humanitarian Office (ECHO), 171
European Union (EU), 7, 68, 86n4, 170
exceptionalism issue, 16
exiles: *gusanos* and *mariposas,* 35, 39n15; on ideology, 16. *See also* Miami Cubans

family violence, 170–71
farmers markets, 74
Fast for Life (Pastors for Peace), 130
Federación de Estudiantes de la Enseñanza Media, 33
Federation of Cuban Women (FMC), 100, 103, 155n12, 161, 171
Federation of University Students (FEU), 33
financing of NGOs, 165, 167
food and beverage industry, 72t
food production, 92
foreign contacts, 186
foreign currencies, 4
foreign direct investment (FDI), 68–73
foreign investment, 65, 68–73, 96
foreign NGOs: Afro-Cuban religions, 147; autonomy issues, 170–71, 178, 185, 187; capacity and intent, 187; in Central America, 176; challenges summarized, 7; consensus lacking, 165–65; continued presence, 164; cooperation with domestic NGOs, 109, 187; Cuban partners, 167, 171–72, 184; debates over civil society, 47; economic reasons for, 164; effect on traditional civil society, 174;

future of, 177–79; how they operate, 166–67; lack of offices, 169; official treatment, 168–70; participatory community planning, 103, 106; reception, 168–70; religious, 146–47; solidarity versus cooperation, 184; sustainability issues, 177–78; terms of reference, 167; views of, 106, 164–65. *See also* Cuban NGOs; NGOs (nongovernmental organizations)
foreign policy: before 1991, 6; radicalism, 3
foreign trade, 66, 68–73, 84
formal economy, 5
France, 70, 118
Freemasonry (Masons), 141, 164, 168–69
free-trade regimes, 67
Freire Fernández, Ángel, 149, 156n27
Fresa y chocolate (film), 11, 166
Fundación de la Naturaleza y el Hombre, 105
funding: CEA, 55; *Temas* journal, 51. *See also* financing of NGOs

Gaceta de Cuba, La, 41, 49, 51, 62
gardens, community-based, 91, 111n1
Gay and Lesbian Association of Cuba, 11, 166
GDIC. *See* Grupo para el Desarrollo Integral de la Capital
Gilbert, Steve, 172, 173, 174
González, Elián, 33
Gramsci, Antonio/Gramscians, 43, 45, 50, 55, 57–58, 61
Granma, 41, 52, 56
grass-roots participation, 1, 57, 10, 27, 29, 91, 178, 179, 183, 186–87
Great Britain. *See* United Kingdom
Greenpeace, 121
gross domestic product, 3–4
Group Ministerial de Trabajo con las Comunidades, 99, 107
Grupo para el Desarrollo Integral de la Capital (GDIC), 91, 101, 102, 103, 106, 107, 108, 177
guerrilla experience, 15, 25
Guevara, Che: command economy, 1; ideas marginalized, 3, 27; on New Man, 132; nonorthodoxy, 22; on solidarity, 116

Habanera, 56
Habitat-Cuba, 105, 111n10, 112n13, 173, 177
Haiti, 30
Hart, Armando, 27, 53, 56, 57

Havana: centralization, 93; as current focus, 18; economic crisis, 92–93; growth and investment, 93; neighborhood development, 93; Pogolotti neighborhood, 90–92; poverty, 99; strategic planning, 108–9; unemployment, 97

Havana Ecopolis, 172–73

Havana hotel bombings, 31

Havana street disturbances (1994), 28, 29–30

Hegel, G.W.F., 43

Helms-Burton Law (1996), 6, 31, 48, 67, 125, 127

Hermanos al Rescate incident, 31, 57

Hernández, Rafael, 49–50, 51

historical experience of Cuba: imagined community, 35; weak state structure, 21

home ownership, 94

homosexuals, 11, 166

house renting sector, 79, 80t

housing, social inequalities, 93–94

human rights organizations, 12, 34

Human Rights Watch, 162

ideology: evolution of, 14–16; exiles on, 16; nationalism, 23

Ifá divination, 150–51

illegal activities, 5

income tax, 83–84, 162

individualization, 29

informal economy, 5

informality, Havana, 18

Initiative for the Americas, 67

institutionalization, 22–23; Afro-Cuban religions, 14; Communist Party, 2–3; *Revolución* and state, 31

Instituto Cubano de Amistad con los Pueblos (ICAP), 128

Instituto Cubano de Arte e Industria Cinematográficos (ICAIC), 26

Instituto Cubano de Radio y Televisión (ICRT), 44

intellectuals, debates over civil society, 54–57, 60

intellectual workers, 87n8

internationalism: nationalism, 24; radical foreign policy, 3, 38n9; solidarity, 16; solidarity missions, 127–28

Italian Catholic Church, 146

Italian NGOs, 172–73

Italy, 70

Jehovah's Witnesses, 143, 153, 155

Jewish community, 142, 146–47, 149, 155n15

jineterismo, 18, 32, 80–81, 81t

John Paul II (pope), 14, 33, 145, 152, 169

joint ventures, 68–70, 71t

Juan Marinello Center for Research and Development of Cuban Culture, 58, 62n10

Kardecan spiritism, 141

Kohan, Néstor, 58

labor, division of, 118, 119

labor movement, 119, 162–63

labor unions, 56

laissez-faire, 122

land tenure, 74

Latin America: armed revolution policy, 3; investment, 70

Latin American School of Medicine, 128

Laurenzi, Fabio, 172

Law 54 of 1985, 12, 165

Law 91 of the People's Councils, 107

leadership. *See* vanguard, political

legitimacy, 37, 42

Leroux, Pierre, 117–18

Letra del Año (Year's Letter), 150–51

liberalism, 57, 60, 59, 173

liberation theology, 144

Literacy Campaign, 9, 22

local governance, 94–96

local initiatives: focus and processes, 91; success, 8

local level: devolution of autonomy, 8; effects of Special Period, 99–101; meaning of, 95

Lunes de Revolución magazine, 26

Luxemburg, Rosa, 57–58, 62n6

malnutrition, 127

Mandela, Nelson, 128

manufacturing, 69, 69t

market mechanisms adopted, 4, 46, 65–66; regulation, 83

Martí, José, 15, 38n7, 168

Martínez Heredía, Fernando, 58

Marx, Carlos, 43

Marxism/Marxism-Leninism, 14, 42, 43, 50; "critical Marxists," 50, 57; "of suspicion," 53; religious believers, 141–42; socialist "alternatives," 59

Masons. *See* Freemasonry (Masons)

mass organizations: Big Seven, 161; Raúl Castro on, 53–54, 56; change in identity, 162; as civil society, 126; as civil society actors, 160, 161–63; civil society debate and, 52; emergence of, 161; freedoms for, 143; labeled NGOs, 185; listed, 82, 111n2, 126, 180n1; local level functions, 100–101; para-statal, 171, 181n12; as participatory mechanisms, 22, 24–25; as preferred approach, 163–64; religious beliefs, 143; traditional, 161

Metropolitan Park of Havana, 90, 107

Mexico, 70

Miami Cubans, 36, 84. *See also* exiles; migration

microbrigades, 94, 102

microfacción affair, 27, 38n13

migration, early departures, 2

militias, 9, 22

Ministry of Culture, 51

MINVEC (Ministerio para la Inversión Extranjera y Colaboración Económica), 167, 168

mixed enterprises, 65, 96

mobilization: early years, 9; Elián campaign, 33–34; ignored features, 28–29; minimal, 29; patterns, 22, 24; Special Period, 29

mode of production, socialist, 45

Movimiento Cristiano Liberación, 150

Municipal Administrative Council (CAM), 95

municipal administration councils (MAP), 94

Municipal Assembly of People's Power, 95

municipality, lack of resources, 96, 98, 100

Murillo, José (Pepe), 170, 171–72

Muslims, 151

Nación y Emigración conferences (1994–1995), 36

National Assembly of People's Power, 94

national identity, *santería*, 151, 157n37

nationalism, 6, 22, 23; meanings of, 23–24; *Revolución* concept, 31

national liberation movements, 128

National Network on Cuba (NNOC), 130–31

Nation of Islam, 151

negotiation, process of daily, 11

neighborhood-level planning, 101–4

neighborhood movement, 91–92, 101, 107–9

neoliberal discourse, 47, 48; civil society as neoliberal concept, 52; free trade paradigm, 67; solidarity of Cuban state compared, 120; state functions and NGOs, 124

new economy, 96, 97

New Man, 25, 132

NGOs (nongovernmental organizations): controversial nature, 111n10; cooperation with state, 183, 187; criticism, 124–25; debate over civil society, 47; economic impact, 124; growth of, 124, 126; managed environment, 179; models of governance and, 126; new actors, 163–65; new research on, 160; official status, 165–66, 168, 169; pyramid graphics, 173, 174f; religious, 149, 153–54; requirements listed, 165; social development policy, 175–77; state approval for projects, 167; trends summarized, 11–12, 187; U.S., 125; U.S.-supported terrorism, 125. *See also* Cuban NGOs; financing of NGOs; foreign NGOs

Nicaragua, 144

Ñico López Party School, 52

nongovernmental organizations. *See* NGOs

"non-proletarian" social layer, 83

Office of Religious Affairs, 142, 145–46, 149–50

oil supplies, 66, 87

Operación Milagro, 128

opportunists purged, 3

opposition activists: factors attenuating, 36; Havana, 18

oppressed, solidarity of the, 119

Organizaciones Revolucionarias Integradas (ORI), 26, 38n11

orisha worship, 147

Ortega, Cardinal, 150, 152–53

Padilla case, 38n12

paladares (private restaurants), 5, 79, 84

palo monte, 141, 148, 154n6

para-statal mass organizations, 171, 181n12. *See also* mass organizations

Pardo Valdés, Gustavo E., 169

participation, 8, 24, 28, 61n2

participatory community planning, 103, 105, 108

participatory democracy, 86

Partido Socialista Popular (People's Socialist Party, PSP): ideology, 15, 38n5; leaders, 3; vanguard trends, 2–3

Pastors for Peace, 129–30, 146

Payá, Osvaldo, 7, 37n1, 150, 176

Paz y el Tercer Mundo, 171

Pensamiento Crítico, 55, 58

Pentecostalists, 140, 151, 152

People's Councils (Consejos Populares), 8, 10, 29, 91, 101, 133; changes, 107–8; described, 104; Havana, 109, 111n8; *lo local* redefined, 104; participatory decision making, 107; role and effectiveness, 105; Special Period, 104; strategic community planning, 109

People's Power, 10

People's Socialist Party. *See* Partido Socialista Popular (PSP)

Pérez, Hassan, 33

Período Especial en Tiempos de Paz (Special Period in Peacetime). *See* Special Period

petty entrepreneurs, 4, 65

Platt Amendment, 15, 21, 23, 38nn2–3

pluralism, 35, 86

PM (film), 26

Poder Local (Local Power), 29

Pogolotti neighborhood, 90–92, 96, 109

political culture, 35

political participation, 8

political parties, registration, 12

political spaces, 10–12, 186

political sphere, 60

political system: centralization, 94–95, 105, 183, 186; characterizing, 10; described, 82; as *sui generis*, 185; underlying patterns, 184

pope's visit, 14, 33, 145, 152, 169

Popular Councils. *See* People's Councils

poverty, in Havana, 99

President's Commission for Assistance to a Free Cuba, 6, 126, 156n29, 176

Prieto, Abel, 51, 58

private sector: agriculture, 75, 76t, 77t; restrictions on, 84; Special Period measures, 96; trends, 81, 81t, 83

private spaces, 42–43

pro-democracy movement, 7, 176

Protestant denominations: cooperation with state, 151; early, 141, 154n7; growth, 155n15; illegality, 143, 155n13; membership, 155n14;

publications, 156n31; social projects, 146, 153; sympathy with Revolution, 144, 152; ties to U.S., 141, 142, 154n7

Protestantism, early, and capitalism, 121

proto-capitalist layers, 84

provincial administration councils (CAP), 94

Provincial Secretariat of People's Power, 107

Proyecto Varela, 7

public services, 96

public spaces, 42–43

public sphere, 60

purchasing power, 5

race, religion and discrimination, 151–52, 157n35

racial segregation, in housing, 94

Rastafarianism, 151–52

ration books, 5, 96

raw materials shortages, 92

Reciprocity Treaty (1934), 21, 38n3

Rectification campaign, 3, 23, 27, 38n8, 44–45

recycling programs, 90, 91

Register of Associations, 149

regla de ocha, 141, 154n6

reglas conga, 141, 154n6

religion: as an ideology, 143; role of, 12–14

religious believers (*creyentes*), 12–14, 84

religious groups, 142–45; cooperation with state, 151; counterrevolutionary stance, 142, 149–50, 155n10; freedom of action, 154; impact of Revolution, 142, 155n9; opening, 11; spaces for believers, 12–14, 84, 154n3; state and, 141, 154; threat of political activism, 149; U.S. on, 141, 154n5

religious tolerance, 13, 83

remittances, 98

residential location, 14, 38n4

resistance, interstices between state organizations, 10

restlessness among Cuban population, 186

Revolución: changing concept, 30–31; as *Patria,* 31–32; patterns of mobilization, 22; reassessing, 186; self-definitions, 22; Special Period, 31; use of term, 17, 31

Revolutionary Offensive of 1968, 1

right-wing international political discourse, 48

Rivero, Otto, 33

Roca Rivas, José Eugenio, 171

Roque, Martha Beatriz, 38n1
Rousseau, Jean Jacques, 119

Salvation Army, 121
San Lázaro pilgrimage, 150, 156–57n33
santería, 141; appeal of, 146, 155n19; Catholics
on, 152–53; co-optation, 157n34; dominance
of, 12; expansion of, 147; hiding practices,
143; income and foreign exchange, 147–48;
national identity, 151, 157n37; social element,
145; Special Period, 13. *See also* Afro-Cuban
religions
Save the Children U.K., 168, 169, 170–71
secularism, 13, 144–45
"siege," 23
siege mentality, 35
self-determination, 130, 131
self-employed: *cuentapropismo*, 78–81; Revolutionary Offensive of 1968, 1; seller category,
79; Special Period, 4, 65; trends, 79–80, 80t
small business, 1, 4
Smith, Adam, 119
social capital, 110
social classes, 83
social development policy: approach for
proposals, 179; decision making, 175; NGOs
and, 175–77
social development projects: apprehension
over, 170; common goals, 172–73; global use
of term "civil society," 47; NGO projects,
164, 167, 172; successful, 177
social inequalities, 83–84; among neighborhoods, 99; dual economy in Havana, 96–97;
housing, 93–94; safety net and, 110
socialism: alternative discourses, 59–60;
debates over, 17, 44–45, 47; Leroux on, 118;
NGOs in Cuba, 178; roots in civil society,
50; solidarity, 122
socialist civil society, 54, 56
social mobility, 21
social policy: Canadian view, 127; macro approaches, 110; urban inequalities, 110
social sciences, debate over civil society, 55,
59–60
social services: coverage, 83; dependents,
81; early changes, 2; policy changes, 108;
religious groups, 146, 149, 156n28; social

solidarity principle, 65; Special Period, 4,
5, 46
social solidarity, 85; as economic principle, 65
social spaces, 10–12, 188
social welfare policy, 118, 120
solidarismo, 28, 29, 186
solidarity: academic, 137; awareness of social
change, 121–22; charity compared, 117–18,
120, 135; Che Guevara on, 116; concept summarized, 15–16; cooperation *versus*, 183–84;
in Cuban Constitution, 128; four uses of,
118–21; international, 134; Liebknecht on,
116; as moral concept, 118–19, 121; NGOs
in Cuba, 178; origins of term, 117, 135;
relevance, 125; as social cohesion, 120; state-
endorsed, 134; as state responsibility, 122,
123; three-dimensional view, 122–23, 123f;
use of term, 116–17. *See also* charity
solidarity activism, 122, 134
solidarity movement in Canada, 116
solidarity organizations, 123–24, 131–36; Canadian people-to-people, 131–36; solidarity
with Cuba, 129–31
South East Asian economic crisis, 85
sovereignty issues, 130, 131
Soviet bloc: collapse and interest in Gramsci,
45; collapse and religion, 140; comparing
Eastern Europe to Cuba, 47; economic consequences of collapse, 66, 92, 160; economic
relationship with, 1–2, 72; loss of paradigm,
45; special relationship, 6; trade collapse, 3
spaces: adherence to system, 10–11; range of,
10–12
Spain, 70, 70t
Special Period: academic circles, 184; alternative socialist discourses, 159; austerity
measures, 4, 65; constitutional changes,
82–83; crisis of change, 4; crisis of values, 14,
28; debates over civil society, 41, 163; effects
on neighborhoods, 96–98; factors leading
to civil society debate, 46; increase in civil
society organizations, 164; leadership in, 28,
29; municipalities, 95–96; neighborhood
movement, 92, 103; NGO participation, 179;
People's Councils, 104; political and social
spaces, 10; pressures for change, 183; racism,
151; religious practice/groups, 140, 145, 149,

152; *Revolución*, 31; role of civil society, 5, 179; social services, 4, 5, 46, 127; Soviet collapse, 66; spiritual aspects, 13; use of term, 19n1. *See also* economic crisis of 1990s

standards of living, 99

state: informal resources, 37; political functions, 32; reconsidering concept of, 37; use of term, 17

state, solidarity of the, 120, 122, 124

state adaptation to change, effects on civil society, 1, 183

state-civil society separation, 22–23, 126; Cuban model, 184–85; functioning, 174–75

state organizations, 82

strategic community planning, 108

Suárez Salazar, Luis, 55

sugar: harvest of 1970, 26; quota system, 38n3; UBPCs, 75

Support for Democratic Transition in Cuba (USAID, 1997), 6, 175–76

syncretic cults, 144, 150, 151, 152

Table de Concertation de Solidarité Québec-Cuba, 131

Talleres de Transformación Integral (Neighborhood Transformation Workshops), 8, 102; La Guinera, 111n6; listed, 111n7; Pogolotti, 90, 91

taxation policy, 83–84, 162

technocrats, 3

Temas (journal), 41, 50–52, 56, 58, 60, 62n9

tenement removal, 102

terminology issues, 8, 17

think tanks, 162. *See also* Centro de Estudios sobre América (CEA)

tiranía (tyranny), 23

Torricelli-Graham law, 30, 48, 106; described by titles, 66–67; opposition to, 125

tourism, 85, 87n7; access to hard currency, 97, 99–100; children working, 98; foreign direct investment, 69t, 69, 71, 81t; Havana as center, 97; race, 87n9; social problems, 98, 145

Trabajo Comunitario Integrado: Proyecto de Programa (1996), 107

transport sector, 79, 80t

Tribunas Abiertas (Open Platforms), 9

UBPCs (Basic Units of Production), 73, 74t, 75, 78

Último Jueves group, 58

unemployment, 97

Union of Communist Youth (UCJ), 13, 32, 33, 133, 143

United Kingdom, 70

United Nations, 106

United States: axis of evil, 34; Bush I administration, 66; Bush II administration, 34, 36, 85; Clinton administration, 85; on fostering civil society, 48, 52–53, 124–25, 176–76; hostility before 1991, 6; infiltration via NGOs, 172; Miami Cubans, 36; paradigm assumptions, 20–21; policy of 1990s and nationalism, 31–32; pressure after 1991, 6–7, 66–67; prospect of intervention by, 30, 125–26; regime change policy, 48; on religious groups, 141, 154n5; religious groups used, 149; Track II policy, 48, 106, 111n12. *See also* exiles

United States Agency for International Development (USAID), 6, 125

United States Interests Section (State Dept.), 34

Universal Declaration of Human Rights, 120

urban agriculture movement, 91

Urban Reform (1959), 94

vacated properties of émigrés, 2

Valdés, Dagoberto, 150, 156nn31, 32

Valdés Hernández, D., 49

Valdés Paz, Juan, 58

Valdés Vivó, Raúl, 52, 53

values, crisis of, 14

vanguard, political: absence of major splits, 27; base limited, 21; cultural vanguard and, 26–27; meetings in Tarará, 26; on participation, 24; "siege," 22; Special Period, 28, 29; trends, 2

Varela Project, 37–38n1, 150

Venceremos Brigade, 129

Venezuela, 70, 70t, 85, 86n, 136

veterans, 9, 32

Virgen de Caridad del Cobre procession (1961), 142

voluntary work, 32

volunteer work brigades to Cuba, 131–36

Walker, Lucius, 130
Washington consensus, 124
welfare state, 120
work, concept of, 132

Yoruba Cultural Association (ACY), 140, 147–49, 150

Yoruba religion and culture, 147–48, 151, 156n24
youth: churches, 14; Elián campaign, 33–34; late 1980s, 9; marginalization, 81, 83; mass organizations, 33; religious interest, 145; role of state, 5–6